IMAGES
of America

JAMES CITY COUNTY

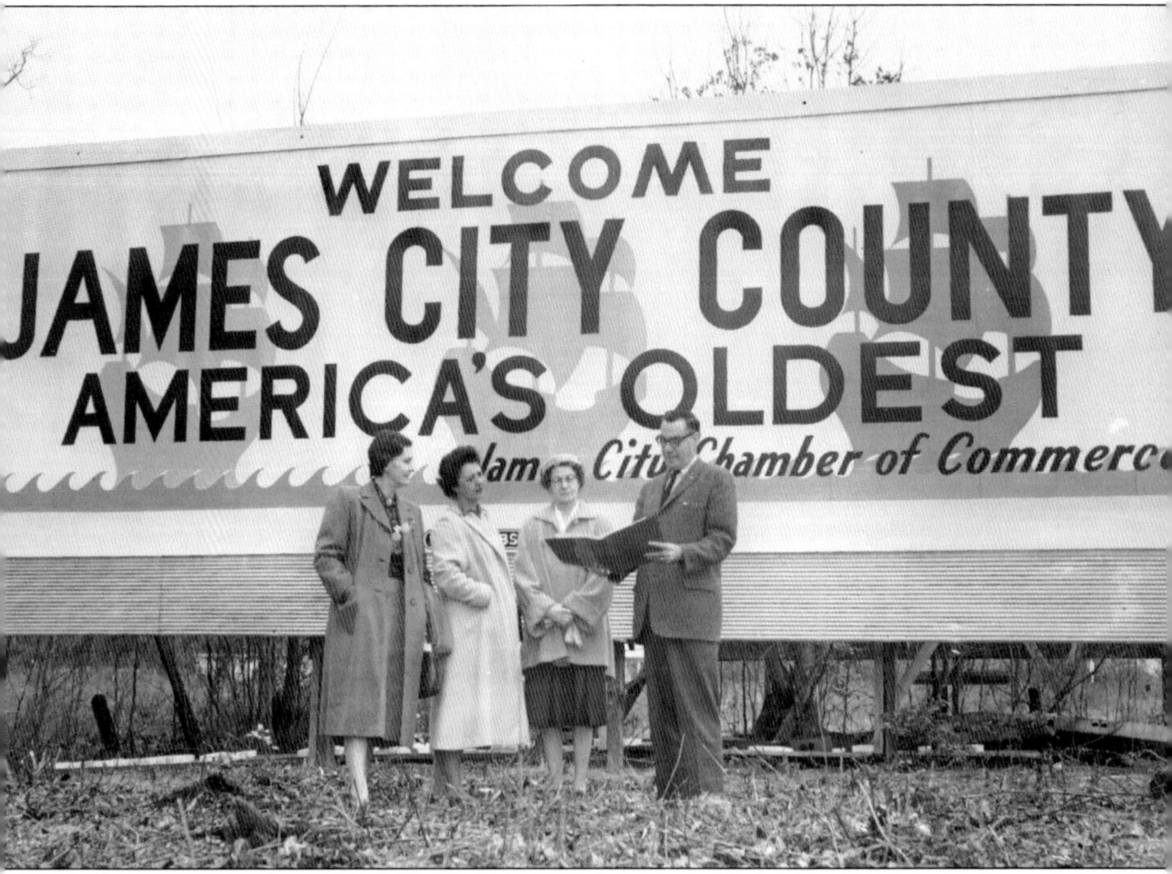

"James Citie" developed on the western end of Jamestown Island, the site of the first permanent English settlement in the New World. Established as a business venture, Virginia became a royal colony in 1624. Settlement spread to the mainland and other parts of eastern Virginia until it was necessary to subdivide the colony into eight counties, of which James City County was one, in 1634. Virginia's first statehouse and many Jamestown buildings were burned in 1676 during Bacon's Rebellion, a populist uprising. During the mid-20th century, tourists drove through rural James City County on their way to see archaeological excavations at Jamestown Island, celebrate the 350th anniversary of the Virginia landing at Jamestown Festival Park, and admire the restoration of Williamsburg, Virginia's second capital city, formed from James City County and York County as a separate municipality in 1699. A billboard in western James City County welcomed history enthusiasts to "America's Oldest" county. From left to right, Caroline Dozier, Nettie Hazelwood, Mabel Hazelwood, and chamber of commerce executive secretary Andy Maloney posed in front of the sign for a *Daily Press* photographer. (SH.)

On the Cover: Alfred Benson was station agent with the Chesapeake and Ohio Railway Company at its Lightfoot depot in James City County from 1909 until 1953. This photograph was probably taken about 1910 by Albert J. Levorsen, who lived nearby. According to an article in the January 20, 1982, *Virginia Gazette*, L. T. Hankins suggested the name Lightfoot when the community post office was opened on January 25, 1882. Hankins was the first postmaster of the facility, located in Six Mile Ordinary, a Colonial and early American hostelry sited at a crossroads six miles from Williamsburg along the Old Stage Road, or the road to Richmond. Hankins and A. B. Tuttle acquired a deed to the building and 70 acres from Lightfoot Taylor in 1881. (DBW.)

IMAGES
of America

JAMES CITY COUNTY

Sara E. Lewis

ARCADIA PUBLISHING

ISBN 978-0-7385-6850-8

Published by Arcadia Publishing
Charleston, South Carolina

Printed in the United States of America

Library of Congress Control Number: 2008934658

For all general information contact Arcadia Publishing at:
Telephone 843-853-2070
Fax 843-853-0044
E-mail sales@arcadiapublishing.com
For customer service and orders:
Toll-Free 1-888-313-2665

Visit us on the Internet at www.arcadiapublishing.com

This book is dedicated to the citizens of James City County, whose ancestral heritage on farms and crossroads dates to the first county's early days.

Contents

Acknowledgments 6

Introduction 7

1. First Settlement to First County 9
2. Colonial County 17
3. First American Century 25
4. Circa 1900 39
5. Toano 57
6. Rural Communities 77
7. The World Wars 95
8. A Moment at Mid-Century 105
9. Traces of the Past Surround Us 121

Acknowledgments

This book was compiled with help from many people who share an interest in the families, farms, and future of James City County. Their heritage has been largely overshadowed by the preservation, re-creation, and promotion of Jamestown and Williamsburg, the Commonwealth of Virginia's first and second capital cities. As a popular history intended for general audiences, the photographs and text presented here are drawn from oral legends, written memoirs, newspapers, and scholarly research. While all provided insight, the book *James City County: Keystone of the Commonwealth* by Martha W. McCartney, published by the James City County Board of Supervisors in 1997, is especially acknowledged for providing important facts. *Velkommen til Norge (Welcome to Norge)*, by Nancy Smith Bradshaw and Frances Huckstep Hamilton, includes more about James City County's Scandinavian settlement. Interested readers can consult these volumes for more information. Special thanks are extended to Donna Tyssen Garrett and Fred Boelt as well as other members of the James City County Historical Commission for their advice and critique of this independent work. Local history collector Doris Benson Wildenberger has been especially generous to offer photographs from her considerable collection as well as her time and interest to this project. In addition, individuals and organizations who contributed photographs and information include the APVA (Association for the Preservation of Virginia Antiquities) Preservation Virginia/Historic Jamestowne, Billy Apperson, Andy Bradshaw, Nancy Smith Bradshaw, Ruth Marston Carter, the Chesapeake and Ohio Historical Society, the Colonial Virginia Chapter–American Red Cross, Glennis Hazelwood Davis, Rosilind Ratcliff Dodd, Michael Flanary, Steve Flanary, Bert Geddy, Willard S. Gilley, Sam Hazelwood, Lois Hornsby, the James City–Bruton Volunteer Fire Department, John Henry Jenson, Lafayette Jones, Irene Lee, George and Dot (Madsen) Marston, Carl "Shorty" Meadows, Kathy Cooke Palmer, Peggy Price, Shirley Robertson, Osborne Taylor Sr., Rosemary Van Houten, David Ware Jr., Martha Ware, Steve White, Norma Davis Wyatt, and Col. and Mrs. (Margaret Walton) Richard F. Wilkinson.

Key

Fred Boelt (FB)
Andy Bradshaw (AB)
APVA Preservation Virginia/Historic Jamestowne (APVA/HJ)
Ruth Marston Carter (RMC)
Chesapeake and Ohio Historical Society (COHS)
Colonial Virginia Chapter–American Red Cross (CVC-ARC)
Glennis Hazelwood Davis (GHD)
Steve Flanary (SF)
Donna Tyssen Garrett (DTG)
Bert Geddy (BG)
Willard S. Gilley (WSG)
Sam Hazelwood (SH)
James City–Bruton Volunteer Fire Department (JC-BVFD)
Library of Congress (LOC)
George and Dot Marston (GDMM)
Carl "Shorty" Meadows (CSM)
Osborne Taylor Sr. (OT)
Ware family (WF)
Steve White (SW)
Doris Benson Wildenberger (DBW)
Col. and Mrs. Richard F. Wilkinson (RFW)
Author's photograph (SEL)

INTRODUCTION

James City County's greatest claim to fame is Jamestown, the fort and island "citie" that was the first permanent English settlement in the New World. Jamestown and then Williamsburg, which was formed from a portion of James City County and York County, were Colonial Virginia's first and second government seats. This publication includes a few photographs of Jamestown and Williamsburg but not many, since these are available in numerous other publications. Rather, this short compilation features a sampling of the people and places that illuminate rural James City preceding its growth as a predominantly exurban area. Since the story of James City County beyond the Colonial capitals is little known to the millions who visit and to the thousands who have settled here, this publication offers them a taste of the history of the living county beyond the renowned museums.

Beginning shortly after the Jamestown outpost was founded in 1607, the surrounding land was granted to adventuring settlers who were mostly English emigrants. Some were members of the middle to minor gentry, and others had mercantile connections. However, the land that became James City County was largely populated by less well-positioned individuals who were increasingly crowded out of the Old World. Those with land paid for indentured servants and slaves who were needed to acquire more land and to labor on homesteads and in tobacco fields.

By 1634, the Virginia Company's venture had become a royal colony with a population of approximately 5,000. Due to the necessity of governance, Virginia's first counties were drawn up so courts would be accessible to the colonists. Virginia's first eight counties were Accomack, Charles City, Charles River, Elizabeth River, Henrico, James City, Warwick River, and Warrosquyoake (Isle of Wight). James City County's seat at "James Citie," or Jamestown, was also the Virginia colony's first administrative center.

Virginia's second capital city was named Williamsburg, and it was founded in 1699. It was built at Middle Plantation, located about six miles northeast of Jamestown on a ridge midway between the James and York Rivers. Early James City County counted upon Williamsburg's urban amenities while today's City of Williamsburg appreciates the resources of a more populous James City County. Since the early days, government buildings, school systems, and many local services have been shared. Williamsburg has annexed portions of James City County through the centuries, with the last annexation in 1983.

From early in the 17th century until the American Revolution, James City County's approximately 150 square miles of land included a few large plantations and many small farms. Landowners, indentured servants, and slaves lived and worked on the land that brought forth crops for subsistence and income. By the middle of the 18th century, James City County's cropland was exhausted of nutrients as a result of tobacco cultivation, and large planters pushed west. Other farmers consolidated early land grants and remained in the area. Some slaves were freed and settled in identifiable communities.

A few descendants of James City County's earliest settlers, black and white, still live in James City County. A legacy surrounds us in place names that have survived. For example, the Green Spring house and surrounding plantation of 17th-century governor William Berkeley has left a mark on the county. The historic site is preserved, but the names Berkeley and Green Spring on signposts, stores, and neighborhoods carry tales and spirits forward. A 19th-century owner of the house and land, William Ludwell Lee, left another legacy. This descendant of Berkeley's second wife bequeathed freedom to his slaves at his death in 1803 and gave them a tract of his land, the Hot Water tract that is today's Freedom Park, where they established a community. Descendants of those free blacks still live in the Centerville Road area and throughout the county.

James City County's first families endured two wars fought on the home front. The skirmishes and the aftermath of the American Revolution and the nearby Battle of Yorktown resulted in property damage and disease. Thousands of American, French, and British soldiers camped here and moved through the area, using up large amounts of food and timber, and spreading epidemics.

James City County residents who survived required more than a decade to recover from the spoil. Then, between 1861 and 1865, the Civil War once again brought soldiers and devastation. Union troops stationed in Hampton fought to capture the Confederate capital of Richmond. James City County was directly in the line of fire. Union troops held the city of Williamsburg. Encampments and crisscrossing of soldiers made the populace anxious about the welfare of their homes, farms, and families. Afterward, wounds to the people, buildings, and environment required time to heal.

The devastation wrought by the American Revolution and Civil War, as well as new technology, changed the character of the county. A unique community created by the post-bellum state of affairs was Norge. Around 1896, a Chesapeake and Ohio (C&O) Railroad executive and entrepreneur of Norwegian descent noticed an area of largely abandoned or cheap farmland midway along the spur of railroad line that ran southeast along the Virginia Peninsula from Richmond to Newport News. He speculated that if these lands were inhabited and farmed, more people and crops would need to be transported by the railroad. He promoted the land to Midwestern families who had come to America from Norway and encouraged them to resettle in James City County, where the weather was less harsh. Today the Norge community is still occupied by many third- and fourth-generation descendants of the original Scandinavian resettlers.

Other distinct communities include Grove, originally part of the extensive plantation land of the Burwells of Carter's Grove and Kingsmill Plantations; Croaker, a crossroads between the homesteads of independent and comfortably prosperous farmers in the northern portion of the county near the York River—where the croaker fish was plentiful; and Chickahominy, near the site of an 18th-century shipyard and a 19th-century brick-making company on the Chickahominy River, a tributary of the James River.

The photographs in this book capture images of the county beginning about 125 years ago, when photography became a useful medium. They celebrate the resilience of the people of James City County who farmed the land, harvested the rivers, and built rural communities. Photographs commemorate the rural way of life. They show the proud faces of those who became free and independent Americans here. Photographs spark a memory and preserve information about a way of living on the land that is largely changed today.

Beyond the photographs, traces of James City County's historic past are all around us. We can look for them in fragments of landscape that have thus far escaped the forces of man and nature. We can hear the past echoing from place names. We can see preserved and ruined structures or their archaeological remains. We can respect these things and their significance in the past as well as their meaning for the future.

One

First Settlement to First County

Europeans roamed the coast of North America for centuries before the Virginia Company of adventurers chose to settle at Jamestown in 1607. Like others, they sought resources and riches. Since England had been at war with Spain for many years, they searched for and found a secure site along the James River more than 40 miles inland from the Chesapeake Bay. Chartered as a business venture, the company was challenged from the start. The settlers' trials with Native Americans and the elements have been the subject of much written record, lore, and scholarly research. Briefly, the Englishmen attempted to claim land that was already considered home to the Algonquin Indians. Because the Virginia Company's sights were set on short-term treasure, the early adventurers cajoled the natives for supplies and neglected to attend to the long-term needs of a proper settlement. They were befriended at first, but the area experienced a drought, and extra food was in short supply. The infamous John Smith, who had experience with foreigners and exploration, left Virginia in 1609. Many of the first settlers died of malaria or intestinal disorders. But the settlement held on. Smith foresaw that the colony would reap riches from the fecund earth. When a strain of sweet tobacco was cultivated and took off as the area's primary cash crop, the first citizens of England's Virginia colony discovered their gold. Women, slaves, and representative government arrived in 1619. A well-orchestrated Native American massacre nearly ended the experiment in 1622. The Virginia Company lost its charter in 1624, and the settlement became a royal colony. Ten years later, the crown divided that colony into shires, or counties; James City County was among them. A curious relic from the early Colonial period is the archaeological trace of a stone house that overlooked Ware Creek. Although it may have served as a fortification, its original builder and function remain a mystery. The name Stonehouse, however, lives on in upper James City County as the name of a magisterial district, a planned community, a church, and more.

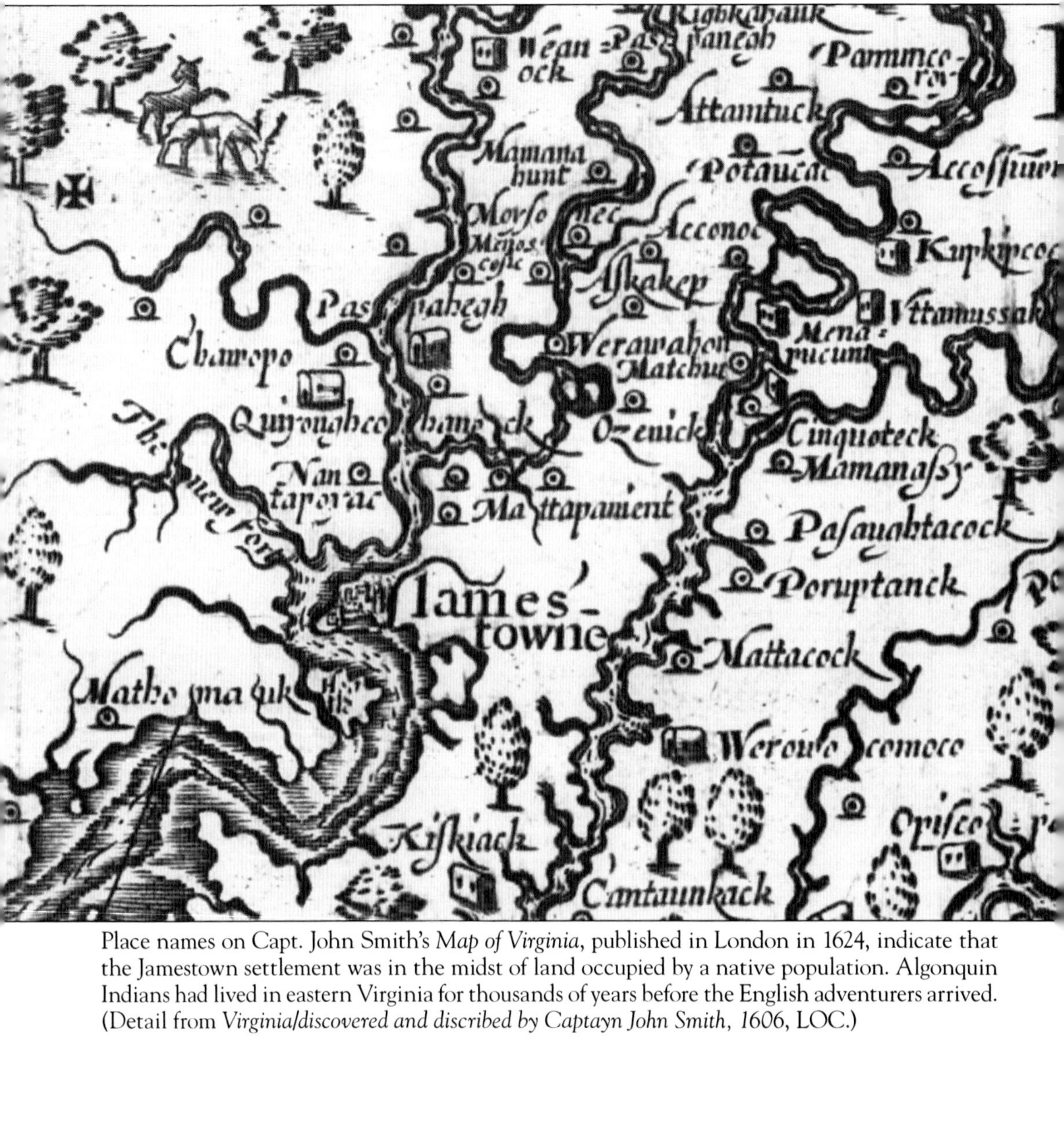

Place names on Capt. John Smith's *Map of Virginia*, published in London in 1624, indicate that the Jamestown settlement was in the midst of land occupied by a native population. Algonquin Indians had lived in eastern Virginia for thousands of years before the English adventurers arrived. (Detail from *Virginia/discovered and discribed by Captayn John Smith, 1606*, LOC.)

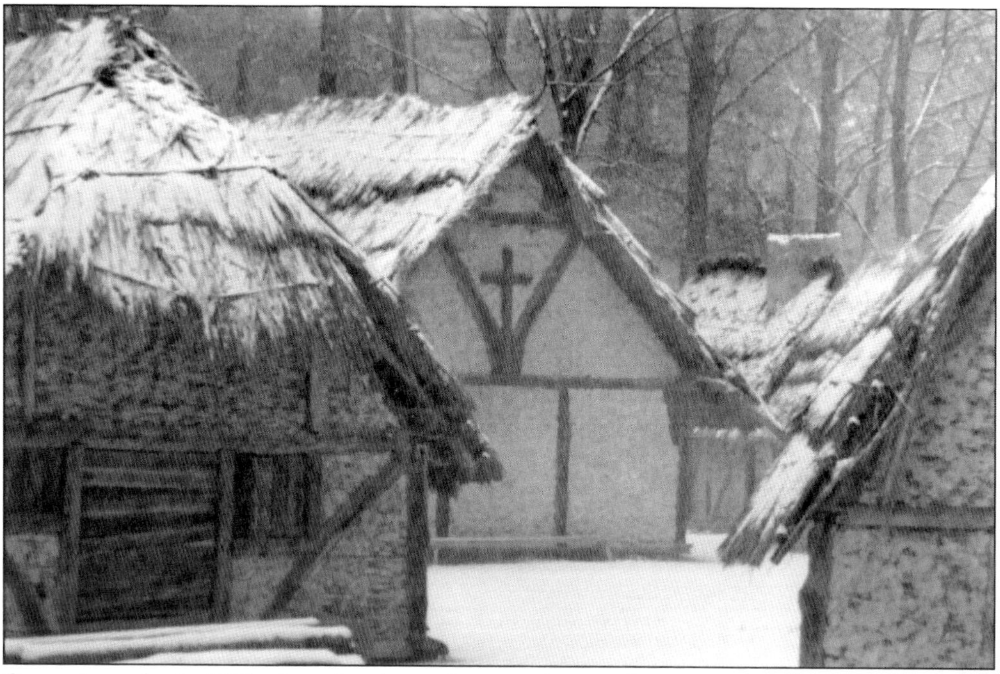

On a winter day in 1978, when the above photograph was taken, a visitor to Jamestown Festival Park could see a re-creation of the fort to imagine where and how the first settlers lived. Today's visitors to Historic Jamestowne can peer into the foundations of the original 17th-century structures. In the photograph below, taken on the 400th anniversary of the landing, visitors watched Jamestown Rediscovery archaeologists who excavated artifacts, including several sword parts, from a subterranean feature inside James Fort. (Above, SEL; below, APVA/HJ.)

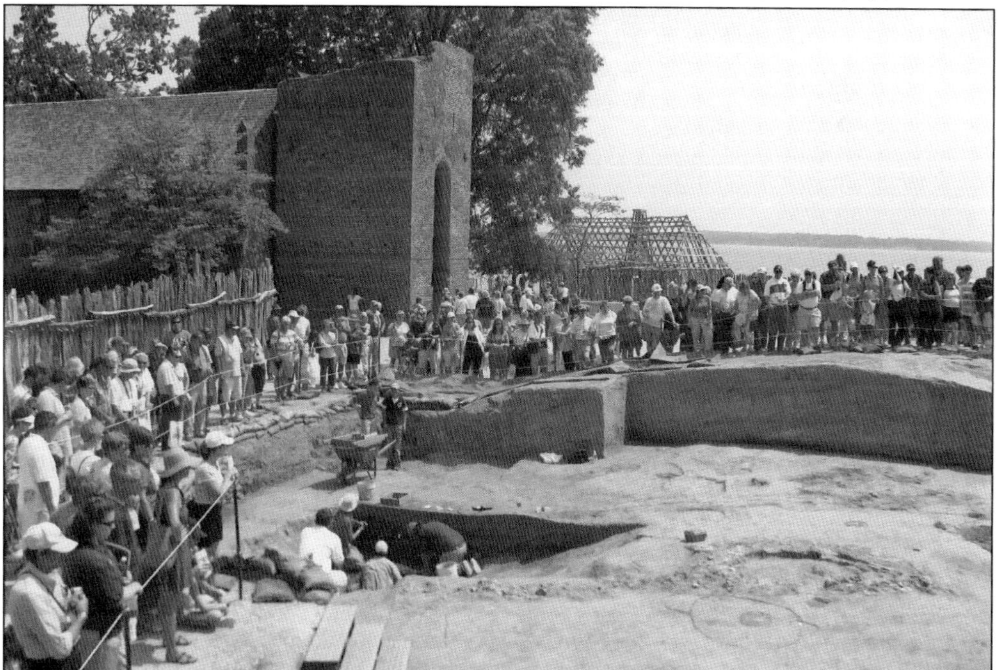

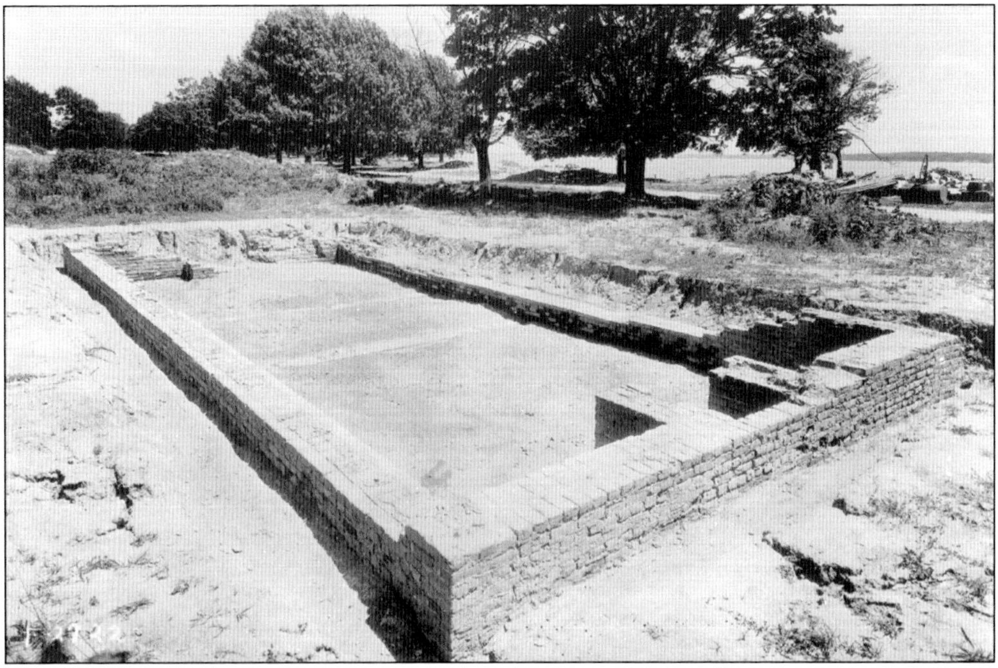

In 1934, three hundred years after James City County was founded, the remains of the New Towne on Jamestown Island were excavated. A National Park Service report accompanying the photograph above states, "The year 1624 marked a new era in the development of Jamestown. A more substantial type of building began to be erected in that section of the city known in this year as 'The New Towne.' This foundation is one of those buildings." (Both, Historic American Buildings Survey, LOC.)

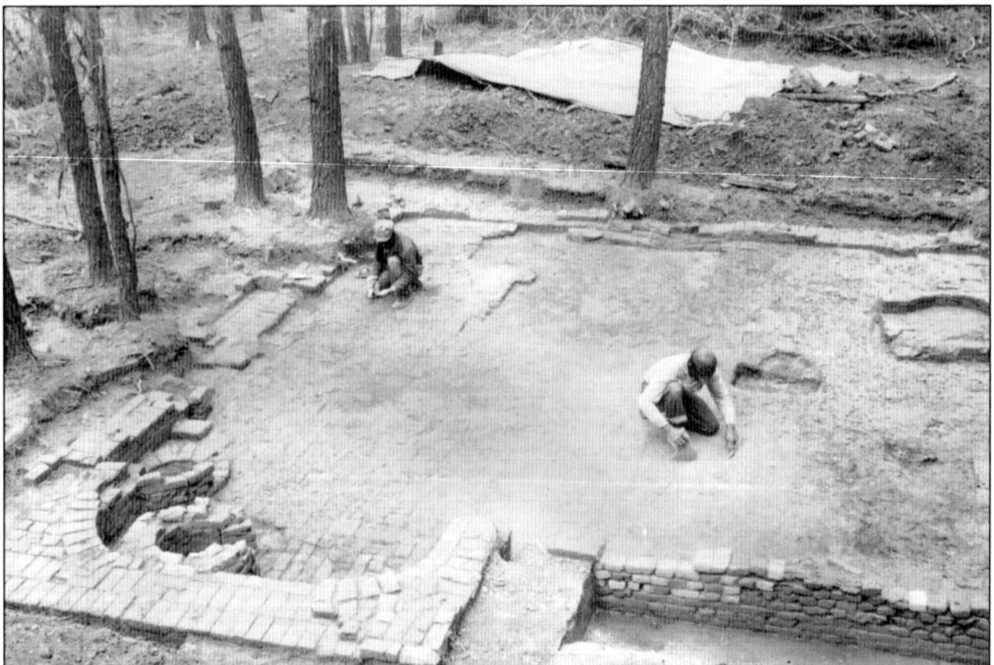

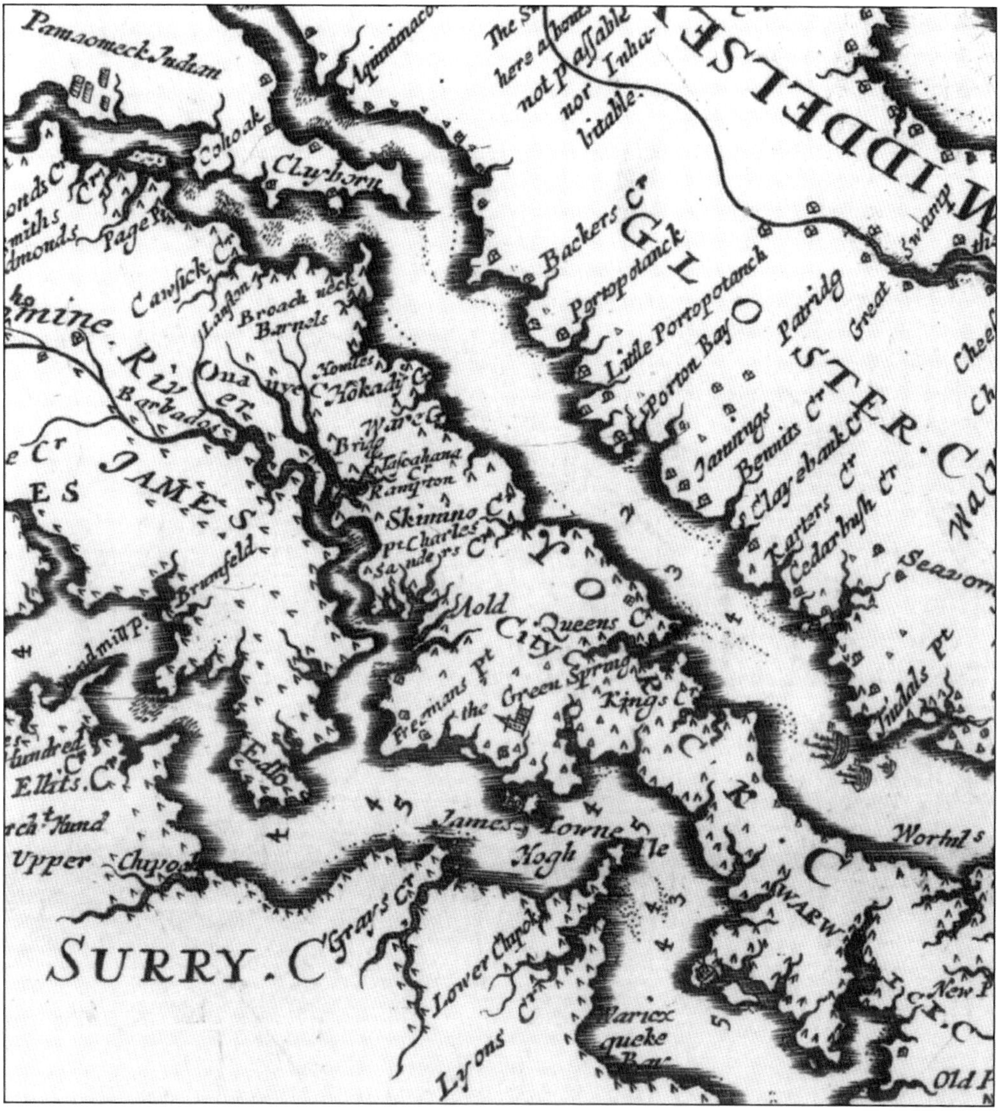

James City County was formed in 1634 when the Virginia colony was divided into eight shires, or counties. James City included what is now Surry County across the James River, as well as part of Charles City County and some of New Kent County, as is suggested in this detail from Augustine Herrmann's 1673 map. A comparison of this map to the one on page 10 illustrates how quickly the county and colony were peopled with newcomers, including landowning middling and minor gentry, the impoverished from the fringes of the British Isles, and African slaves. From 1650 to the American Revolution, more than half of the white immigrants to the Chesapeake region were indentured servants. Millions of Africans were brought to British North America during this period. (*Map of Virginia, 1673*, by Augustine Herrmann, LOC.)

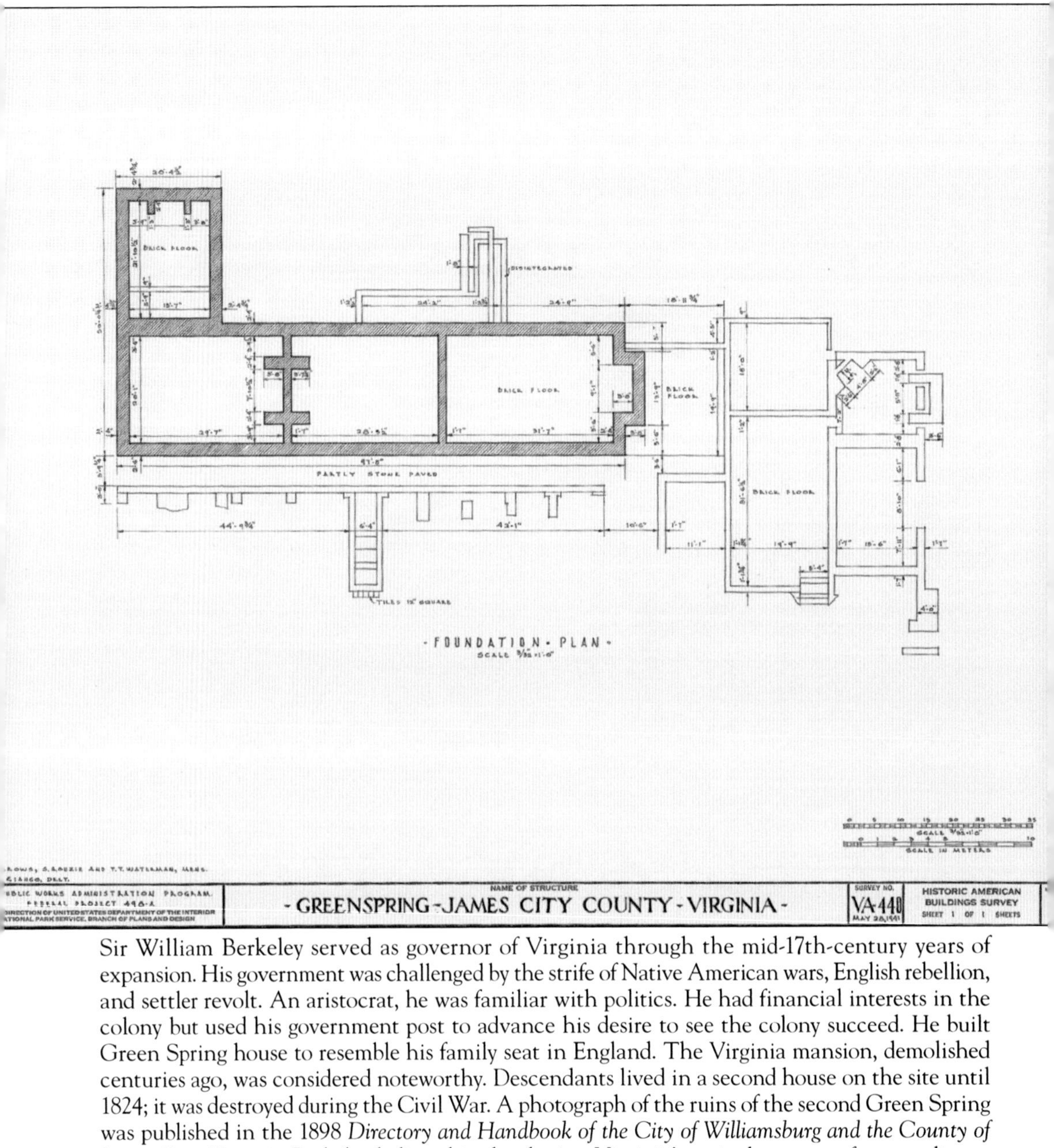

Sir William Berkeley served as governor of Virginia through the mid-17th-century years of expansion. His government was challenged by the strife of Native American wars, English rebellion, and settler revolt. An aristocrat, he was familiar with politics. He had financial interests in the colony but used his government post to advance his desire to see the colony succeed. He built Green Spring house to resemble his family seat in England. The Virginia mansion, demolished centuries ago, was considered noteworthy. Descendants lived in a second house on the site until 1824; it was destroyed during the Civil War. A photograph of the ruins of the second Green Spring was published in the 1898 *Directory and Handbook of the City of Williamsburg and the County of James City, Virginia*. Berkeley believed in developing Virginia's agriculture away from a reliance on tobacco, and the fields around Green Spring were his laboratory. He cultivated substitutes including hemp, flax, rapeseed, dyestuffs, pitch, tar, vineyards, orchards, mulberry trees, silkworms, and pig iron. (Historic American Buildings Survey, LOC.)

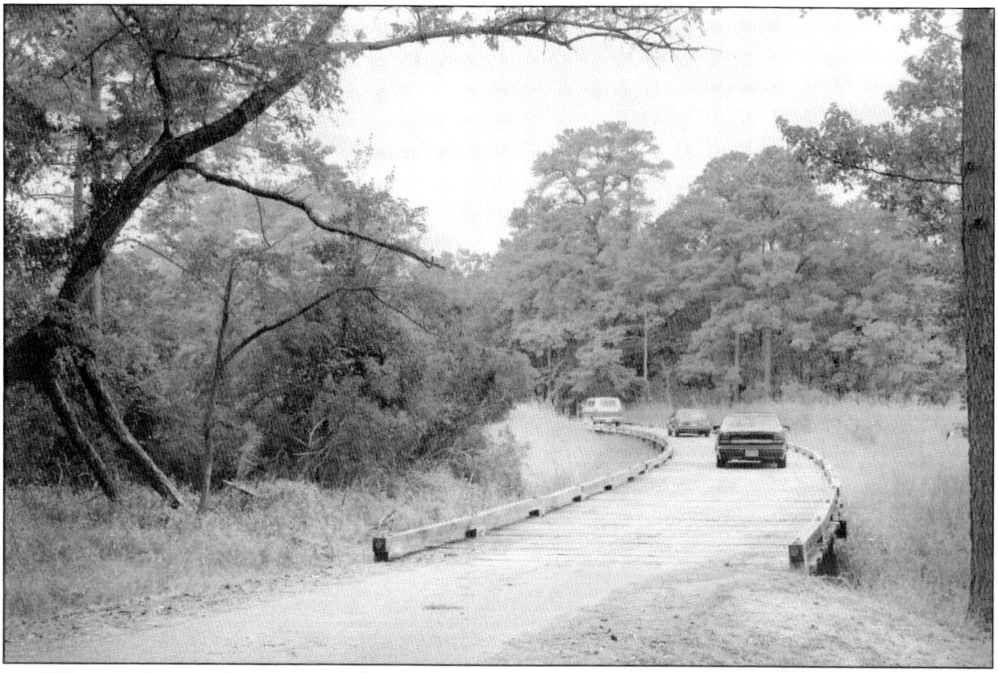

In 1957, a road around Jamestown Island completed the Colonial Parkway project. The parkway and island tour road were built at a time when slower and less congested travel allowed sightseeing by automobile to be viable and popular. It was hoped that automobile tourists would be inspired with awe for Jamestown as an isolated settlement on the edge of the known world. Paintings and signs were posted along the way to interpret historians' visions of the settlers' lives, early commerce, and use of the land. The works of art were painted by Sidney King for the National Park Service. (Both, Historic American Engineering Record, LOC.)

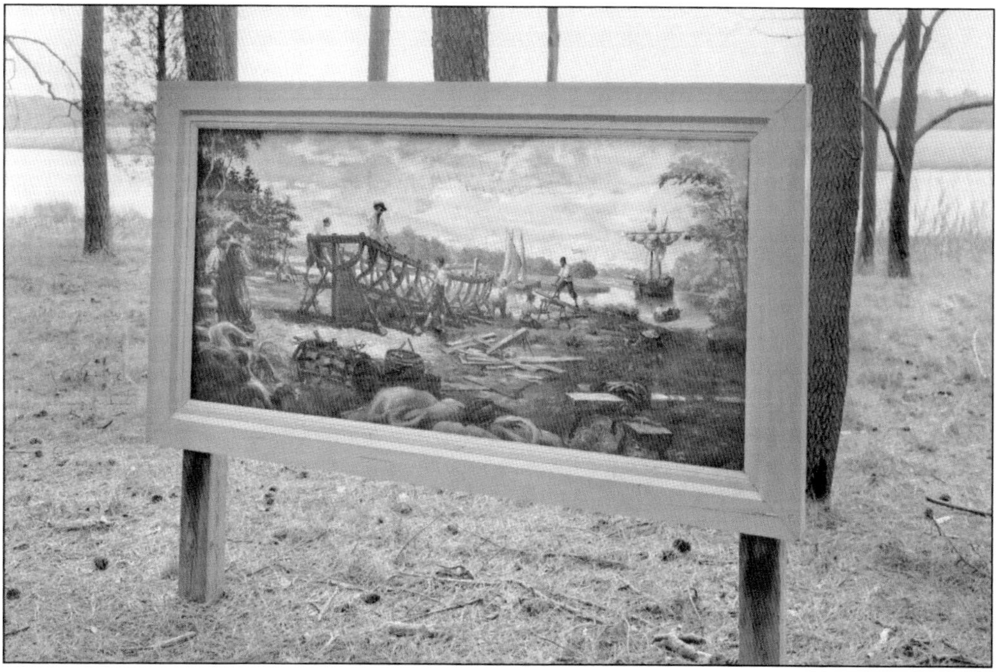

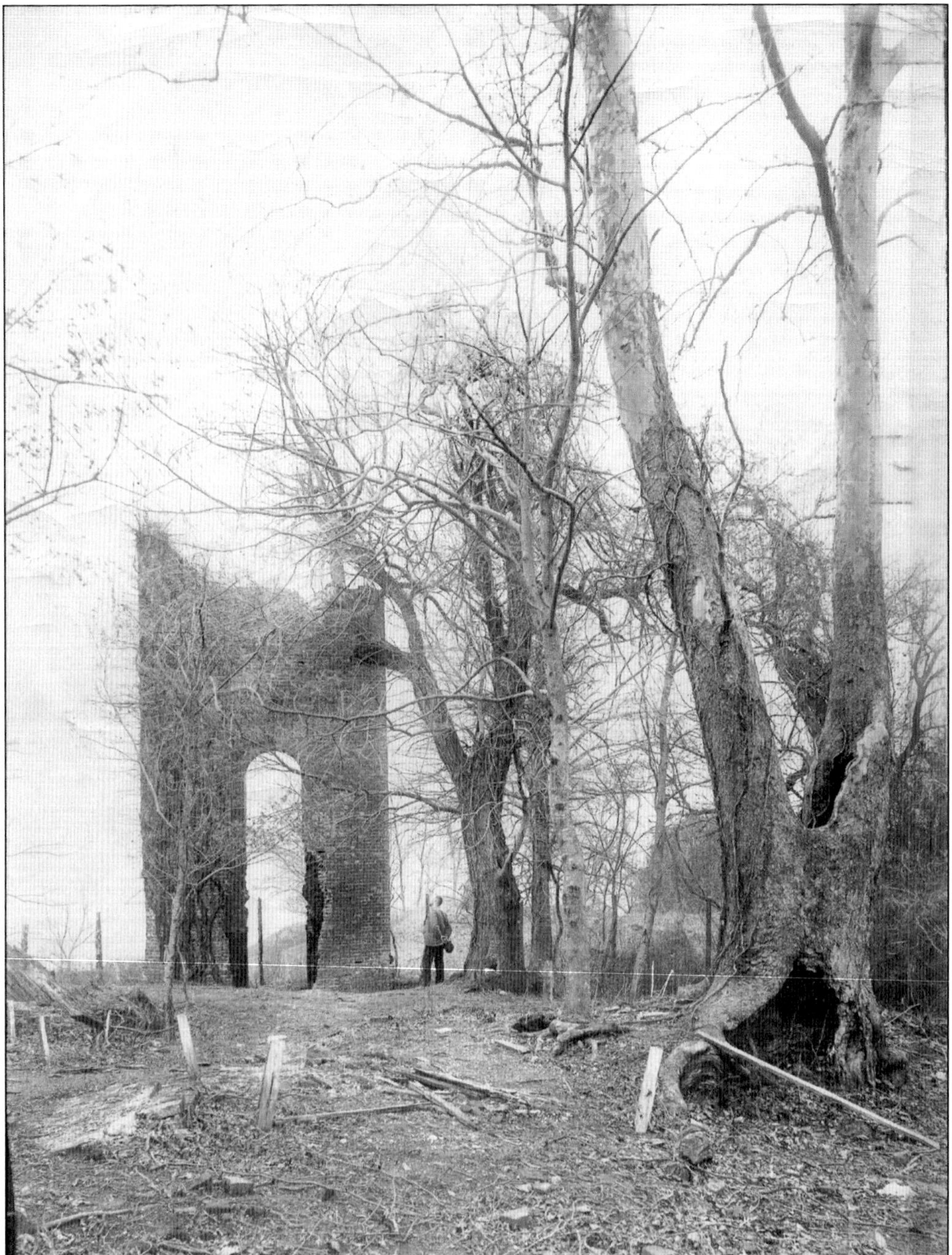

In 1893, the church tower at Jamestown, built in 1639, was the most notable remnant of the first permanent English settlement in the New World. Just before the dawn of the 20th century, landowners Edward and Louise Barney probably recognized the significant approach of the settlement's 300th anniversary in 1907 and donated 22.5 acres of Jamestown Island to the Association for the Preservation of Virginia Antiquities. Dating from the late 19th century, this is one of the earliest known photographs of the historic church tower, the only surviving aboveground 17th-century structure at Jamestown. (APVA/HJ.)

Two

Colonial County

During most of the first Colonial century, Jamestown Island was the center of government activity. Nearby plantations, owned by the county's elite, were spread along the James River between Skiffe's Creek and Warwick County to the east and the Chickahominy River to the west. Massive emigration from England led Gov. William Berkeley to fear rebellion. He said, "Six parts of Seven at least are Poore, Indebted, Discontented and Armed." Planter Nathaniel Bacon, a wealthy man who probably came to Virginia because of a family dispute, rallied the anger of small inland planters against the government. They wanted greater protection of their inland property from the native population. In 1676, Bacon and his supporters plundered James City County estates and slaughtered Virginia Indians. The buildings on Jamestown Island were burned. Government business continued at Jamestown, and it would take two decades to relocate the capital to Williamsburg. Afterward, Jamestown Island was occupied by a few large plantation owners. A century later, visitors to the 1807 bicentennial saw little of early Jamestown. Its material remnants were degraded and overgrown. Inland settlement had spread northwest to what became James City County's western boundary line between the Chickahominy River's Diascund Creek and the York River's Ware Creek tributaries. In the headwaters and central portion of the county, bisected by an ancient Virginia Indian path, James City County was populated by middling to prosperous farmers, as well as the indentured and enslaved who worked for them. Large sections of upper James City County remained rural in fact and in spirit until the last decades of the 20th century. Many of James City County's Colonial homes were recorded by photographers and architects employed by the Depression-era Historic American Buildings Survey (HABS). Their work is part of the U.S. Library of Congress collection, of which a large portion is digitized and available for viewing wherever there is access to the Internet. Unless otherwise noted, all of the photographs in this chapter are from the HABS collection.

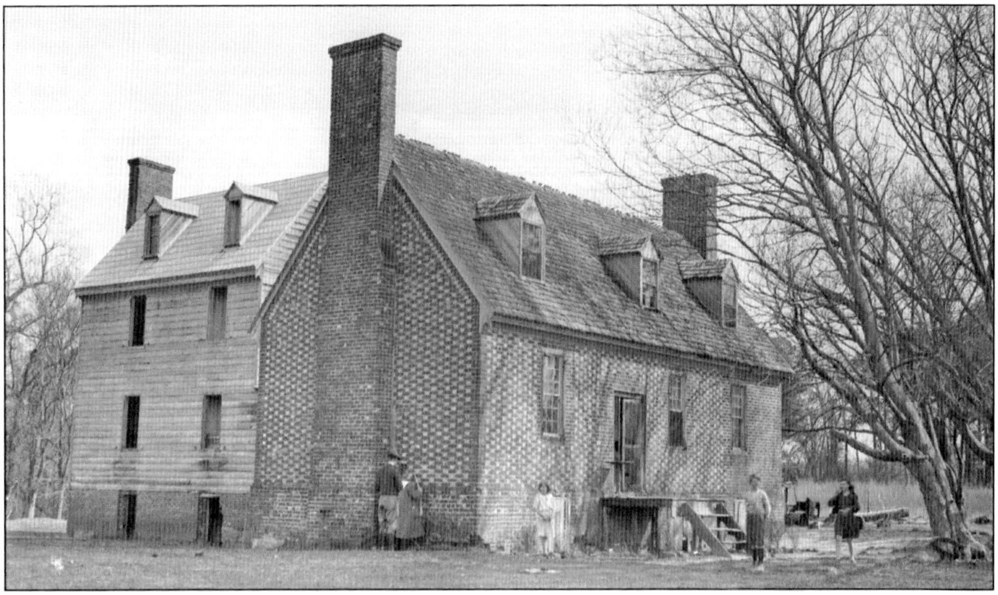

The original portion of this Skiff's Creek–area house dates to around 1750 and the addition to between 1810 and 1820. Tax records indicate that Col. William Allen owned the land in 1768, and it later passed to his son, Hudson Allen. By 1801, Haynes Lee appears as the owner. Col. George Blow purchased the house and farm in 1829, and it was called Wheatland. The house burned during World War II. The brick ruins remained until they were destroyed to make way for an industrial park.

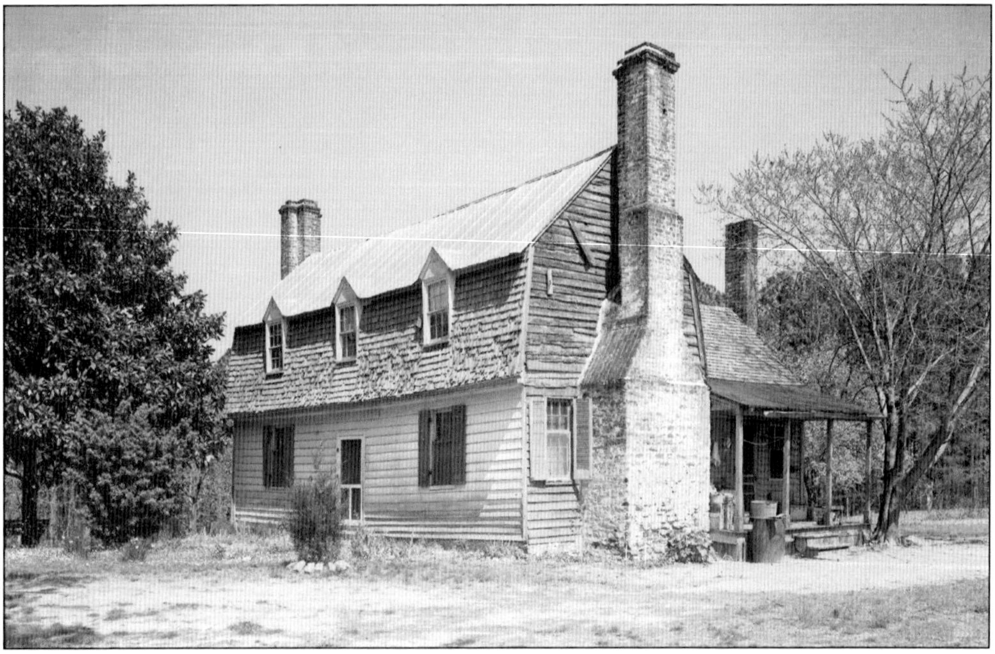

Poplar Hall was located in the Skiff's Creek area. Although HABS notes say the house was built in 1645, it may have been built and improved later. Baker Perkins moved from Warwick County to James City County sometime before 1768 tax records reveal that he owned the property. Perkins lived at Poplar Hall until 1784, and descendants owned the farm until 1880.

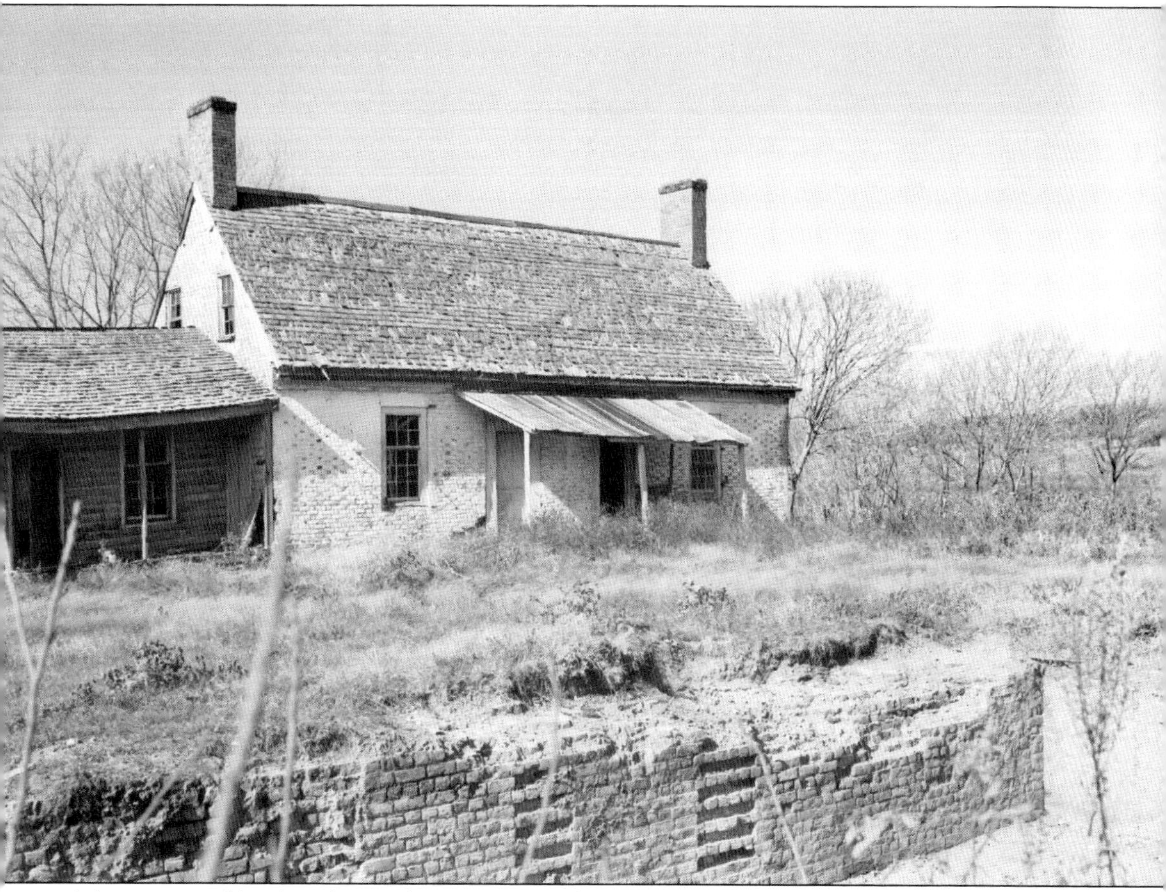

A large tract of land in the southeast portion of James City County was patented before 1637 by Richard Kingsmill and passed by marriage to Lewis Burwell. Kingsmill Plantation was built by a Burwell descendant in the mid-1730s and consisted of a mansion, outbuildings, a garden, and 1,400 acres. "The valuable plantation Kingsmill . . . containing 2000 acres" was advertised for sale in the *Virginia Gazette* on February 24, 1781, as "an elegant and convenient two story brick house, with four rooms on a floor, and every necessary out house thereon." By the time of the American Revolution, many members of the Burwell family had taken up land in Frederick County, Virginia, and moved their slaves west. The Kingsmill plantation house burned in 1843. Only the office and the kitchen were still standing when this photograph was taken.

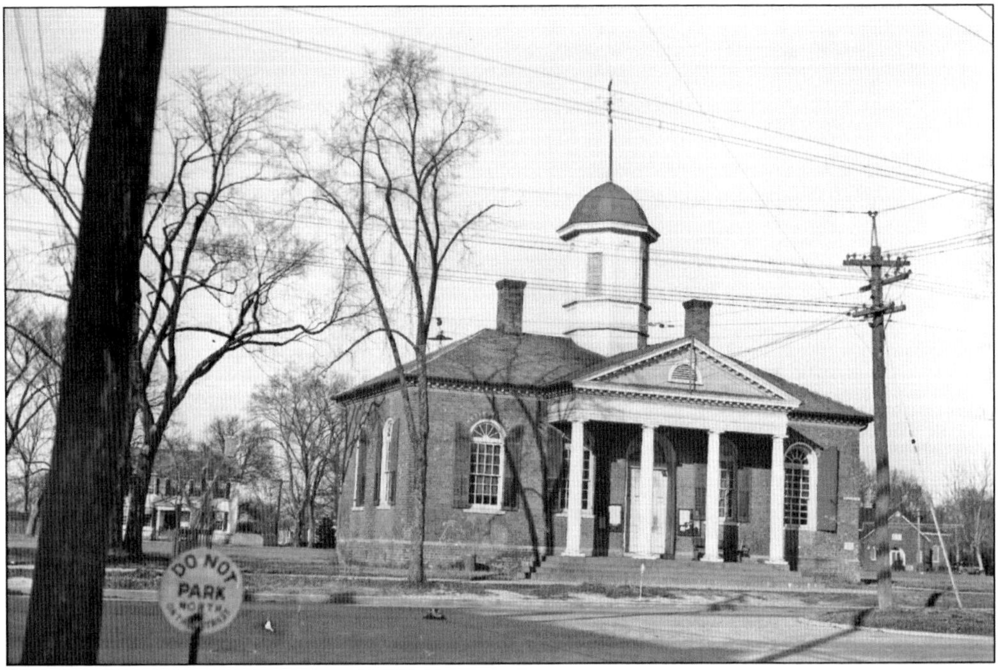

Between 1770 and 1772, a courthouse was built to serve the people of the city of Williamsburg and James City County. The building, which included a courtroom (see page 97) and rooms for justices and juries, as well as an unusual cantilevered pediment, was gutted by fire in 1911. When rebuilt, columns were added under the pediment. The building was restored to its original appearance in 1932 by Colonial Williamsburg.

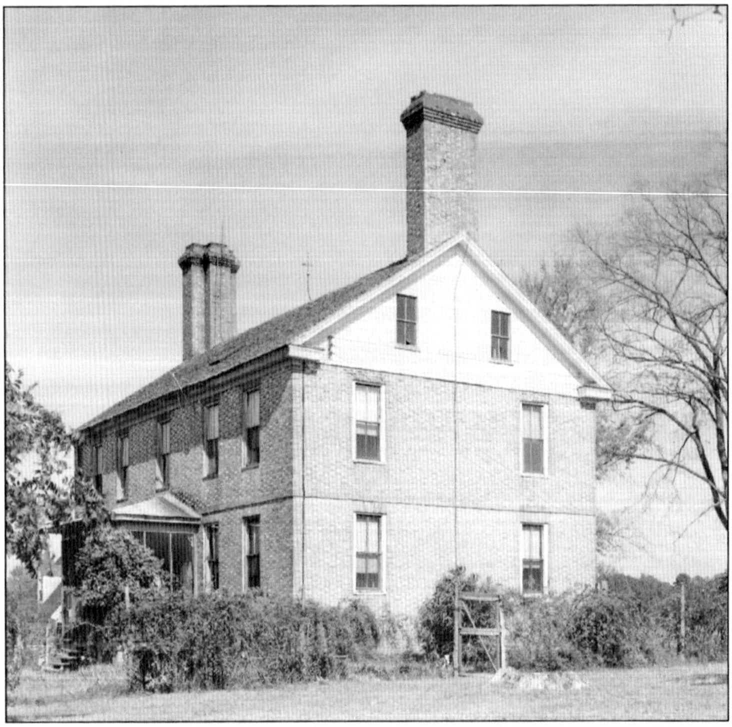

Richard Eggleston acquired grants to land north of Jamestown Island on Powhatan Creek beginning in the mid-1600s. In time, his descendant Elizabeth Eggleston acquired a portion of the land where her husband, architect, builder, and planter Richard Taliaferro, designed their home on the creek's east side in 1740. In the mid-1750s, Taliaferro designed and built the home of his son-in-law, George Wythe, as well as an addition to the Governor's Palace in Williamsburg.

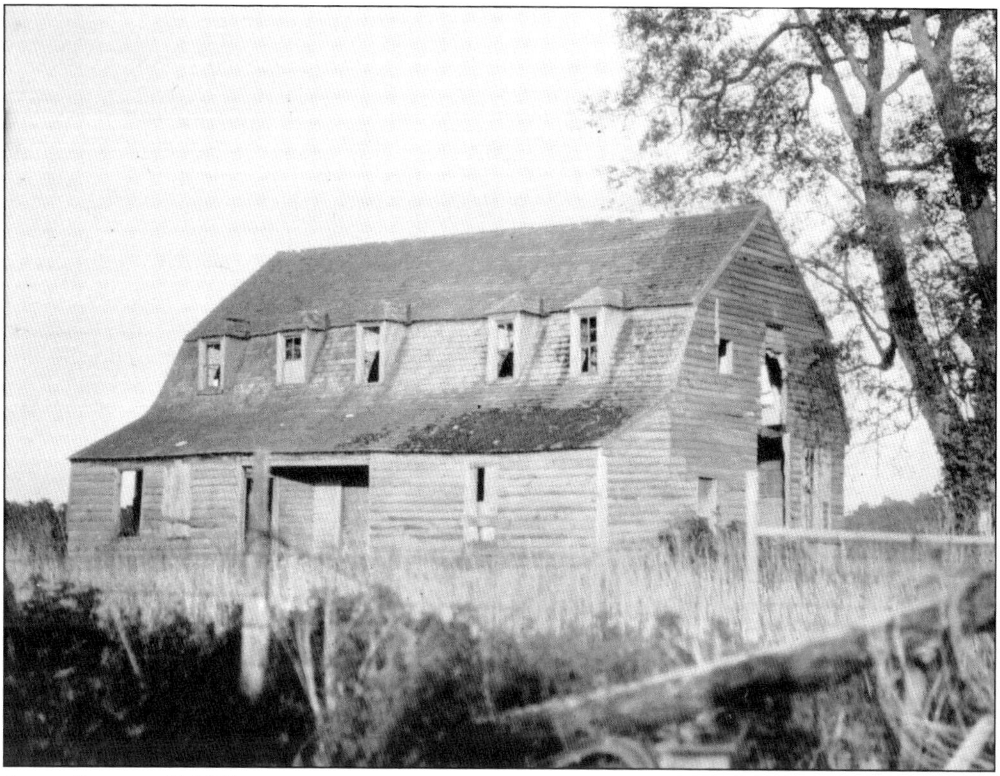

According to a HABS data sheet, "Maine Farm near present St. Georges Farm on the James River . . . was demolished to obtain antique materials for the Williamsburg Restoration. It was a gambrel roof building with hipped roof dormers and projecting end chimneys. It had good simple interior trim, also the original sash and shutters and beaded weatherboarding. The farm is said to have gotten its name from the fact that it was situated on the mainland instead of on Jamestown Island."

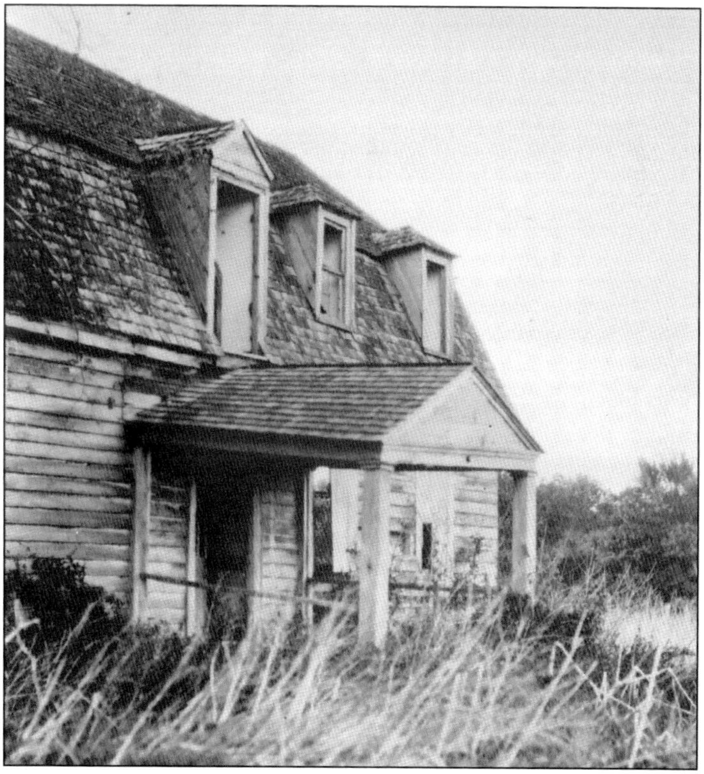

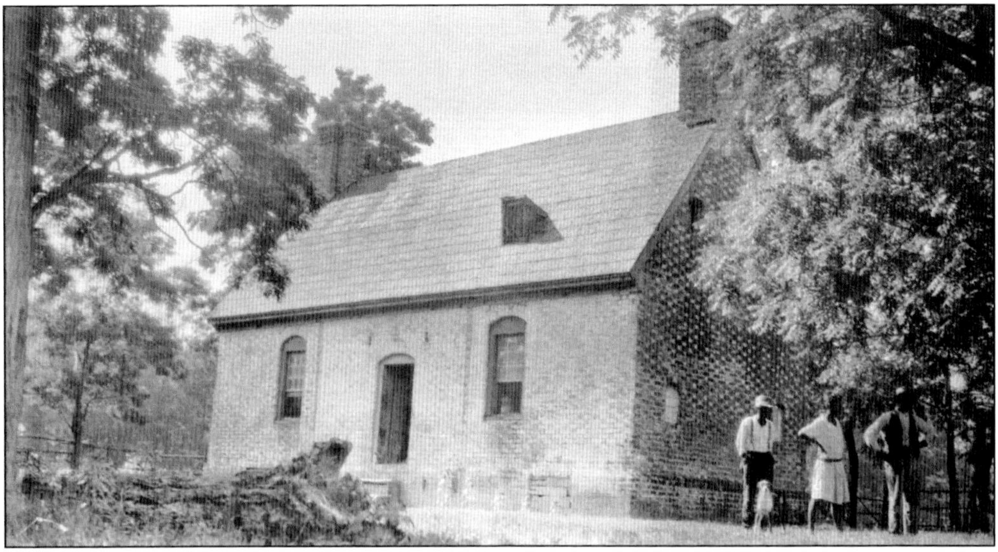

In the mid-17th century, Benjamin Warburton's ancestors lived northwest of Governor Berkeley's land and Green Spring house between Deep and Powhatan Creeks. When he inherited the property, Warburton lived in this typical late-17th-century planter's house. The brickwork is laid in a Flemish bond pattern, where the short ends and long sides of the bricks, called headers and stretchers, were alternated to create a handsome pattern. Today the house is known by the name Pinewoods.

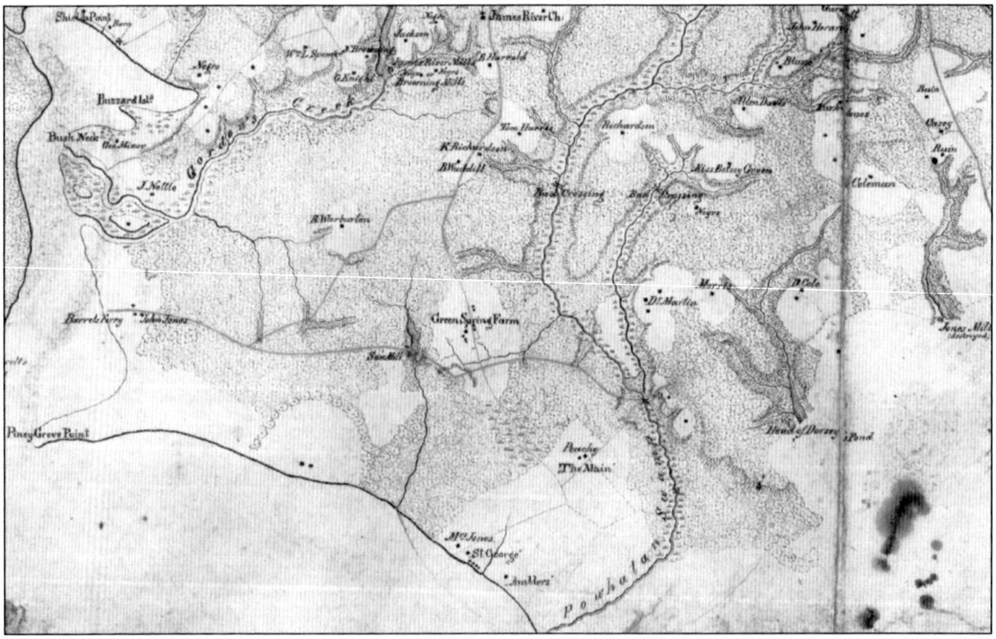

A Civil War–era map notes plantations between the Chickahominy River (left) and the College of William and Mary, east of Jones Mill (today's Lake Matoaka) and Dorsey's Pond (today's Lake Powell) on the right. Most of this James River land passed for 200 years through generations of a few families. However, there was turnover: The name "Dr. Martin" in the map's center indicates that he owned Powhatan Plantation (see page 20). (Detail from *Map of New Kent, Charles City, James City and York Counties, Colonel J. F. Gilmer Chief Engineer*, LOC.)

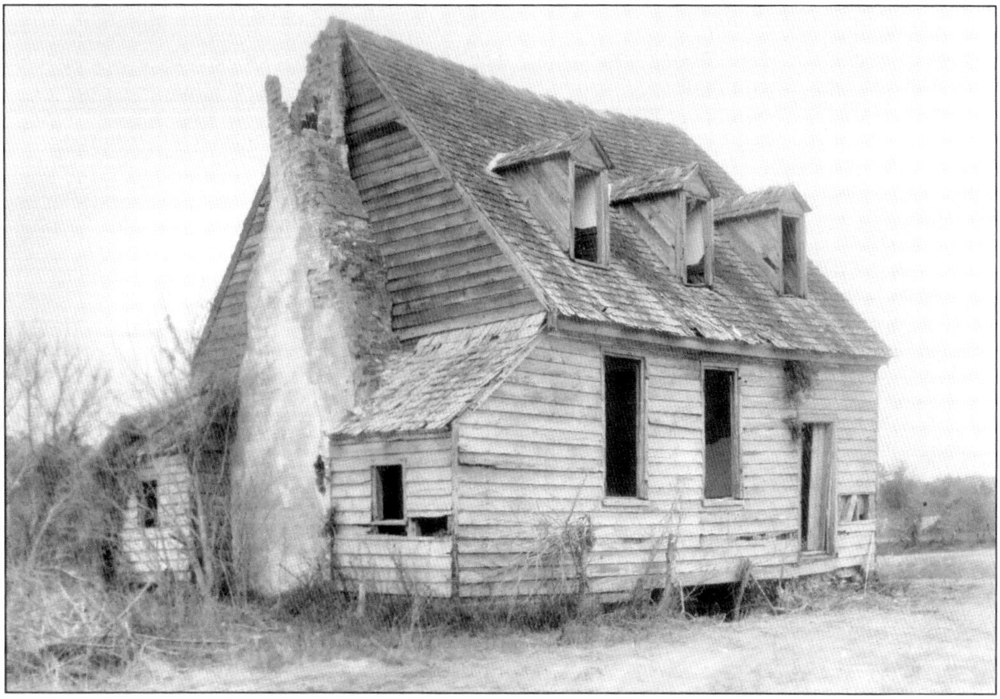

This story-and-a-half gable-roofed house was built about 1700. According to tax records, Edward Richardson purchased this tract from Sylvanus Prince in 1787–1788. The HABS surveyor noted the condition as "ruinous," although the interior trim was thought to be of "considerable interest." The stairway balustrade was described as of "the so-call Chinese Chippendale style." The house was located in the Croaker area but no longer exists. Richardson family members owned considerable acreage and other dwellings in the area.

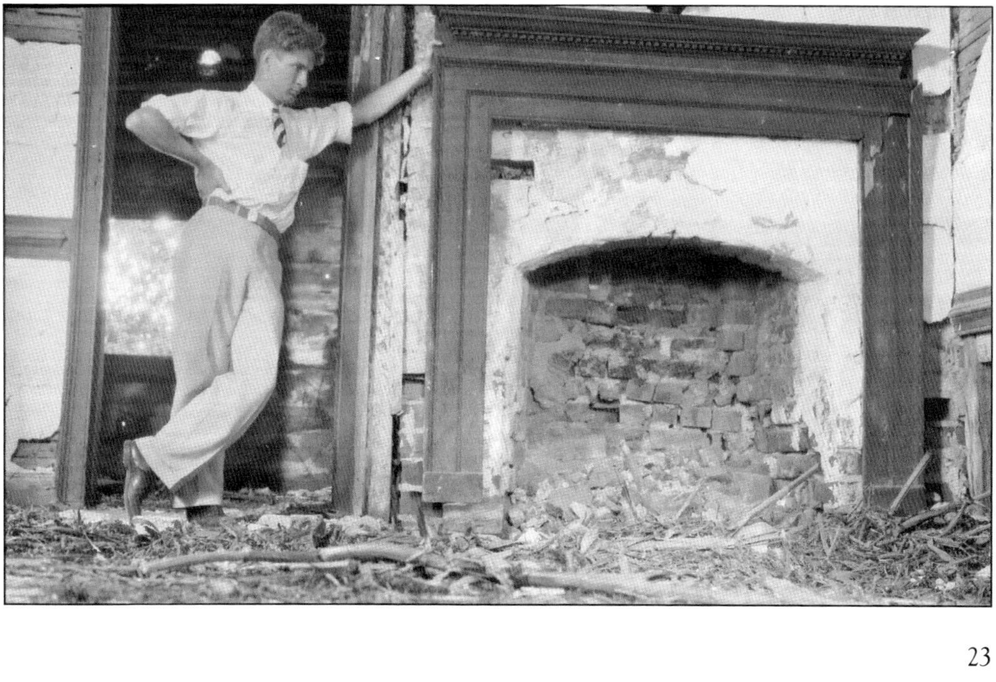

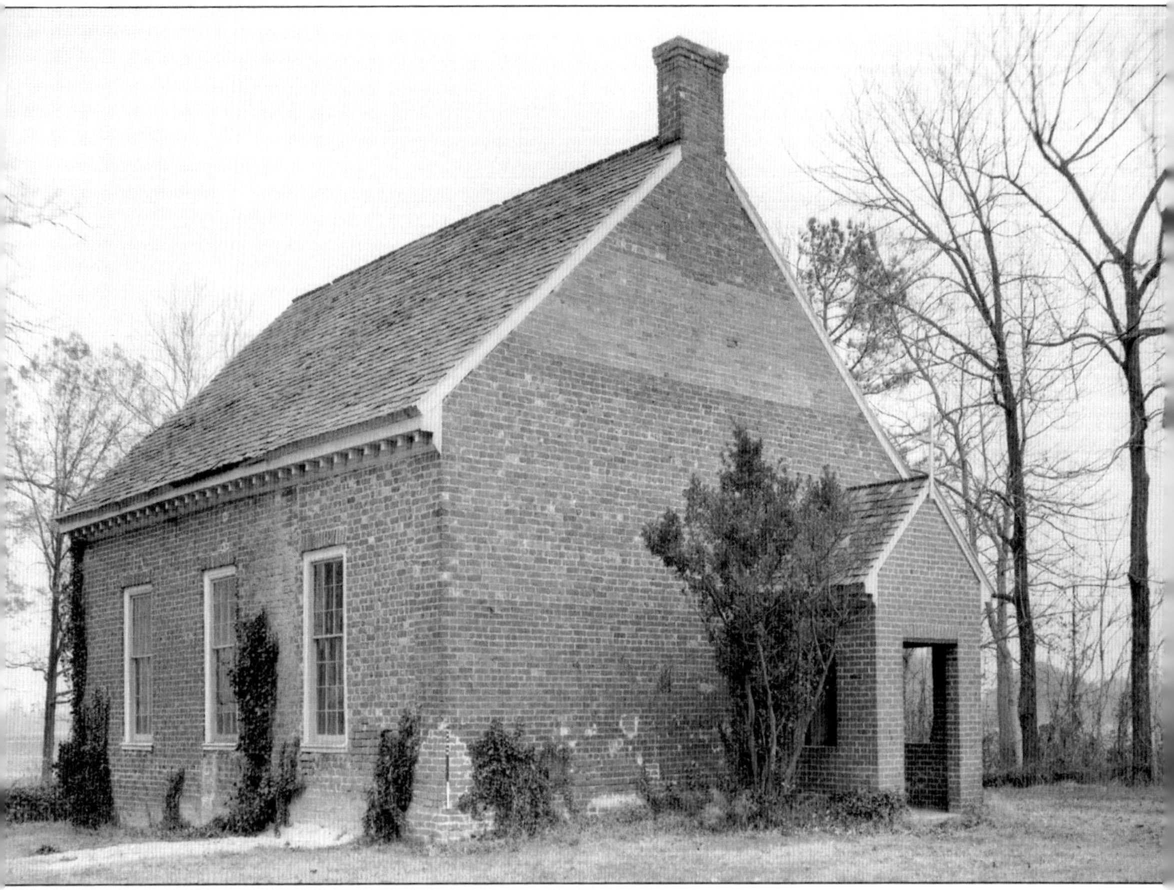

Built in 1734, Hickory Neck Church served as a hospital and encampment site for Continental soldiers during the Revolutionary War. One soldier reported seeing the night sky lit by a blaze from the state's new shipyard on the Chickahominy River, where ships under construction for the Virginia navy were destroyed by the British. From its prime location along the main road east and west, Hickory Neck served as a marker for travelers between Williamsburg and Richmond. After the American Revolution, when the Anglican Church was no longer the official denomination, the building was used as a private academy for area planters' children. The building shown is the north transept, which was added in 1774 to the earlier church. In 1825, it was demolished, and the transept was lengthened and enclosed to serve as Hickory Neck Academy.

Three

FIRST AMERICAN CENTURY

When Virginia's capital moved from Williamsburg to Richmond in 1780, many merchants, attorneys, and others followed. In addition, many tobacco planters moved west to fresh land. In 1781, the last significant battle of the American Revolution was fought in nearby Yorktown. James City County bore the scars of war. In the spring of 1781, the British burned the Chickahominy Shipyard, established to build Virginia's navy. The Marquis de Lafayette and the Continentals crisscrossed the county in that summer. Skirmishes were fought, including one near Centerville and Longhill Roads, which may have given rise to the name War Hill. A prelude to the Battle of Yorktown was fought between Cornwallis and the Continentals at Green Spring. Large plantation holdings were broken up, and by 1800, James City County's small farmers planted corn, wheat, and potatoes instead of tobacco. The economy remained depressed until nearly the middle of the 19th century. Farming methods were improved, and steamboat trade on the James and Chickahominy Rivers stimulated the economy. A town center with homes, churches, stores, and manufacturing grew around Burnt Ordinary. In the pre–Civil War era, James City County farmers used slave labor, although machines such as reapers and threshers would have made them more productive. Among the county's free black population, many had specialized skills and lived in enclaves on Centerville and Chickahominy Roads and in the Ware Creek and Croaker areas. Virginia seceded from the Union in 1861. Some families in eastern James City County fled ahead of advancing troops participating in the Peninsula Campaign, and some former slaves joined their newly freed fellows in Union-held Hampton. Following the May 5, 1862, Battle of Williamsburg, Union troops held the city. The remaining citizens of rural James City County experienced turmoil through the end of the war. Afterward, the local economy lay in ruins as black and white alike eked out a spare subsistence.

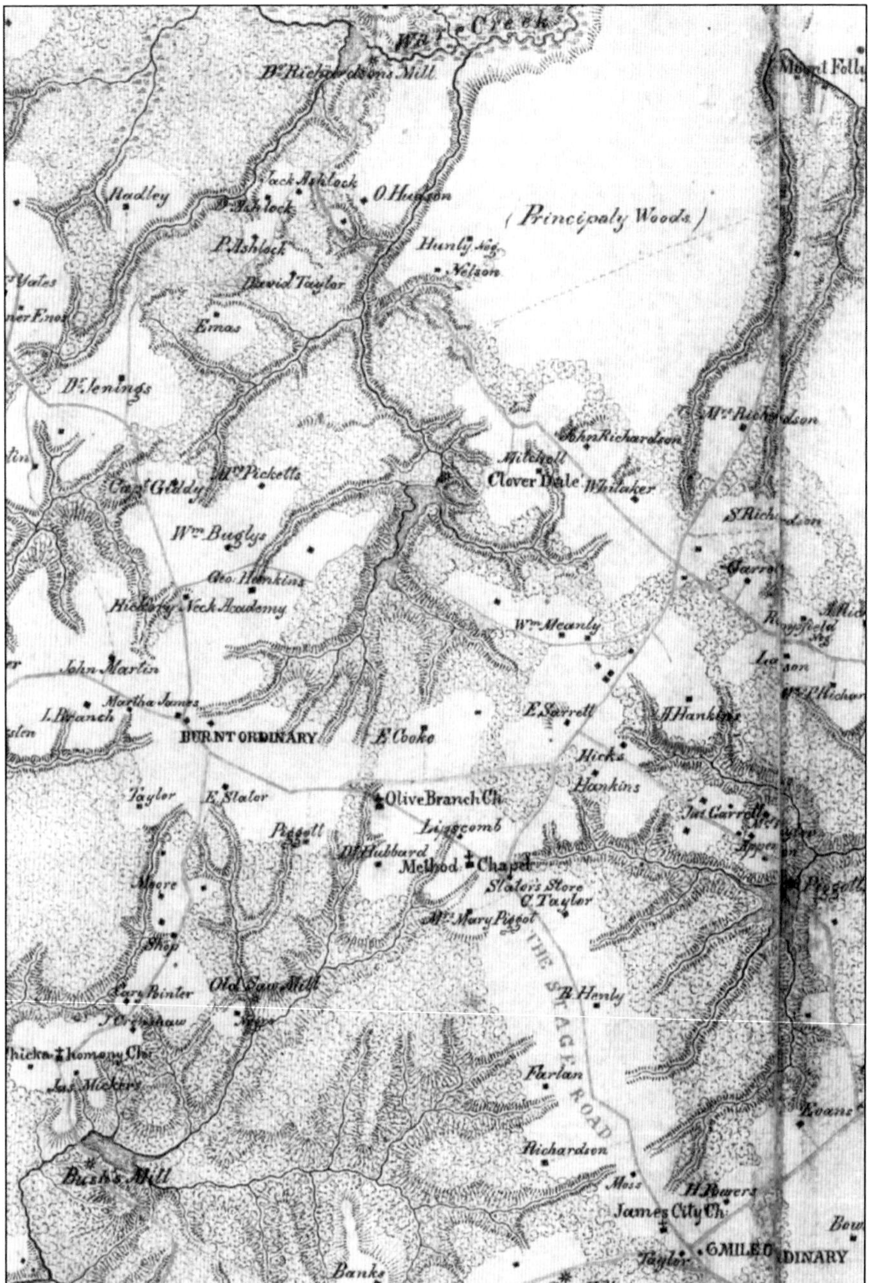

Civil War maps reveal patterns of land ownership before the war. Ware Creek along the top of this map is the northern boundary of James City County, and the Old Stage Road (roughly today's Richmond Road) traces across the map diagonally from top left to bottom right. The road passed Capt. George E. Geddy's house (White Hall), Hickory Neck Academy (Hickory Neck Church), Burnt Ordinary (Toano), Olive Branch Church, Method [*sic*] Chapel (next to James City Cemetery, was moved and is part of Mount Vernon Methodist Church in Toano), James City Church (Smith Memorial Church), and Six Mile Ordinary (Lightfoot). (Detail from *Map of New Kent, Charles City, James City and York Counties, Colonel J. F. Gilmer Chief Engineer*, LOC.)

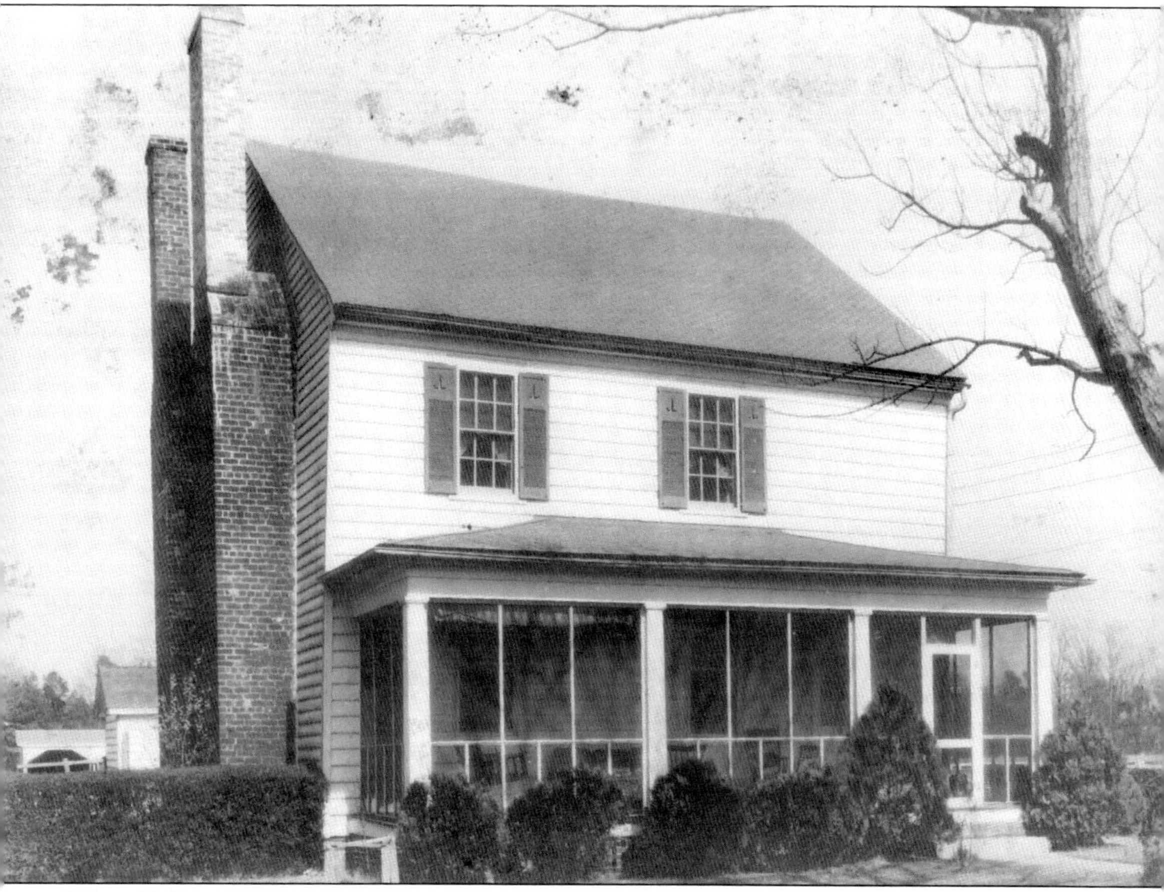

White Hall, built about 1805, is one of the oldest structures in James City County and is currently owned by a descendant of William Geddy, the original property owner. The Geddy family has owned the surrounding land since 1780, and according to the Virginia Register of Historic Places nomination form, the farmhouse illustrates that the quality of housing improved during the early years of the new republic. The Geddy family descends from Williamsburg blacksmith William Geddy and silversmith James Geddy. The "Capt. Geddy" noted on the map on the facing page was George Edward Geddy, a Civil War veteran. (BG.)

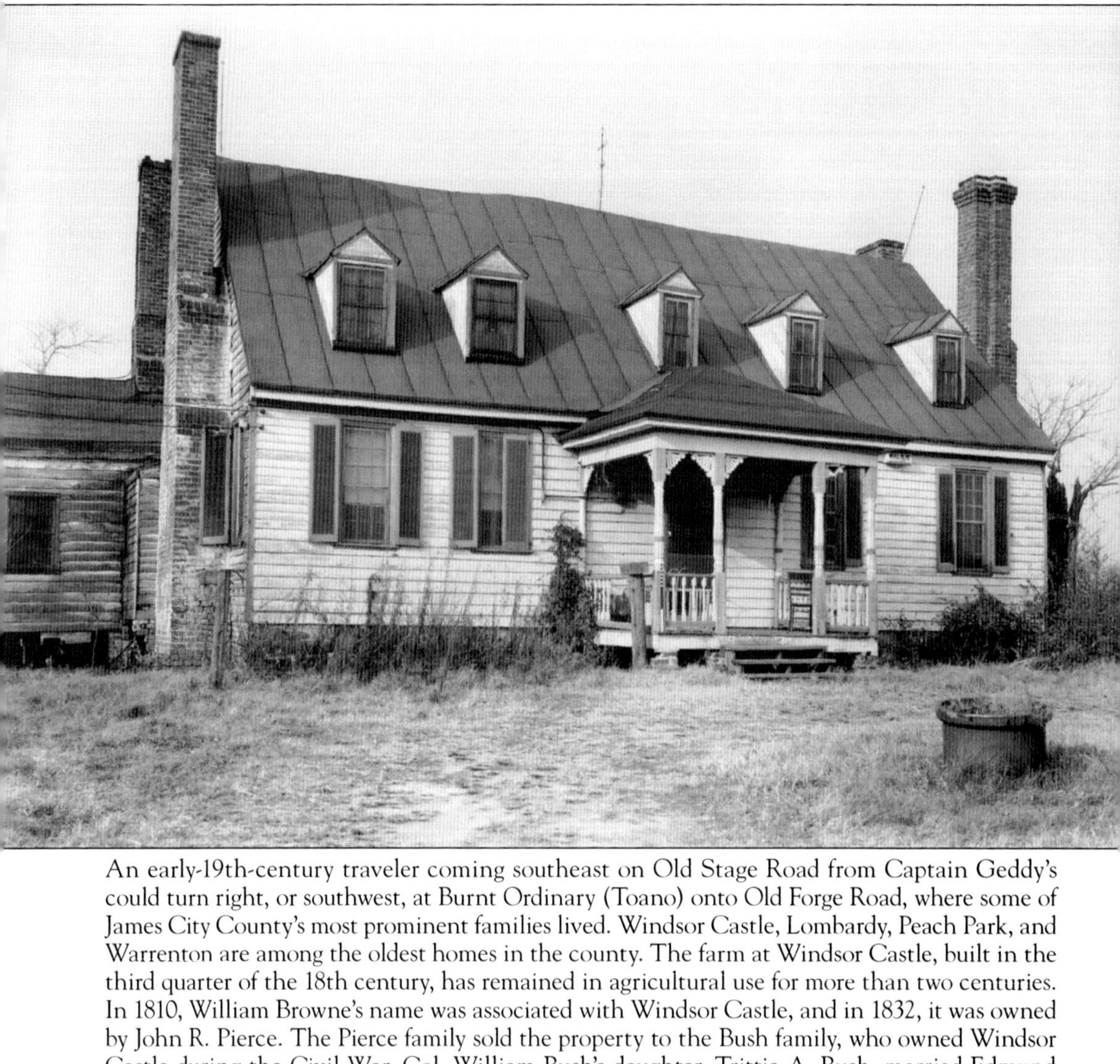

An early-19th-century traveler coming southeast on Old Stage Road from Captain Geddy's could turn right, or southwest, at Burnt Ordinary (Toano) onto Old Forge Road, where some of James City County's most prominent families lived. Windsor Castle, Lombardy, Peach Park, and Warrenton are among the oldest homes in the county. The farm at Windsor Castle, built in the third quarter of the 18th century, has remained in agricultural use for more than two centuries. In 1810, William Browne's name was associated with Windsor Castle, and in 1832, it was owned by John R. Pierce. The Pierce family sold the property to the Bush family, who owned Windsor Castle during the Civil War. Col. William Bush's daughter, Trittie A. Bush, married Edmund Macon Ware. The property has remained in the hands of the Ware family since then. (Historic American Buildings Survey, LOC.)

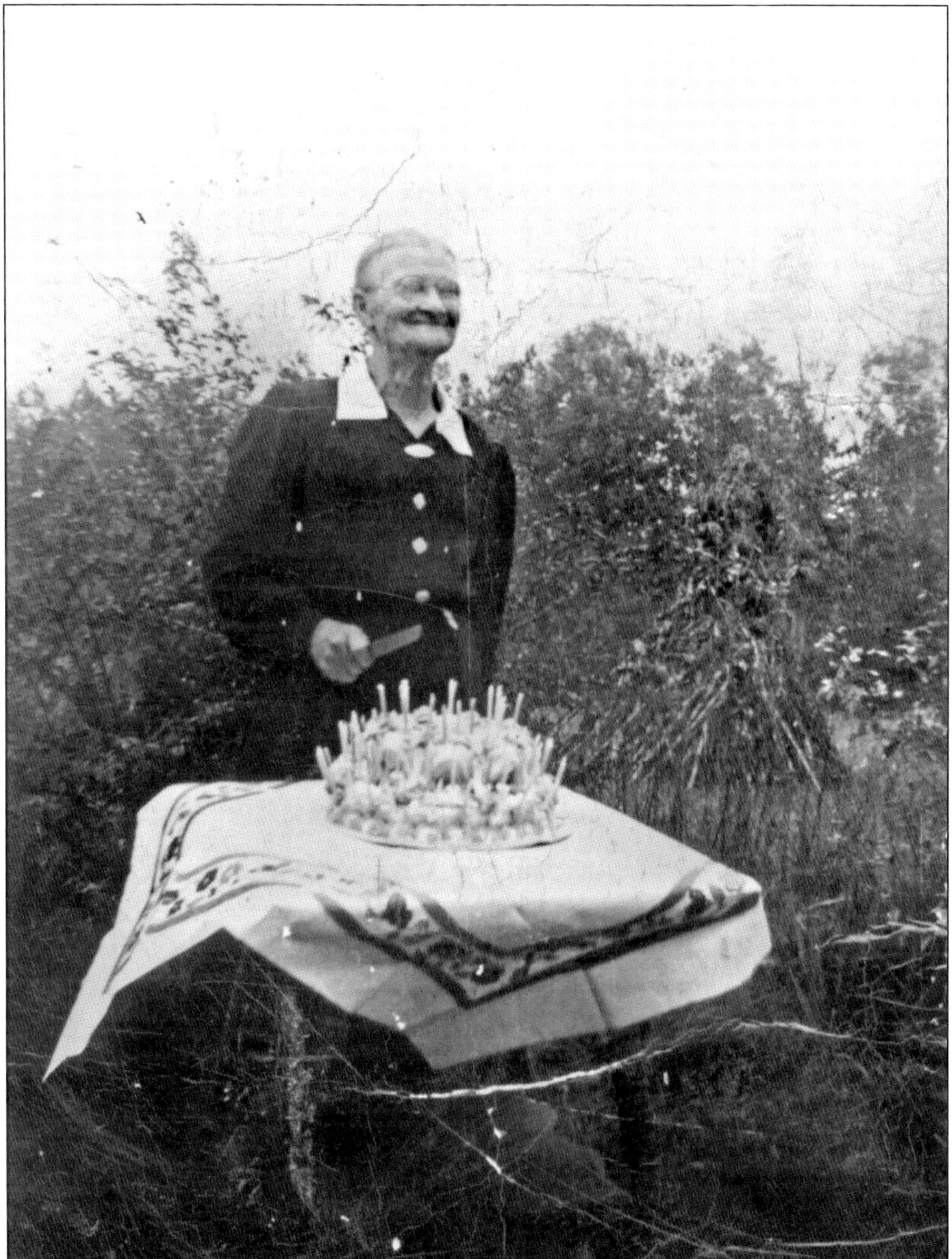

Martha Thomas Hicks Hazelwood (1863–1945) celebrated her 80th birthday in 1943 at her home on Diascund Road (which turns north near Windsor Castle and continues to Richmond Road). During the Civil War, when Union forces occupied Williamsburg, her mother, Martha An Martin Hicks (1831–1916), sewed uniforms for Union soldiers and took fish and vegetables to Williamsburg by horse and buggy for market days while her husband was fighting. The market days were called line days since marketers were stopped at boundary lines on Jamestown and Richmond Roads. There they conducted trade across the line with townspeople of the Union-held city. (GHD.)

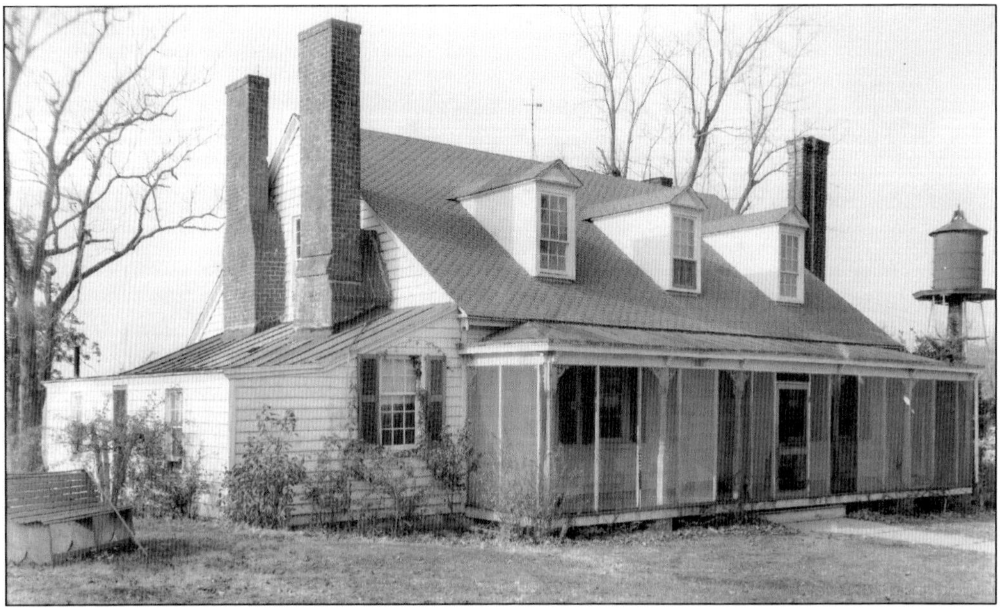

Lombardy was owned by several families through the 19th century, including the Gregorys, Taylors, Warrens, Wallers, Timberlakes, and Martins. Although it was still in the Martin family's hands when this HABS photograph was taken, Lombardy was later sold to the Cottrell family. Their descendants still own the property. (Historic American Buildings Survey, LOC.)

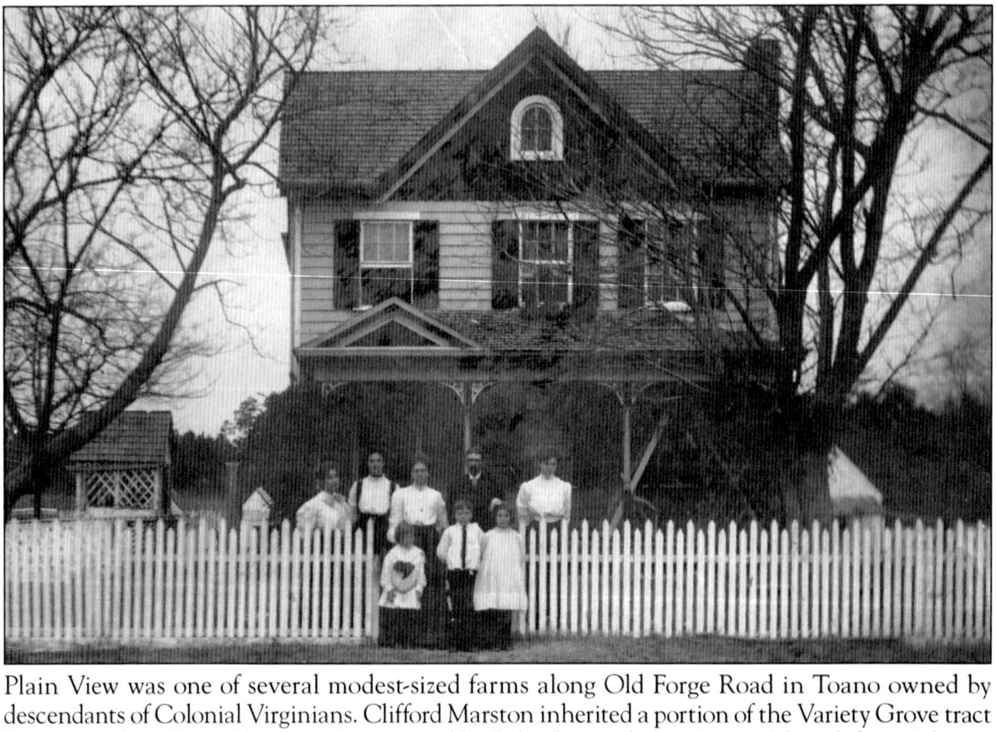

Plain View was one of several modest-sized farms along Old Forge Road in Toano owned by descendants of Colonial Virginians. Clifford Marston inherited a portion of the Variety Grove tract from his father, Dandridge W. Marston, and built his home there. Pictured from left to right are (first row) Marston children Thomas Baker, Perkins, and Lucile; (second row) Alice Ware, Maybelle Marston, Bessie Wynne Marston, Clifford Prior Marston, and Ella Mae Marston. (RMC.)

William Spencer Mahone built this home, located in present-day Norge, in 1840 and sold it the next year to Francis Foster. Wealthy planter Nathaniel Piggott purchased the Foster estate and added it to his considerable holdings in the center of the county. (DBW.)

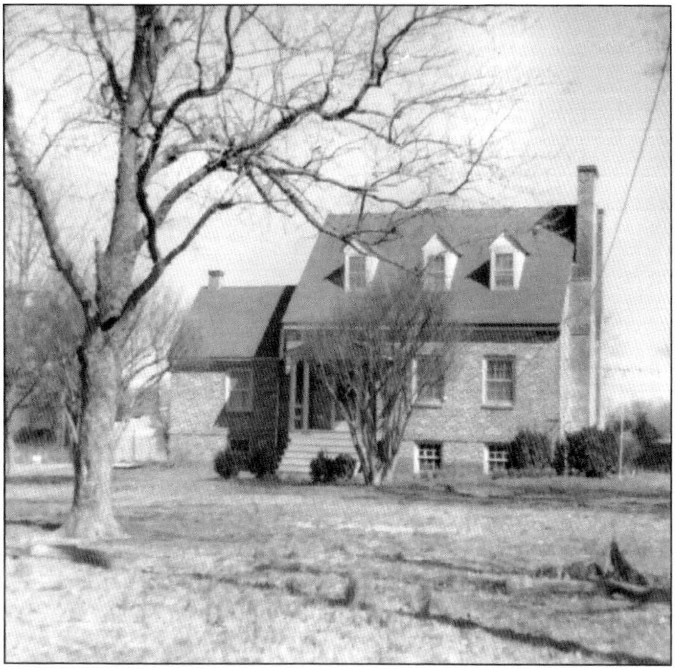

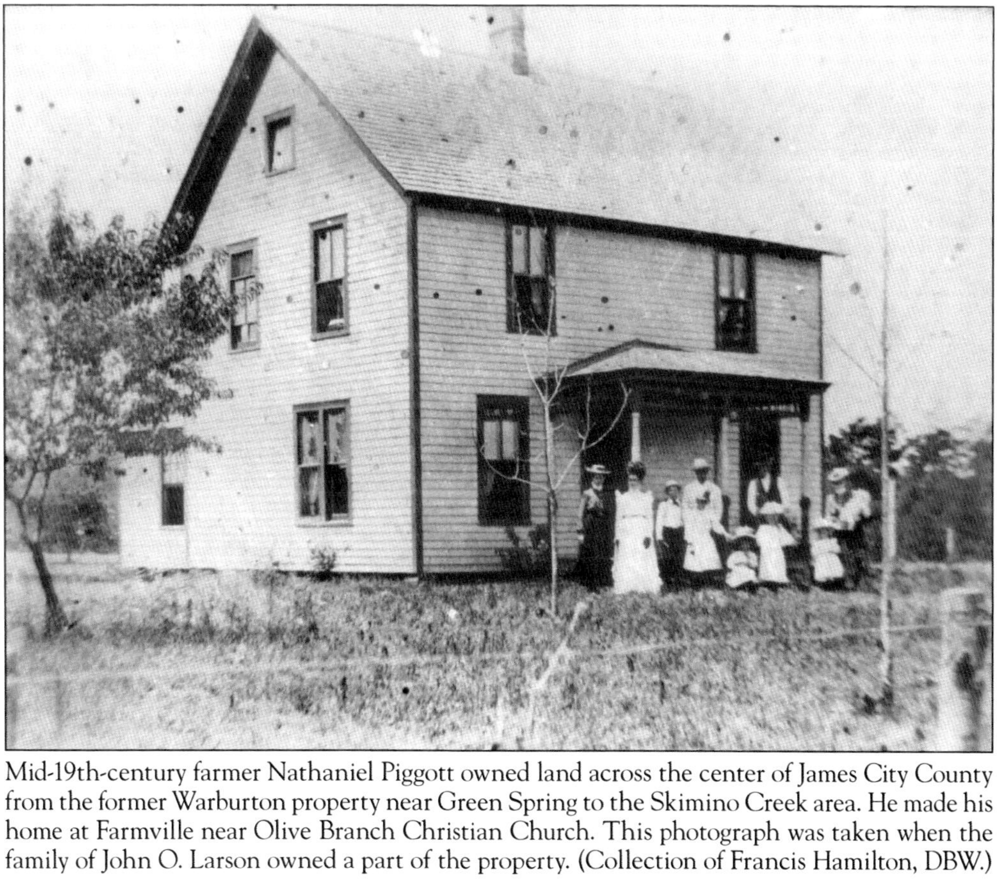

Mid-19th-century farmer Nathaniel Piggott owned land across the center of James City County from the former Warburton property near Green Spring to the Skimino Creek area. He made his home at Farmville near Olive Branch Christian Church. This photograph was taken when the family of John O. Larson owned a part of the property. (Collection of Francis Hamilton, DBW.)

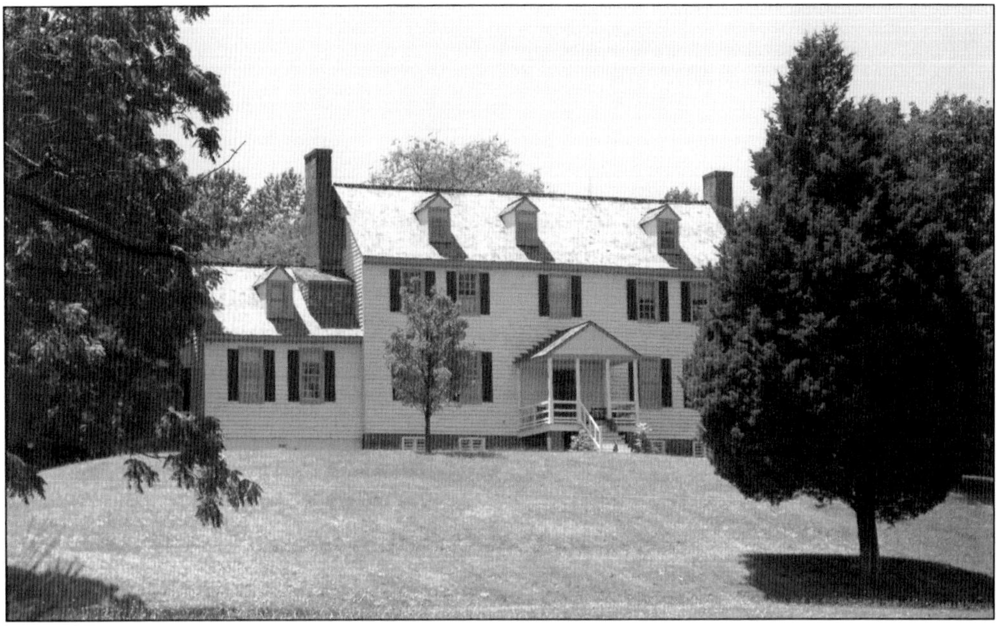

According to tax records, Albert and Zelica Whitaker Hankins's Riverview property on the York River at Skimino Creek increased in value before the mid-19th century. According to Martha McCartney, the Hankinses may have enlarged their home during that period. Just after mid-century, several members of the family died of contagious diseases, and a Civil War legend reveals that they posted a sign warning of smallpox to keep Union soldiers away. (SEL.)

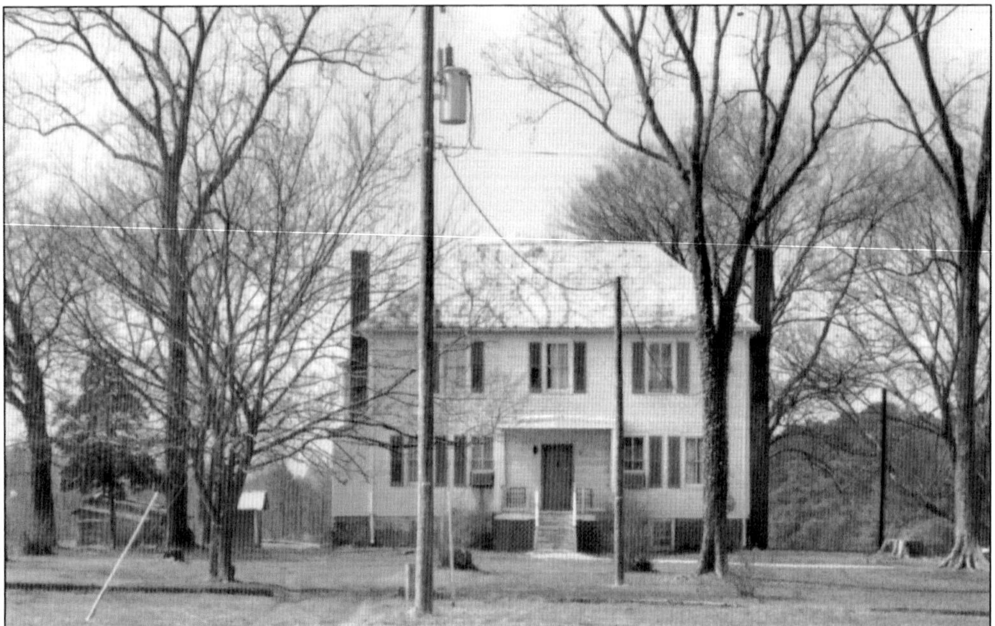

Breezeland was the home of the Farthing family. When farm productivity suffered during the American Revolution, the Farthings were among county petitioners who sought relief from taxes. Members of the longtime James City County family also fought in the Civil War. The house, which was on the south side of Old Stage Road near Lightfoot, is no longer standing. (DBW.)

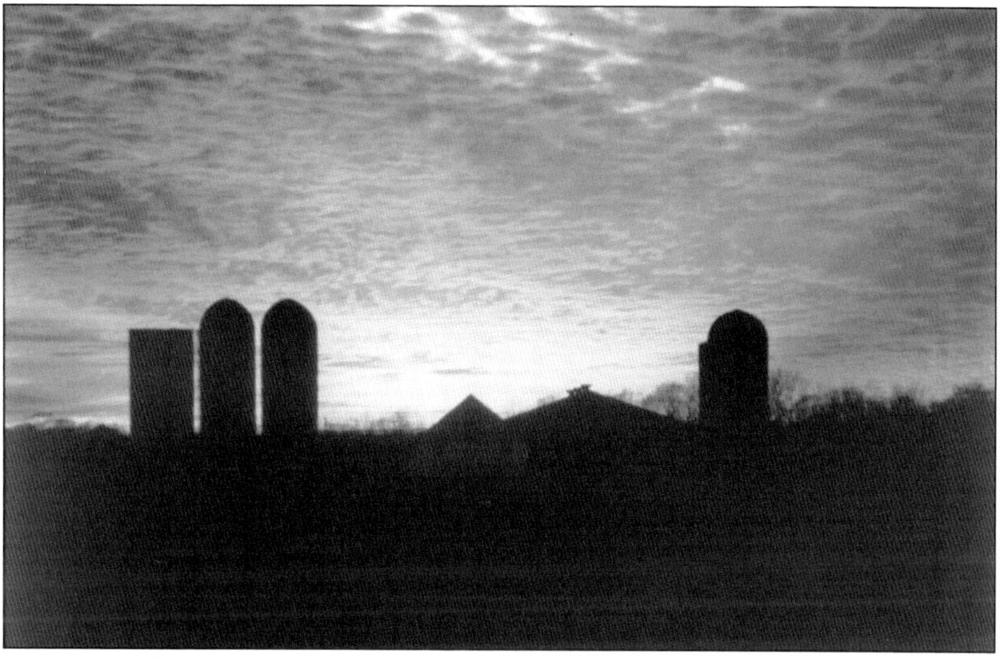

During the early 19th century, Allen Marston began accumulating the acreage that became known as Roslyn. During the 20th century, silos and barns on the property, then known as the Massey Farm (today's Colonial Heritage development), created picturesque views. (DBW.)

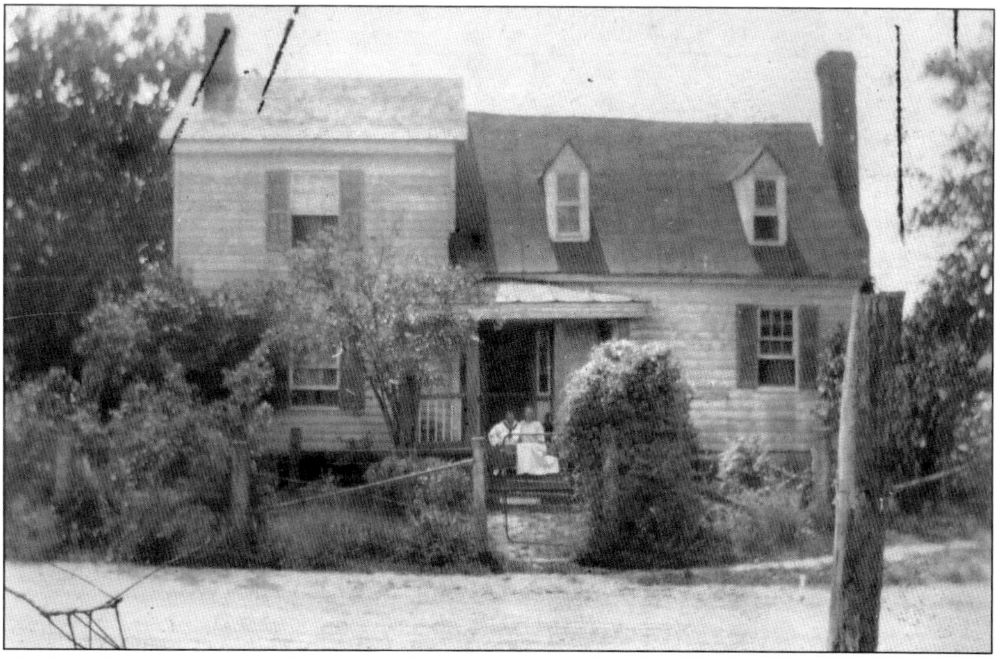

Elizabeth D. Taylor inherited the Six Mile Ordinary farm from her husband, William, who bought it in 1827. She ran a popular tavern there on the well-traveled Old Stage Road. At the end of the Civil War, she could not collect on her accounts. In the late 19th century, Langdon T. Hankins, who had acquired the deed with A. B. Tuttle and ran a store there, advertised that he would exchange merchandise for farm goods. (Collection of Cora Hughes, DBW.)

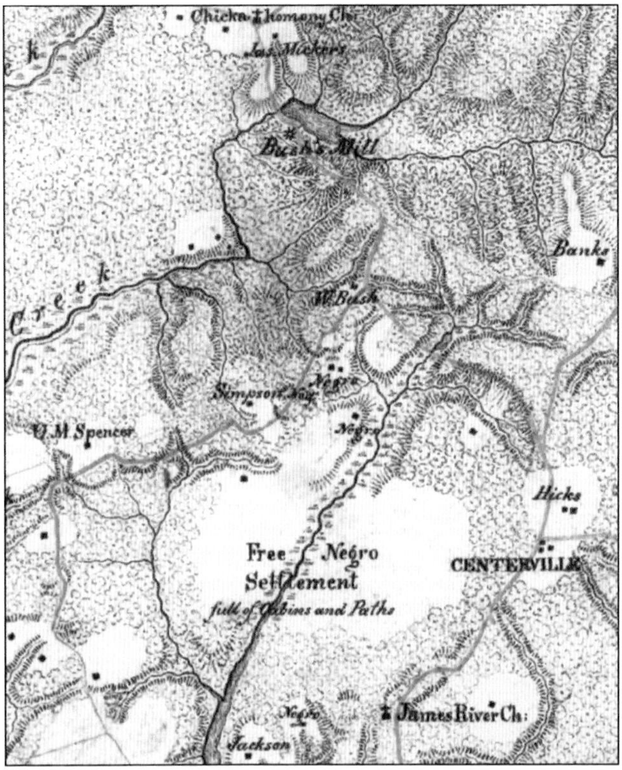

A large tract of land on Centerville Road was occupied by "Free Negroes," according to this Civil War map's maker. William Ludwell Lee, who died in 1803, set his slaves free and provided for them in his will. Today's Freedom Park includes three reconstructed cabins and exhibits that interpret their story. (Detail from *Map of New Kent, Charles City, James City and York Counties, Colonel J. F. Gilmer Chief Engineer*, LOC.)

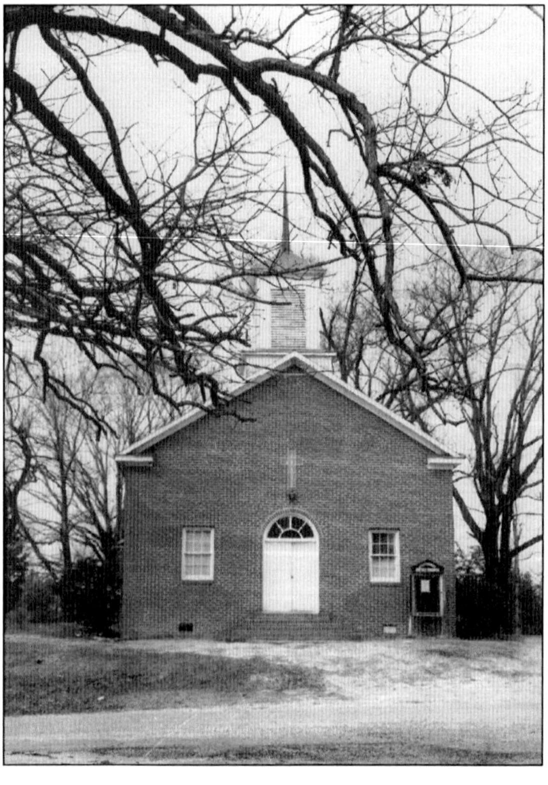

Two miles south of Toano, African Americans founded Chickahominy Baptist Church in 1865 on the foundation of Chickahominy Church, an Anglican house of worship built about 1750. Lafayette's troops camped there on July 6–8, 1781, and the original church was used as a hospital before being burned down by the enemy later in 1781. Remodeled several times, the 20th-century Chickahominy Baptist Church, pictured here, overlies this history. (OT.)

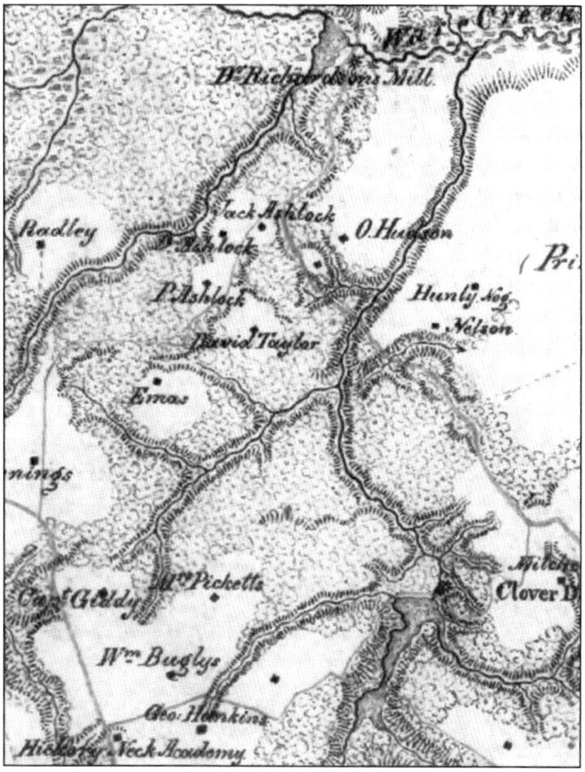

A free African American community was located in the northern end of the county on Ware Creek above Richardson's Mill in the pre–Civil War 19th century. John Ashlock purchased land there in 1817. The Ashlock names appearing on the 1863 Gilmer map, pictured at right, may have been ancestors of Unis Ashlock, seen in the mid-20th-century photograph below. Ashlock posed in front of Hickory Neck Church, which was overgrown and unused at the time. (Right, detail from *Map of New Kent, Charles City, James City and York Counties, Colonel J. F. Gilmer Chief Engineer*, LOC; below, RFW.)

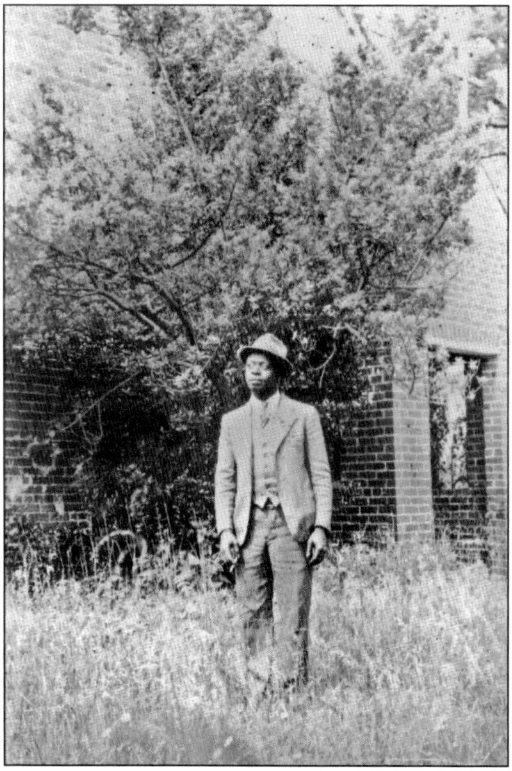

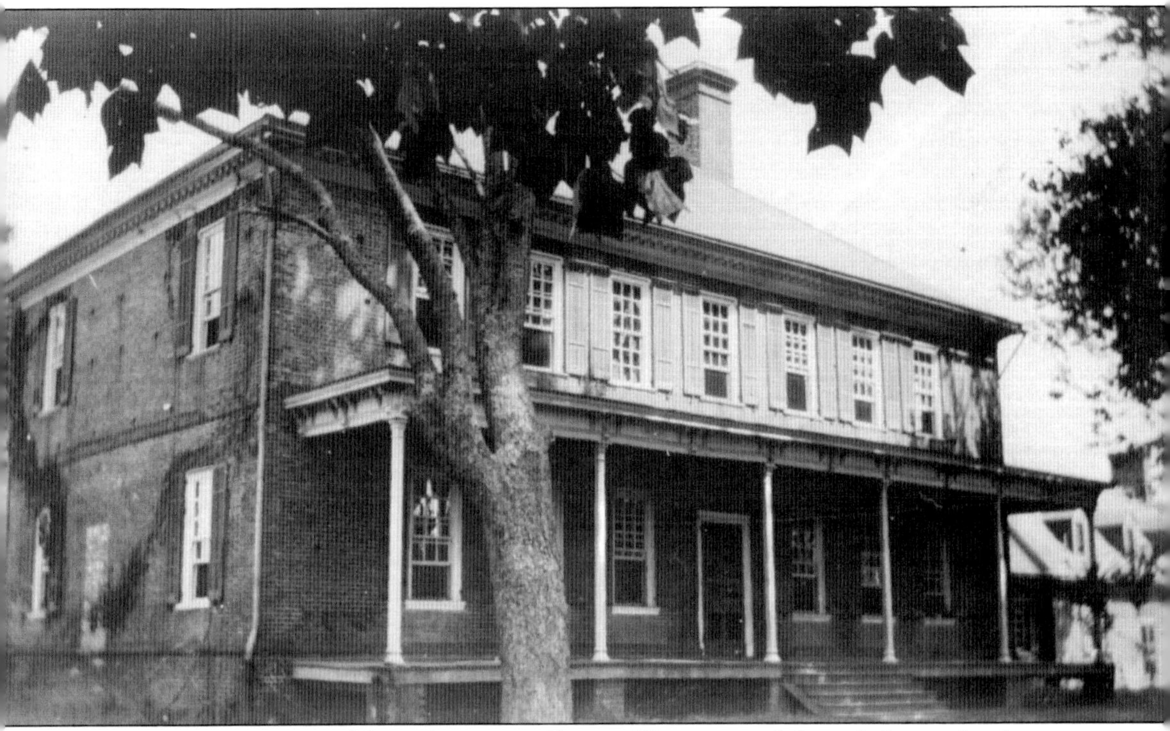

In the second quarter of the 19th century, Thomas Wynne owned Carter's Grove, the plantation built for Carter Burwell, grandson of Robert "King" Carter in the 1750s. Later Lewis Ellison owned it, and a variety of crops and livestock made the antebellum plantation productive. After the Civil War, tenant farmers occupied parts of Carter's Grove and neighboring Kingsmill as part of the Freedman's Bureau program. According to Mary A. Stephenson, "For twenty-nine years following the death of Thomas Wynne, his plantation called 'The Grove' by him was sold six times by . . . guardians of his minor children. None of these sales were ever completed. . . . Because payments were not made as contracted, the plantation was taken back by the Wynne family and resold." The circumstances at Carter's Grove illustrate the dismal economic situation in James City County at the end of the 19th century. (FB.)

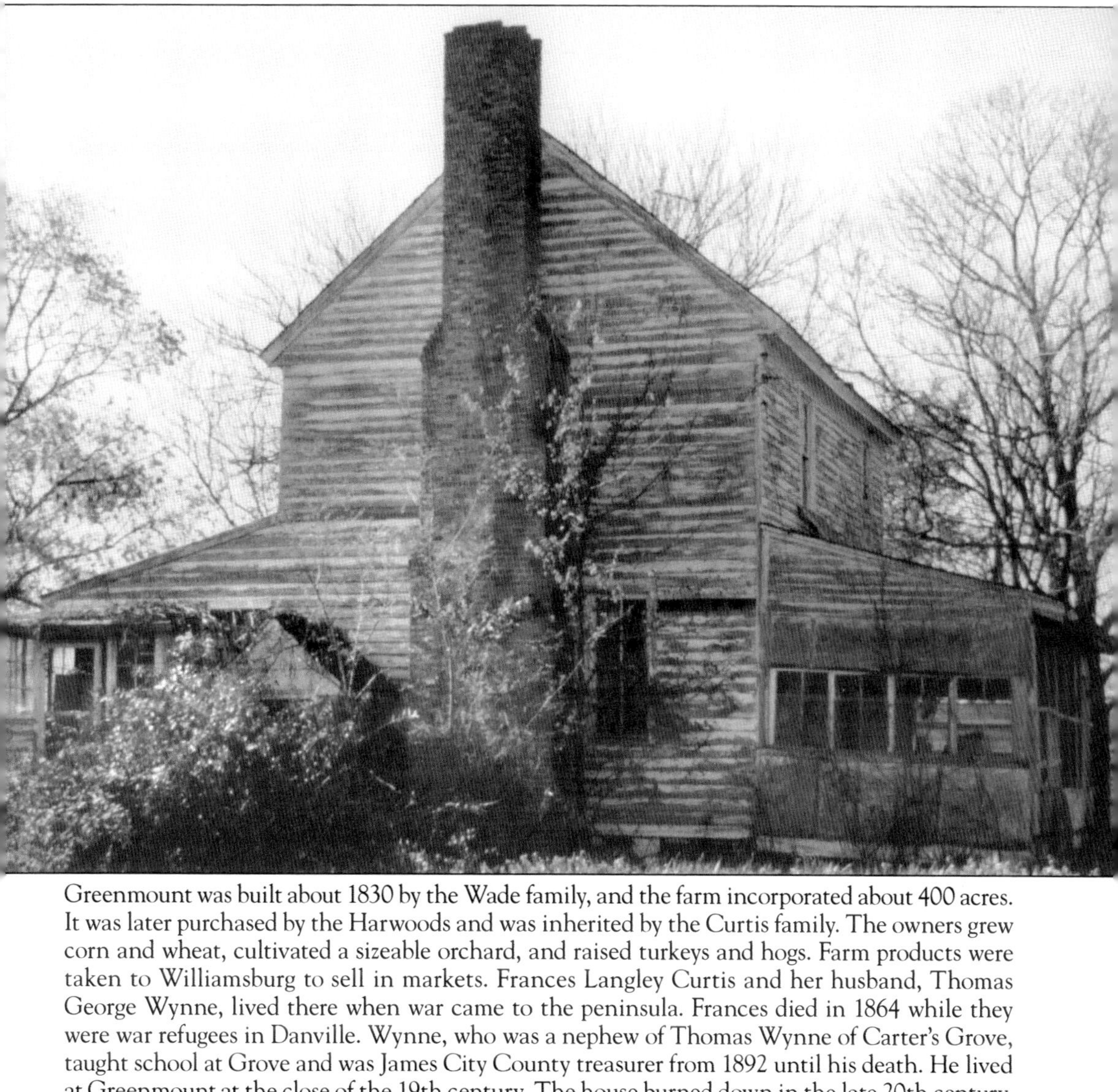

Greenmount was built about 1830 by the Wade family, and the farm incorporated about 400 acres. It was later purchased by the Harwoods and was inherited by the Curtis family. The owners grew corn and wheat, cultivated a sizeable orchard, and raised turkeys and hogs. Farm products were taken to Williamsburg to sell in markets. Frances Langley Curtis and her husband, Thomas George Wynne, lived there when war came to the peninsula. Frances died in 1864 while they were war refugees in Danville. Wynne, who was a nephew of Thomas Wynne of Carter's Grove, taught school at Grove and was James City County treasurer from 1892 until his death. He lived at Greenmount at the close of the 19th century. The house burned down in the late 20th century, and the property is currently an industrial park. (FB.)

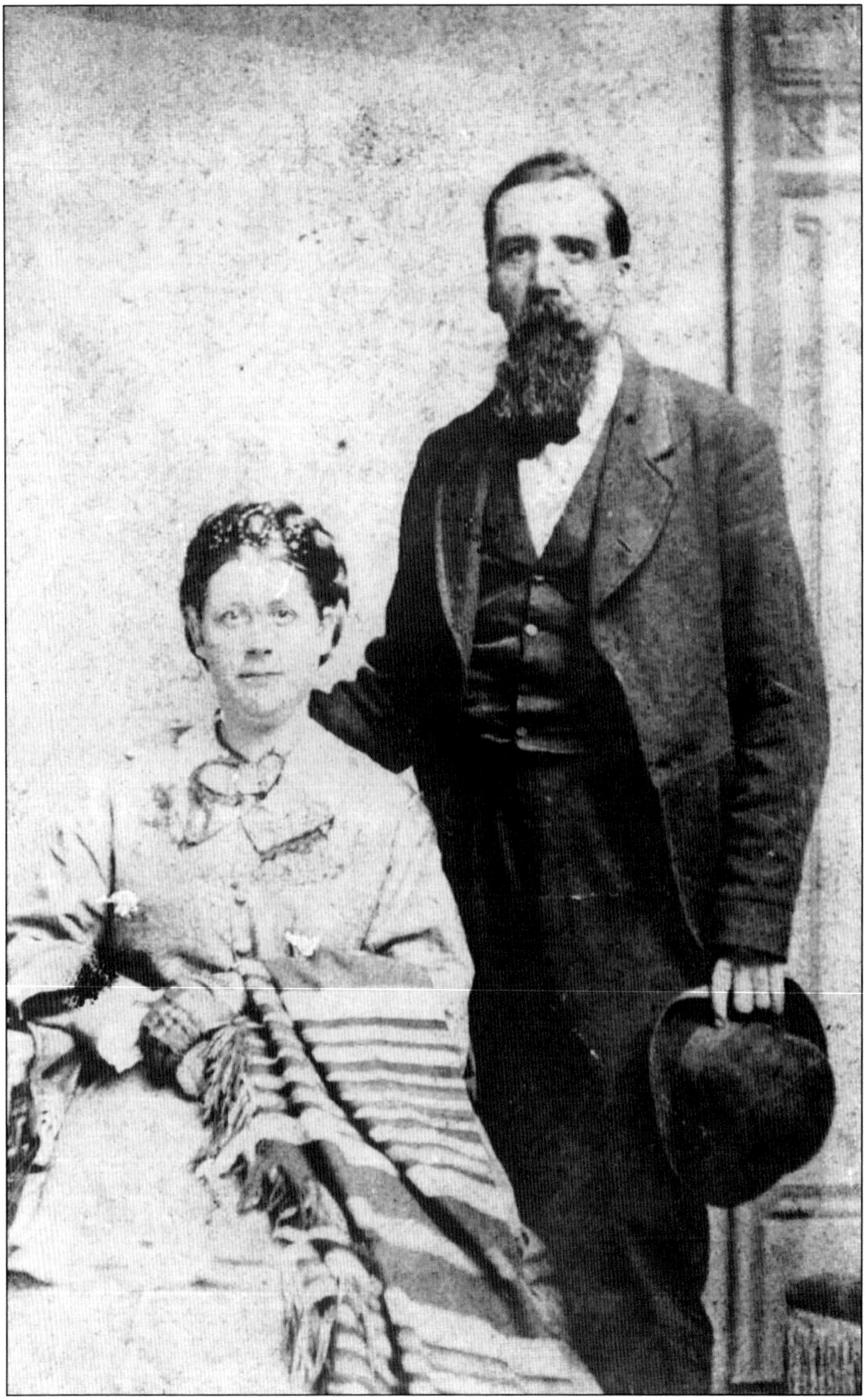

During the Civil War, Lt. Edmund Macon Ware was gravely wounded at Cold Harbor. He survived wounds to his face, arm, and torso, and he lived and later served James City County as a justice of the peace. He was married to Trittie Bush, daughter of William and Matilda Finch Bush of Windsor Castle on Forge Road near Burnt Ordinary. (WF.)

Four

CIRCA 1900

The 1898 *Directory and Handbook of the City of Williamsburg and County of James City* notes that James City County is "26 miles in length and 8 in breadth. The population at the last census was 5,643 including Williamsburg." Williamsburg's "colored residents" are listed by name, but only white heads of household appear beneath James City County post offices. The U.S. Census number would have included both races. The directory also states:

> The public schools . . . are being improved . . . and new ones located wherever required . . . good teachers are employed. There are now about nineteen schools in the county—white 11; colored 8. In the several districts . . . are churches of the various denominations—Episcopalian, Methodist, Baptist and Christian. There is no Presbyterian church building.
>
> Trucking and general farming are the principal occupations of the people. However, thousands of cords of pine, oak and ash wood, and a great amount of lumber are shipped annually from the forests. Toano is a great trucking centre and many car loads of melons, sweet and Irish potatoes, peas and other early varieties of vegetables are shipped to Northern and Western markets, commanding high prices. Of the cereals, corn is the staple product, although wheat, oats, grass, etc., are raised. A large acreage of peanuts was planted the past year. . . . Apples, peaches, pears, plums, grapes, cherries, strawberries, raspberries, etc., do well here.
>
> The nature of the soil is a sandy loam with a clay subsoil, and is susceptible to a high state of cultivation. At least one-half of the total area of 92,377 acres is in timber, part of it original growth. Pine, oak, ash, walnut, chestnut, and hickory abound in the forests.
>
> The fisheries . . . are quite an industry also: Diascund creek is famous for its herring; Chickahominy river for shad and perch; James river for shad, rock and sturgeon, and York river for oysters, trout and numerous other fish, while the ponds are full of chub, perch and other fresh water fish. Plenty of wild game is found in the forests and marshes.

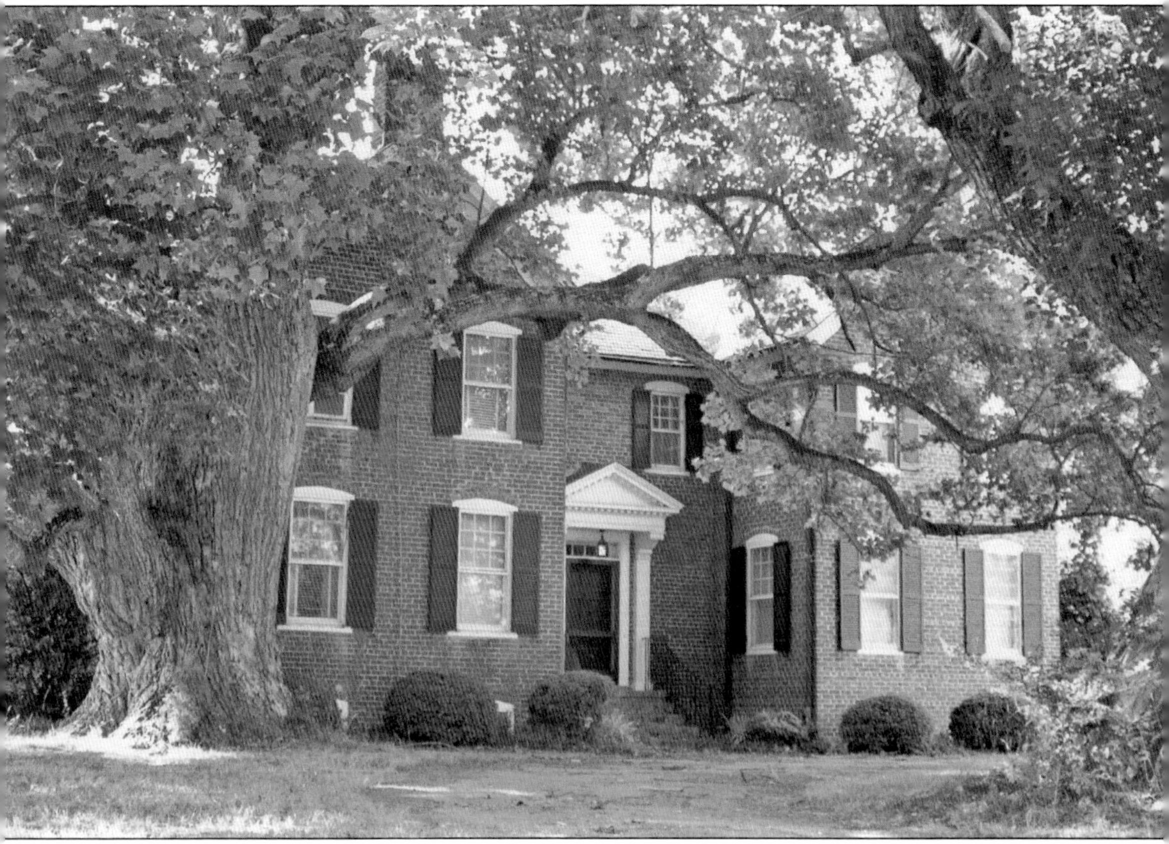

The Ambler family accumulated property on Jamestown Island and the mainland but sold it before the Civil War. Located on property called Ambler's in the 20th century, a part of this house date may date to the mid-1800s. In 1907, while the nation observed the 300th anniversary of Jamestown's settlement in Norfolk, the occupants of this house may have welcomed the building of a hard-surfaced road from Williamsburg to Jamestown for those who wished to see the original site. *Outing Magazine* featured a story written by a motorist who drove from New York City: "Evidently cars as yet are few and far between. . . . the honk of our horn brought folks to their doors and horses and mules resented our approach by backing away and performing other antics." A story about bicyclists traveling to Jamestown was featured in 1896: "We landed . . . at the historic old Jamestown Island, which is now the property of a Northern capitalist. . . . The site of 'James Cittie' has long been plowed over. . . . bricks are turned up here and there, and sometimes a skull . . . At the head of the island is the tower of the old church." (SEL.)

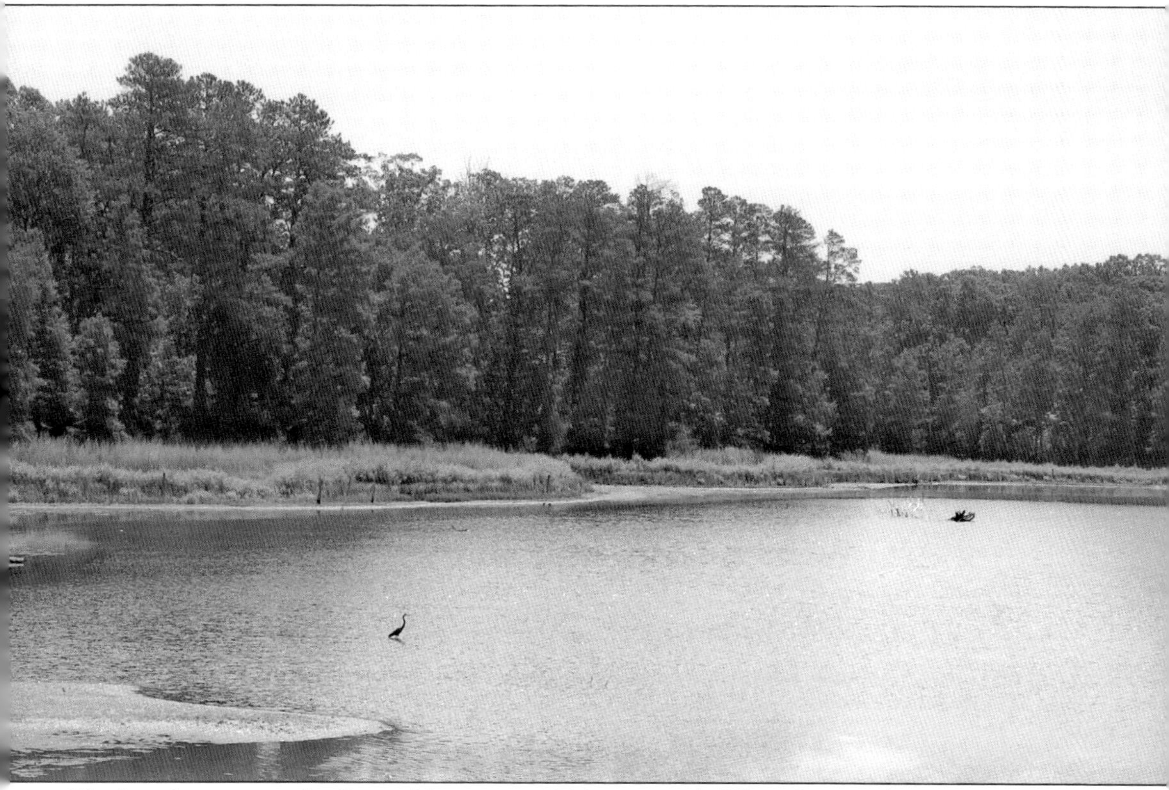

The bicyclists writing for *Outing Magazine* in 1896 continued: "We rode away the next morning, floundering through a morass on the north end of the island and then crossing a long bridge to the mainland. The road wound through verdant river meadows, between the inevitable worm fences decked in flaunting trumpet flowers. . . . Then we turned inland, and passing suddenly again into a primeval forest of pines, a carpeting of brown needles spread down the shadowy aisles, while overhead the somber green boughs arched and met, in an effect quite Gothic. . . . In the midst of the forest we found an ancient mill, and stopped to listen to its clacking wheels and discuss the gentle art of angling with a fisherman. We lingered around the mill-pond, a beautiful sheet of water that mirrored the overhanging pines and drifting clouds, and then we rode over the dam and, after an altogether pleasant turn of five miles, found ourselves in old Williamsburg town." This view of today's Lake Powell, where they may have spied the mill, echoes their observations. (SEL.)

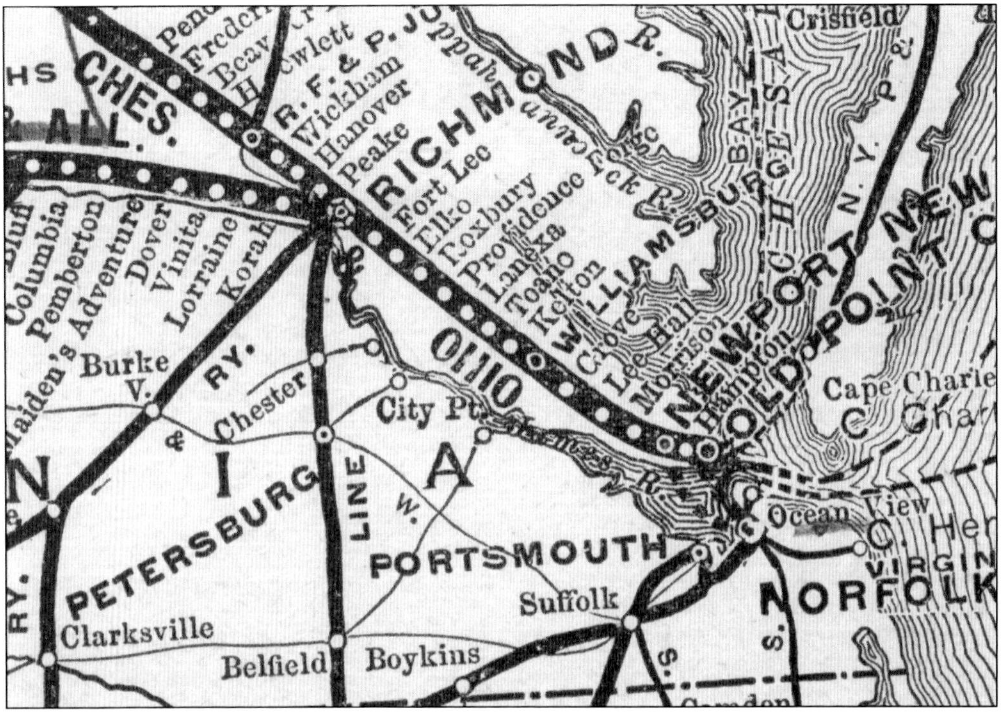

In the 1880s, the Chesapeake and Ohio Railway extended its line along the Virginia Peninsula from Richmond to Newport News. The railroad increased activity in the county, as it did in the nation and world, by providing regular mail and a faster means to transport people and ship farm products to distant markets. The detail of the map, shown above, was taken from an 1895 railroad schedule, and the Lanexa station photograph below was taken in 1915 for insurance valuation purposes. (Both, COHS.)

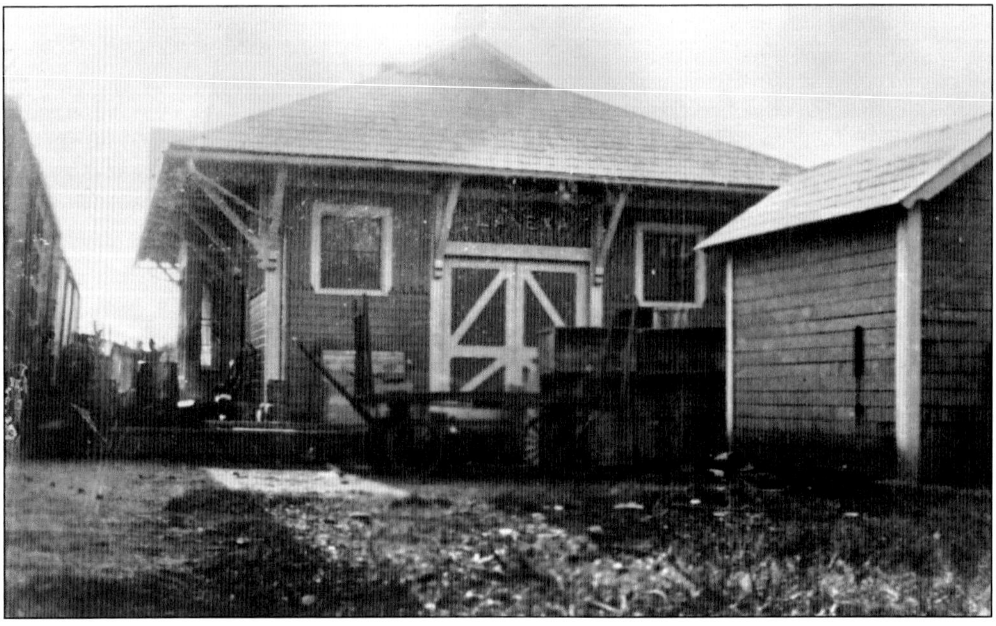

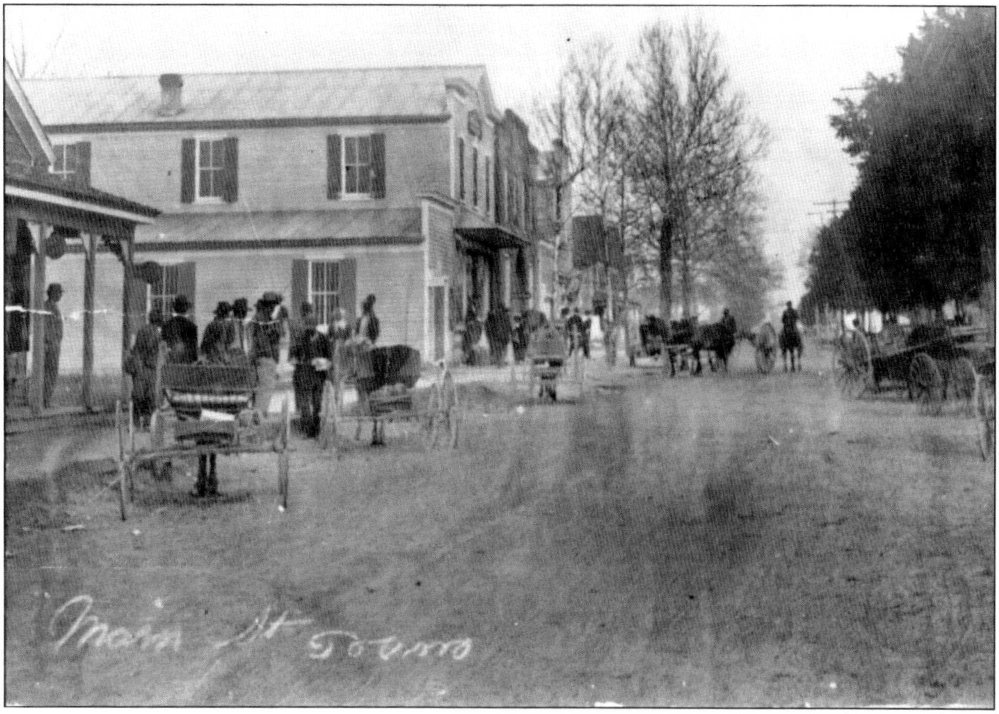

By the time of these early-20th-century photographs, Toano had become the county's primary commercial center and included a depot, a freight station, a barrel factory, a canning factory, a bank, a hotel, and stores. Above, this view is toward the east; several of the buildings on the left, including the bank building, are still standing. Below, the Toano depot, which was demolished in the late 20th century, was built behind these structures according to standardized plans befitting the burgeoning industrial age. (Above, SH; below, COHS.)

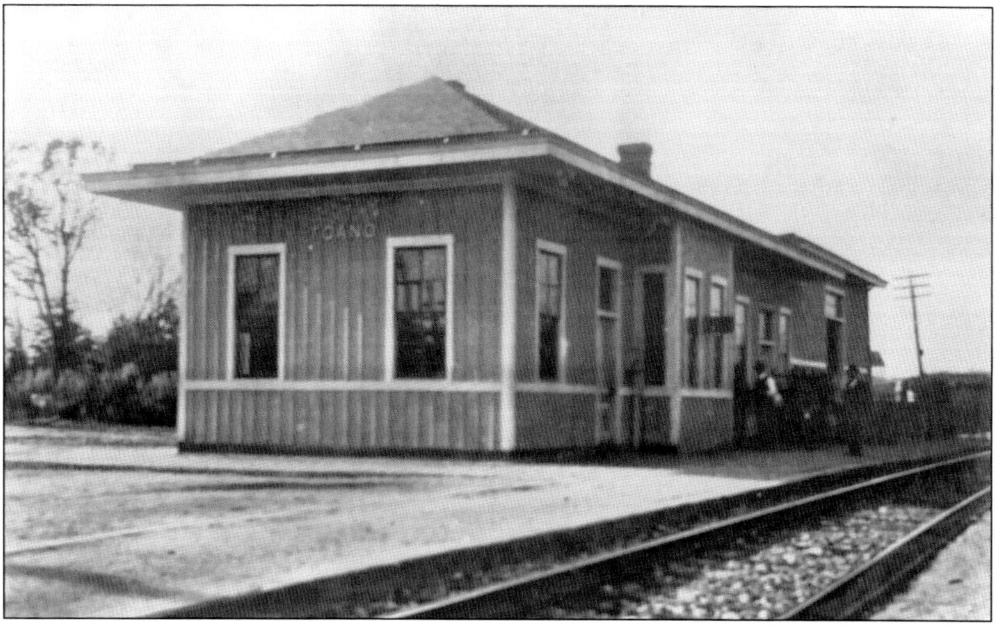

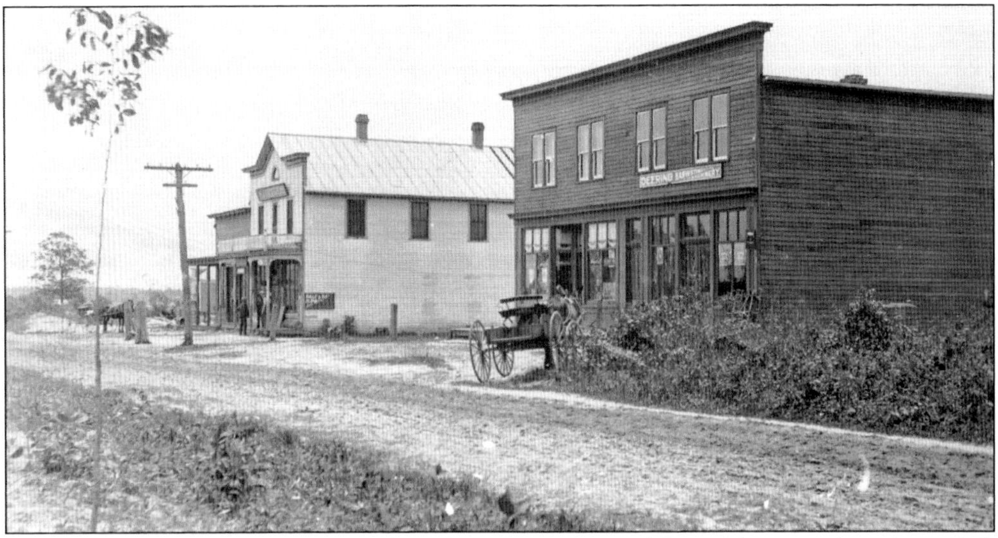

Norwegians who had first emigrated to the U.S. Midwest, followed by Danish and Swedish resettlers, built a community at Norge beginning in 1896. In this *c.* 1908 photograph, the Kinde and Nesseth Store, built in 1903, is on the right, and the Halvor H. Anderson Store, built in 1907, is on the left. The Kinde store included a post office and a bank, and sold clothing, dry goods, groceries, hardware, tobacco, medicine, and other items needed for the home. The Anderson Store was built in two sections with an entrance to a stairway in between. The store owner's family living quarters were upstairs. Area families with a Scandinavian heritage named Bergh, Flatten, and Jennings listed their post office as Toano in the 1898 *Directory and Handbook of the City of Williamsburg and County of James City.* The Norge Depot (pictured below) was located on Peach Street when the photograph was taken about 1910. The train station included a telegraph office. Frances Hamilton, daughter of station telegrapher Irvin Walker Huckstep, formed the Norge Railroad Depot Preservation Association in 1990, and the station was moved to the James City County Library on Croaker Road in 2006. (Above, DBW; below, collection of Frances Huckstep Hamilton, DBW.)

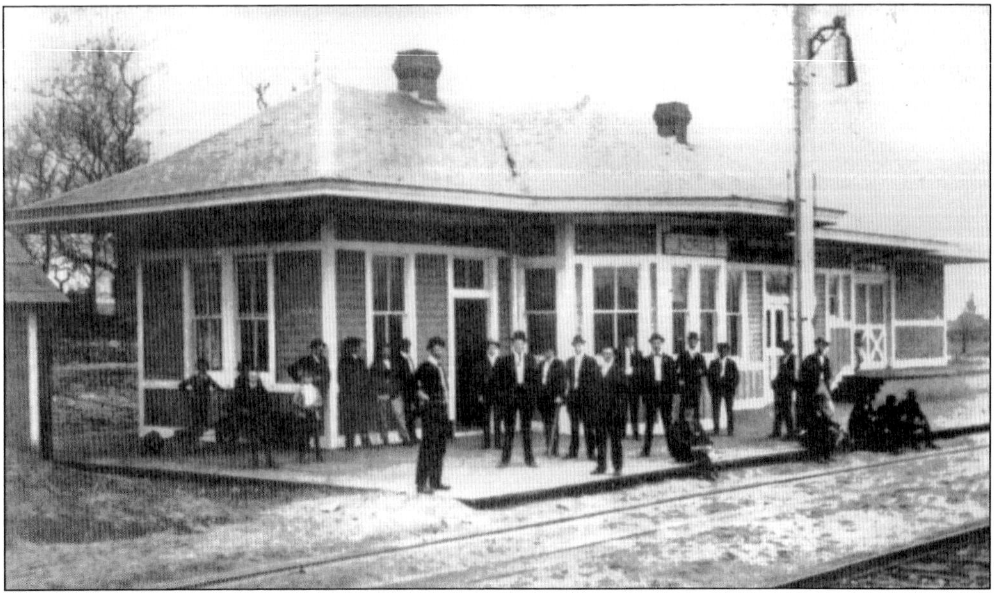

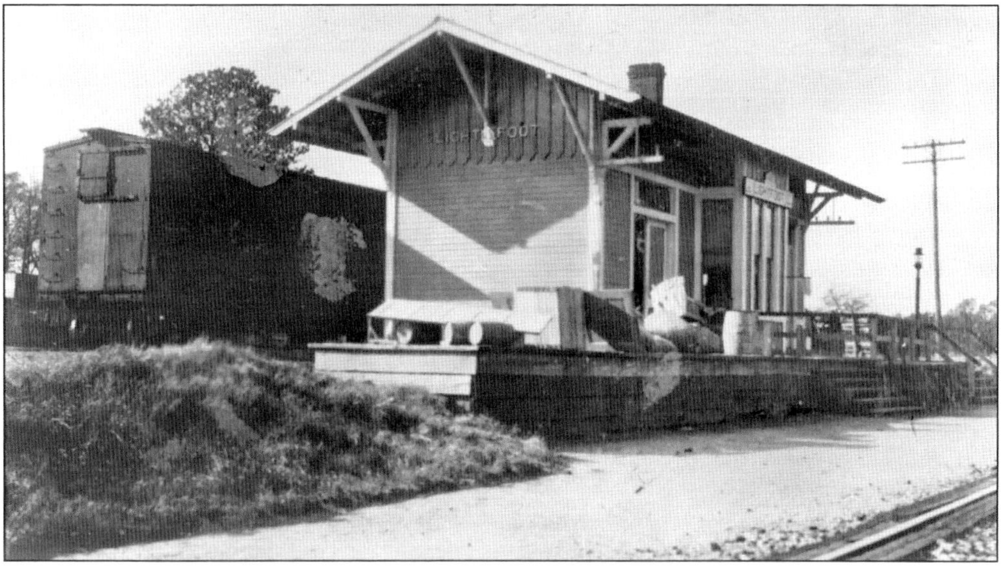

The 1915 insurance valuation photograph (above) shows barrels, sacks, and boxes at the Lightfoot depot with a freight car on the tracks. The depot is listed on C&O passenger schedules as early as 1903. Around 1900, businesses began to locate near the railroad stations, and it may have served as a mail stop earlier. Pictured on the cover, Albert Benson (1883–1956) worked as station agent from 1909 until 1953. His wife, Pernille "Nellie" Gulden Benson, served as Lightfoot's postmistress. Below, in the center from left to right, Amanda Olson, Valborg Christopherson, and Clara Olson were surrounded by children when they posed for this photograph at the Lightfoot depot in 1910. (Above, COHS; below, collection of Barbara Levorsen Quinn, DBW.)

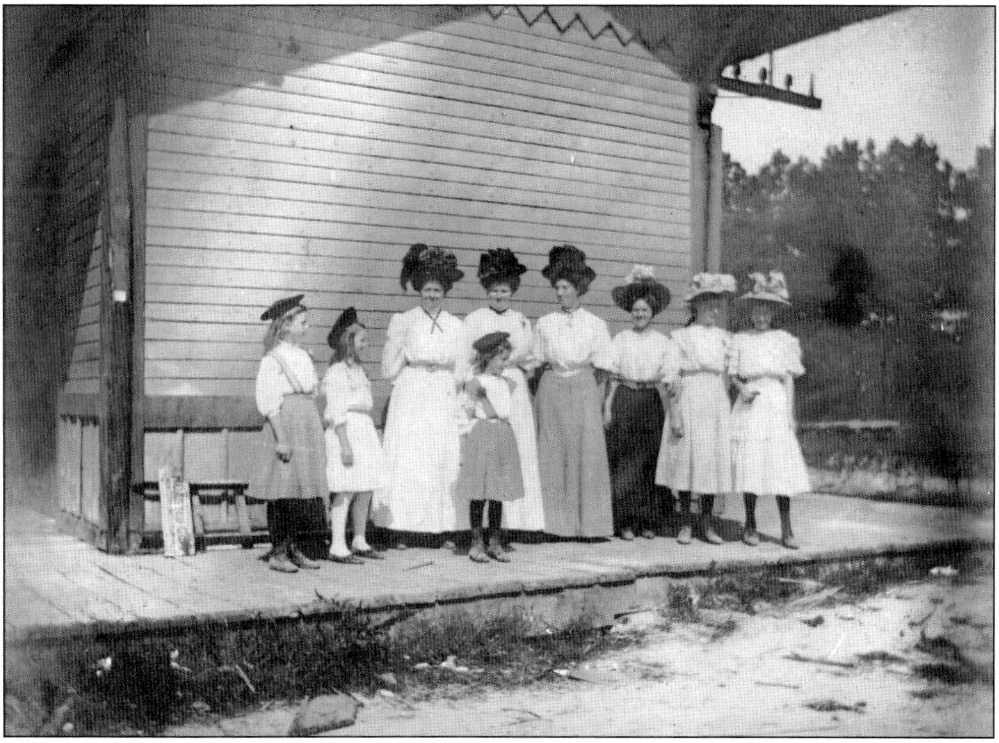

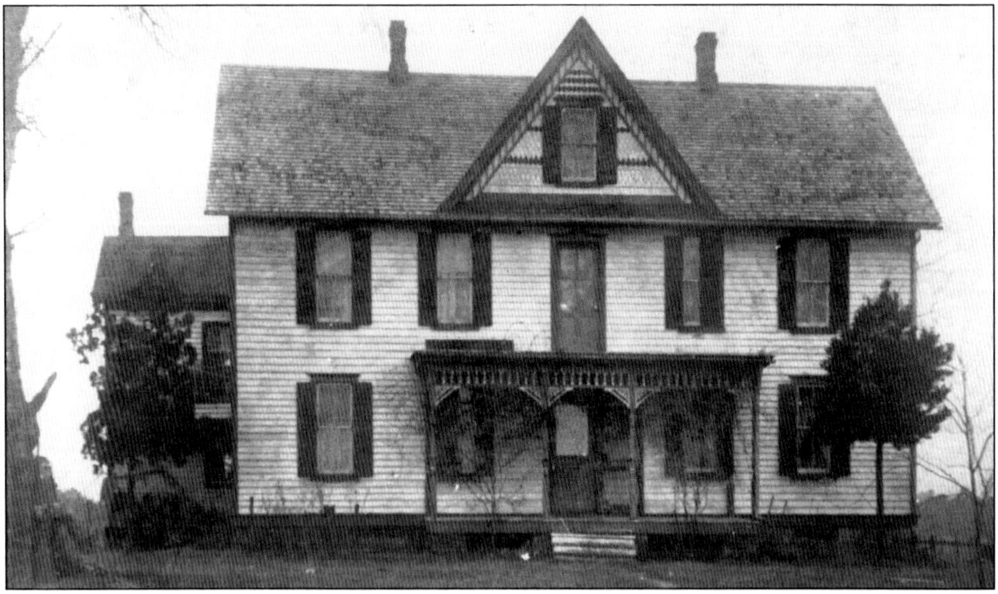

Carl Martin Bergh (1849–1906) was a land agent for the Chesapeake and Ohio Railroad whose home (above) was built in 1900 on land purchased from the R. L. Henley estate. The Norge depot (below) was nearby. He said of James City County's post–Civil War citizens, "Their former wealth and standing was at once blown away. Their cattle, sheep, hogs, and chickens were eaten by the soldiers, their horses and mules were stolen, their hoard of Confederate money was not worth the paper it was printed on." Bergh acquired extensive tracts of former plantation land left fallow in the post-bellum years and then he advertised in Wisconsin, Minnesota, and the Dakotas for people to come to Virginia where the land was cheap and the winters were mild. The railroad needed more customers along the route from Richmond to Newport News in order to make a profit, and Bergh envisioned a town for the Midwesterners midway in James City County. He died in 1906, and his ambitious plans did not fully materialize. (Above, collection of Anna Bergh Ficke, DBW; below, COHS.)

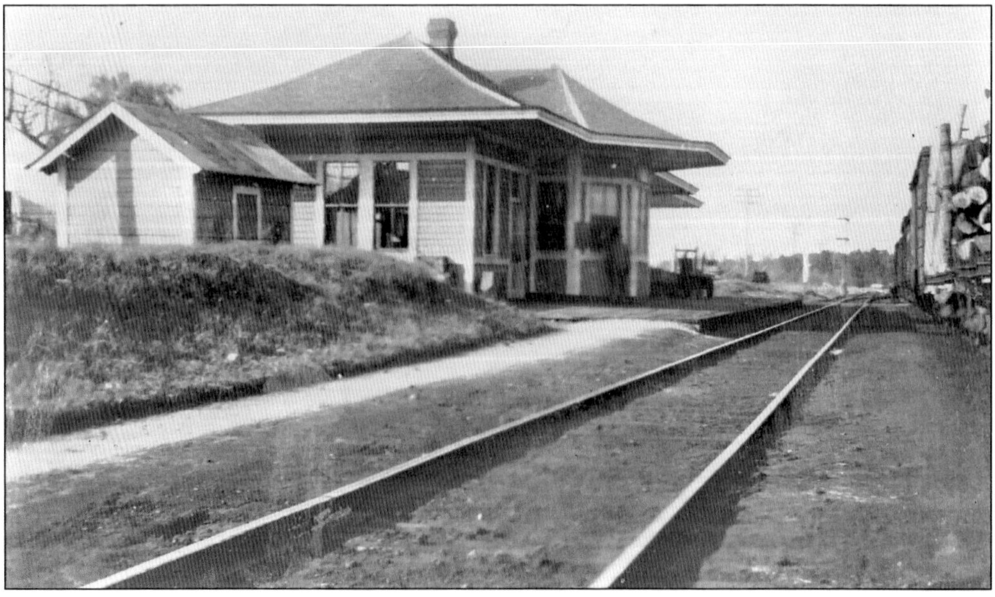

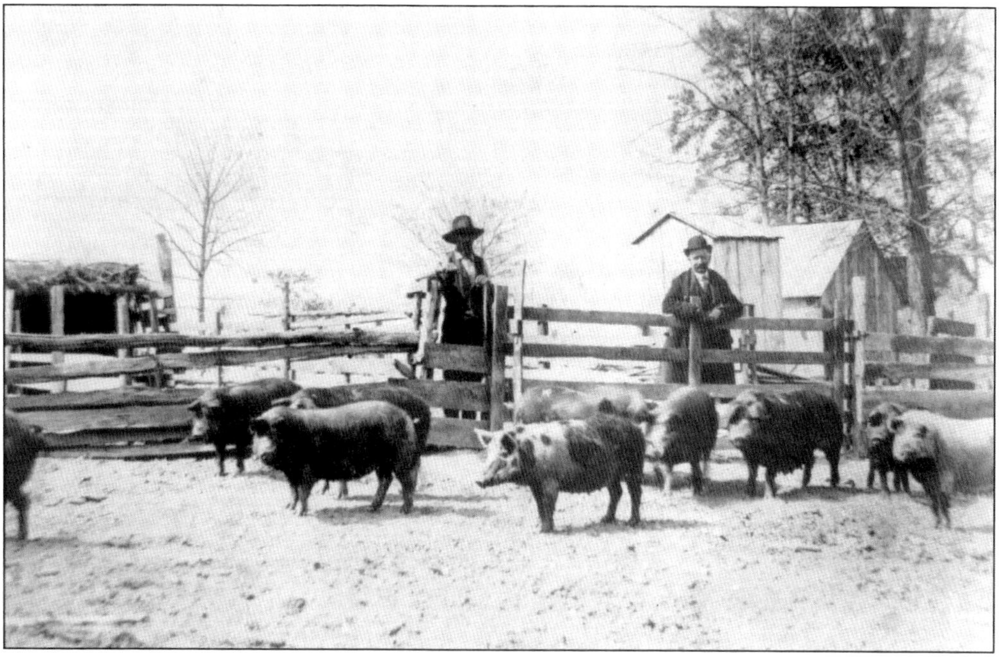

Norwegian emigrant H. J. Kinde (left) is seen above with Carl M. Bergh. Below, others who resettled in the Lightfoot area of James City County gathered in front of the Christopherson home for this playful 1910 photograph, including, from left to right, Bennett Benson, Alfred Benson, Amanda Olson (Hove), Clara Levorsen (Olson), Mabel Christopherson (Dukleth), Clara Christopherson (Munter), Mabel Olson, Olga Christopherson (Atkins), Nora Olson, Joseph Christopherson, Gertrude Tweten, Robert Christopherson, and Hilda Olson. (Above, collection of the Kinde family, DBW; below, DBW.)

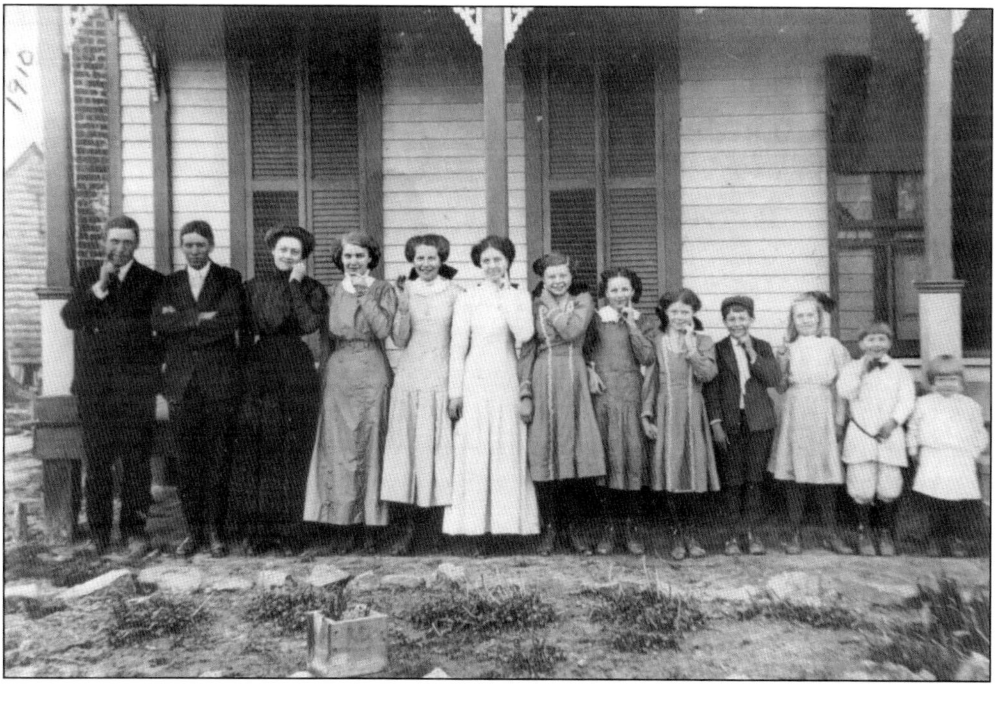

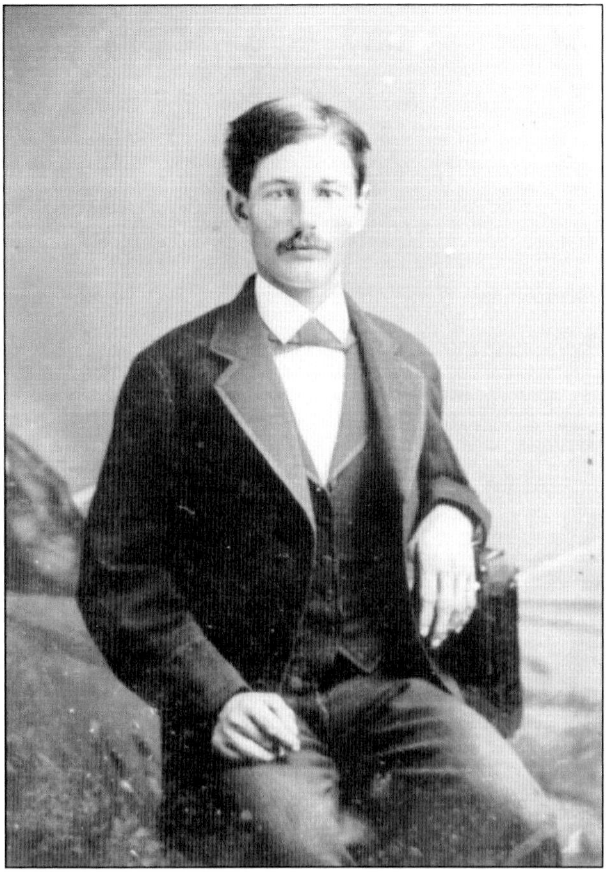

The Southern Land Company of Madison, Wisconsin, advertised four James City County farms on the road to Jamestown (today's Neck O' Land Road) and sold them in 1905 to the Ayers, Mepham, Gilley, and Burleson families. Three of the farms were dairy farms, and one was a general farm. Edwin Gilley, pictured at left, was brother-in-law of C. F. Ayers, who wrote to his friends in Madison that "the weather, the land, the grass, the roads, the fruit, the flowers, and the birds, are all in advance of our most sanguine expectations. . . . White clover is in abundance and has been continuously in blossom since April 20, making it a very good place for bee-keeping. . . . Peaches, apples, cherries and plums are an abundant crop and the fields abound with all kinds of berries. Pears were . . . a heavy crop last year." Gilley farm buildings, pictured below, still stand today. (Above, WSG; below, SEL.)

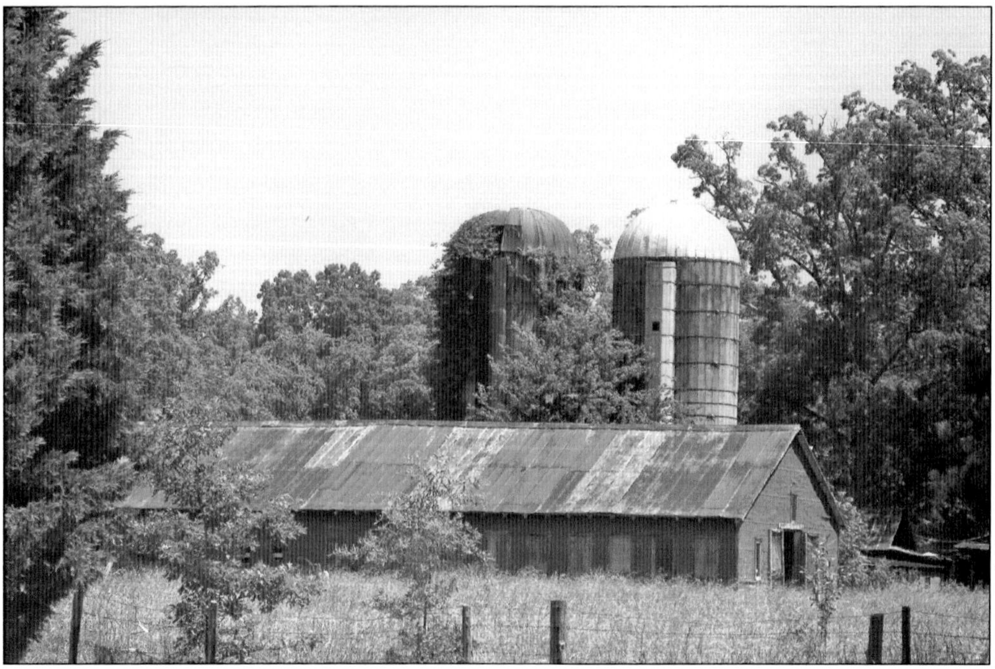

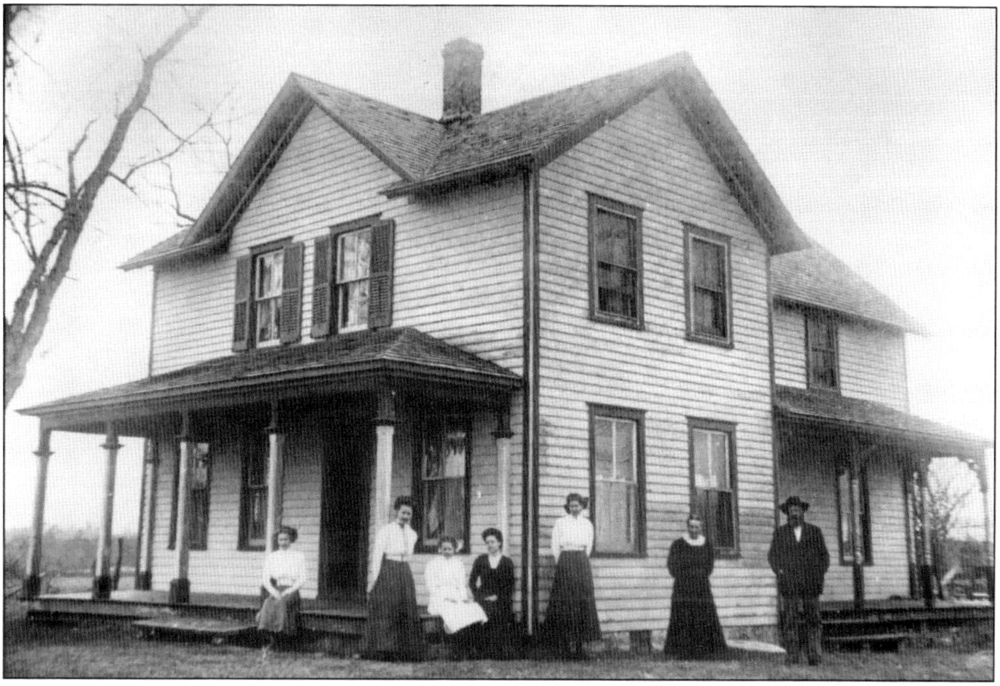

John and Louise Trosvig moved to James City County from Pelican Falls, Minnesota, just after the dawn of the 20th century. A newspaper clipping reprinted in the *Virginia Gazette* in 1975 said, "When Mr. Trosvig first began farming in Virginia he followed the popular practice of raising potatoes." Due to the poor soil and need to add fertilizer, he lost money and "was one of the first to enter dairying in that part of the south." (DBW.)

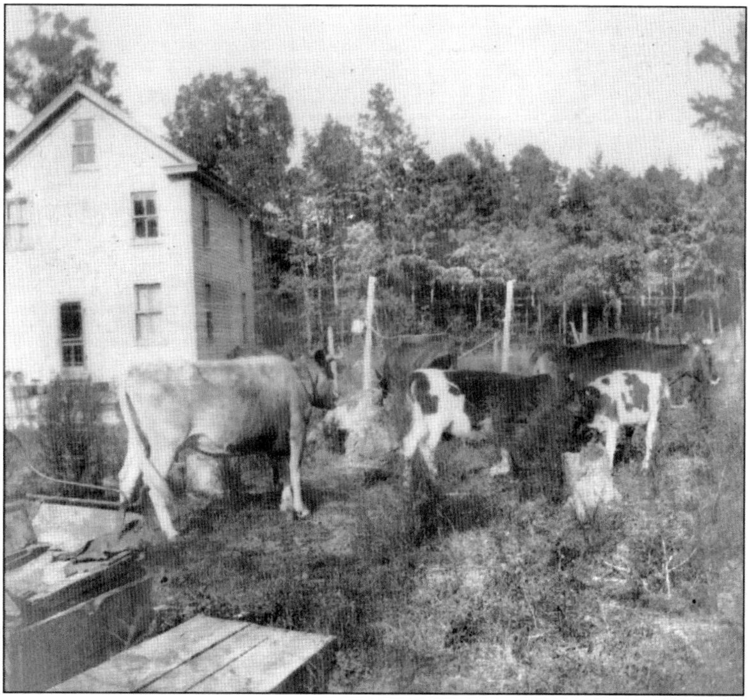

Cows grazed in the William B. Wynne yard in Grove. The 1898 *Directory and Handbook of the City of Williamsburg and the County of James City* lists 24 white heads of household with a Grove Post Office address, including J. R. Wynne, R. J. Wynne, T. G. Wynne, and W. B. Wynne. Other family names listed are Lee (7), Harwood (4), Kirby (3), Booth, Graham, Skillman, Smith, Stryker, and West. (FB.)

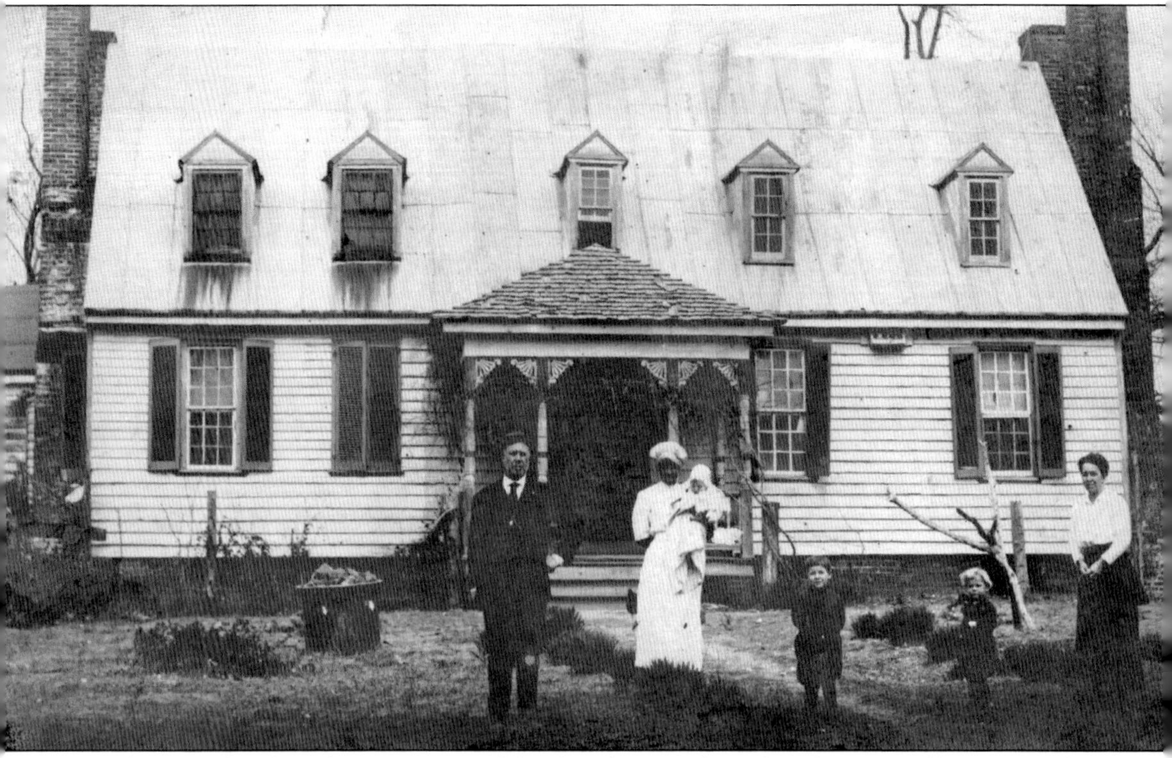

The Ware family and a servant posed for this photograph at their farm on Old Forge Road in 1913. Included (from left to right) are William Walker Ware, a servant holding Mary Kline Vail Ware, C. M. Ware, William Walker Ware Jr., and Mary Vail Ware. The elder William Ware was listed in the 1898 *Directory and Handbook of the City of Williamsburg and County of James City* as deputy sheriff of James City County, and he advertised as a dealer in general merchandise, cordwood, and railroad ties. Although some James City County landholders had seen their pre–Civil War wealth measured by slave ownership, after the war, it was measured in land that could be harvested for timber or leased to sharecroppers. Although slavery was abolished, the difficult economic situation and social hierarchy of the time caused a system to evolve where many blacks left the area for the cities while others continued to live and work near former plantation homes, sometimes for generations. (WF.)

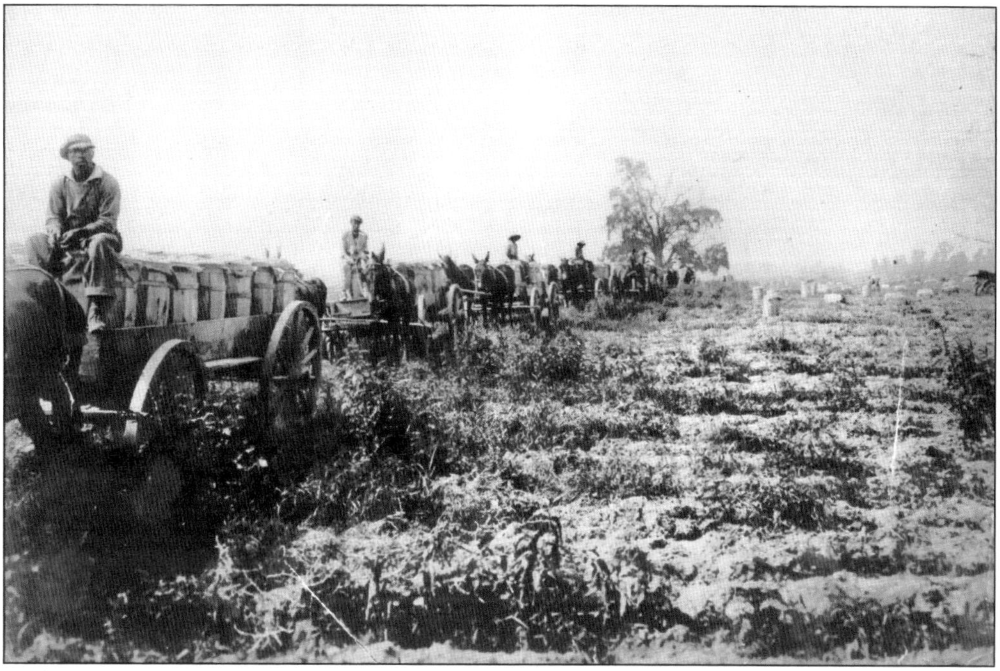

In the 1920s, on the Old Forge Road farm owned by C. C. Branch, the largest in the county, potatoes were harvested and loaded into barrels and wagons by local workers. The Branch operation required thousands of barrels, which were made at the Toano barrel factory. Many train cars brought mules and other supplies. Branch is said to have lost a fortune when two shipments of potatoes sent to Cuba spoiled and were thrown overboard. Many of the African American workers he employed lived nearby, and a photograph of a "Negro house near Toano" can be viewed online in the University of Virginia's Jackson Davis Collection of African American Educational Photographs. Although blacks were free, economics and so-called "Jim Crow" laws separated blacks from whites and regulated their activity within the society of local whites. (Both, WF.)

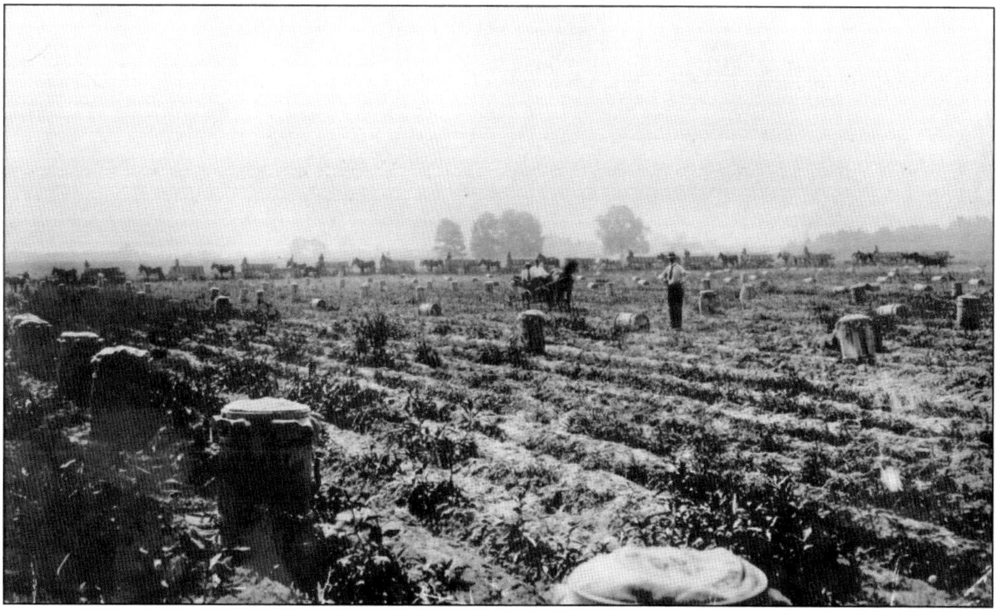

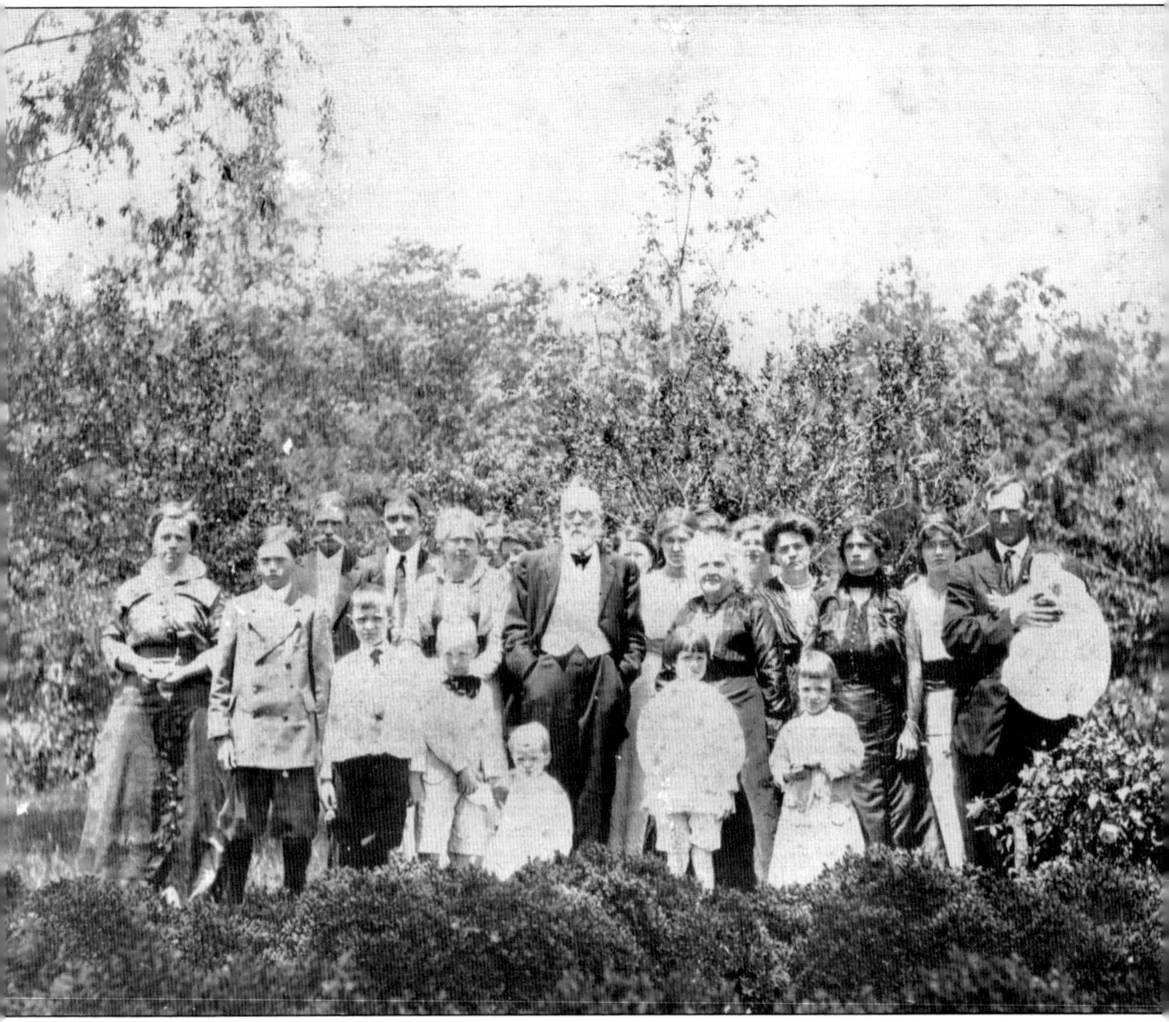

In May 1915, William Baker and Bettie Henderson Wynne celebrated their 50th wedding anniversary at their home on Grove Lane. Wynne owned Locust Grove and Helicon, and purchased 60 acres of the Carter's Grove tract in 1861 but fled ahead of the Union troop advance during the Peninsula Campaign. When he returned, he taught at the Grove School and was station master of the Grove depot. Pictured from left to right are Effie Wynne, Tom Baker Marston, Clifford Marston, Robert Baker Wynne, Baker Perkins Wynne, Hannah Mahala Wynne, Oliver Clifford Hockaday, Carroll Franklin Hockaday, two unidentified, William Baker Wynne, two unidentified, Wynne Noel, Bettie Henderson Wynne, unidentified, Nora Wynne Noel, Anne Cary Wynne, Maybelle Marston Hockaday, unidentified, and Oliver Hockaday holding John Harvey Hockaday. (FB.)

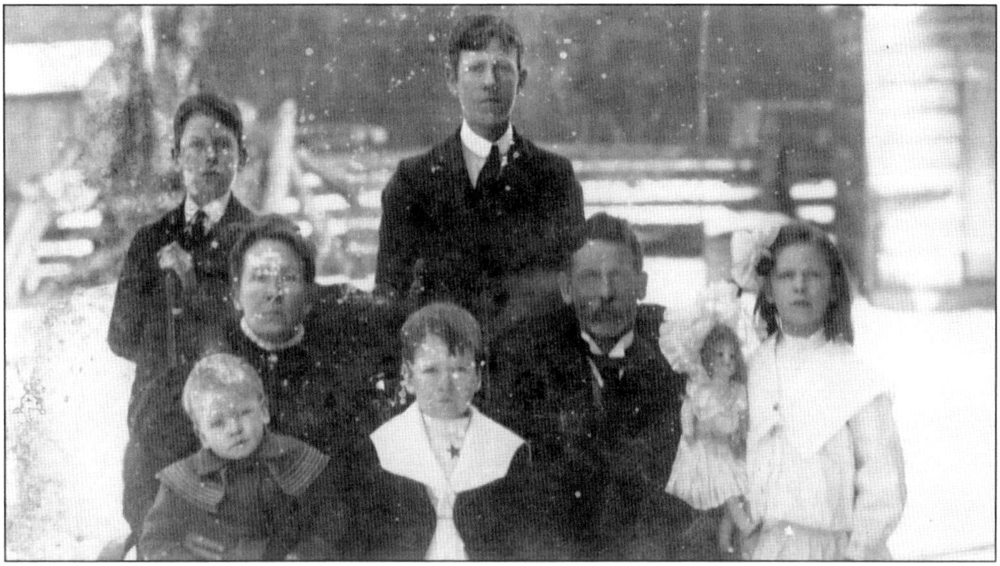

The Geddy family posed in front of White Hall, their home that had been built by ancestors 100 years earlier. Lucy James and Richard Brown Geddy (seated) had five children. Bert (standing, far left) became a partner in the Wilkinson and Geddy Store in Toano, and Otis (standing, center) became owner of the Williamsburg Coal Company. The other children are, from left to right, Frank, Richard, and Lucille Geddy. (BG.)

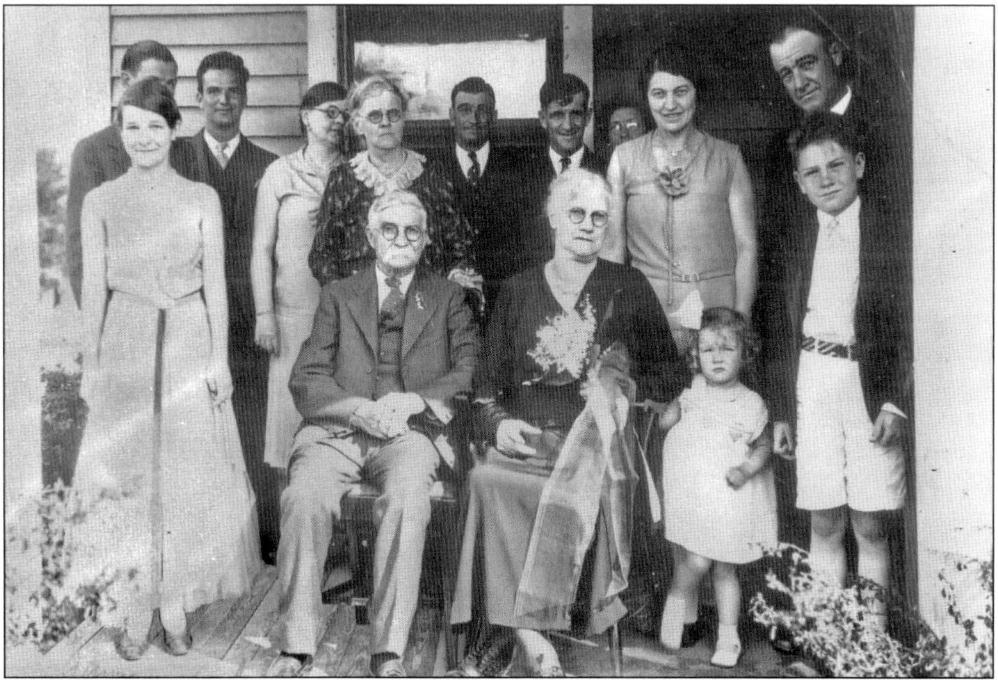

C. F. and Evelyn Ayers celebrated their 50th wedding anniversary in 1931 at their farm on old Jamestown Road (Neck O' Land Road). The seated couple is surrounded by children, grandchildren, and neighbors. Charles Franklin and Mary Gilley stand behind C. F. Ayers. Sons Floyd, Arthur, and Ellsworth are among the well-wishers. Ellsworth Jr. (right, wearing white shorts) died in Italy during World War II. The farm is today's Peleg's Point subdivision. (WSG.)

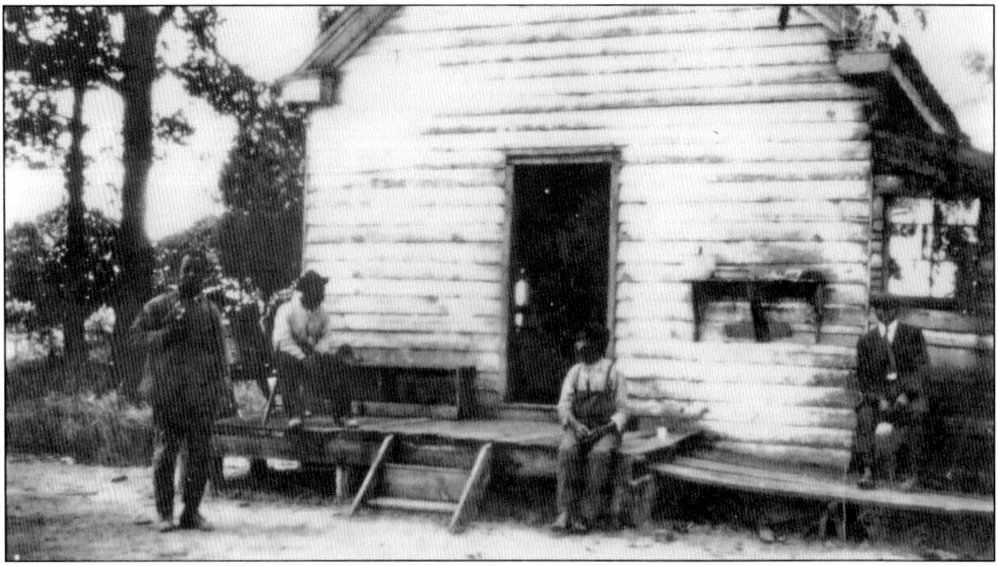

Before public education was established during Reconstruction, white children were taught at home and in private academies while few blacks received any education. In 1870, a Virginia "Jim Crow" law prohibited white and "colored" children from being taught in the same school. Jackson Davis, state agent for Negro Schools for the Virginia State Board of Education, took many photographs of schools between 1906 and 1947, including a one-room school on Maxton Lane in James City County similar to this one. After seventh grade, African American children went to Williamsburg to attend James City County Training School, built in 1924, and later Bruton Heights School, built in 1940. (DBW.)

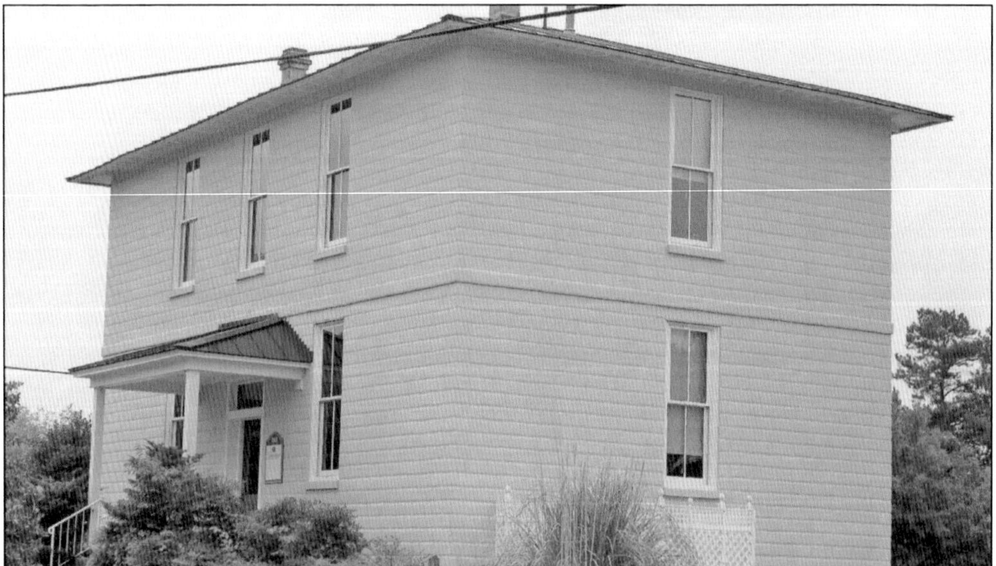

Five Forks School for white children included six grades held in three classrooms. Each two-grade class was taught by one teacher, and the school's three teachers lived in the teacherage next door. Children who lived in the Jamestown Magisterial District attended Five Forks and shared a school system with the City of Williamsburg. They received their high school education at Williamsburg High School. (SEL.)

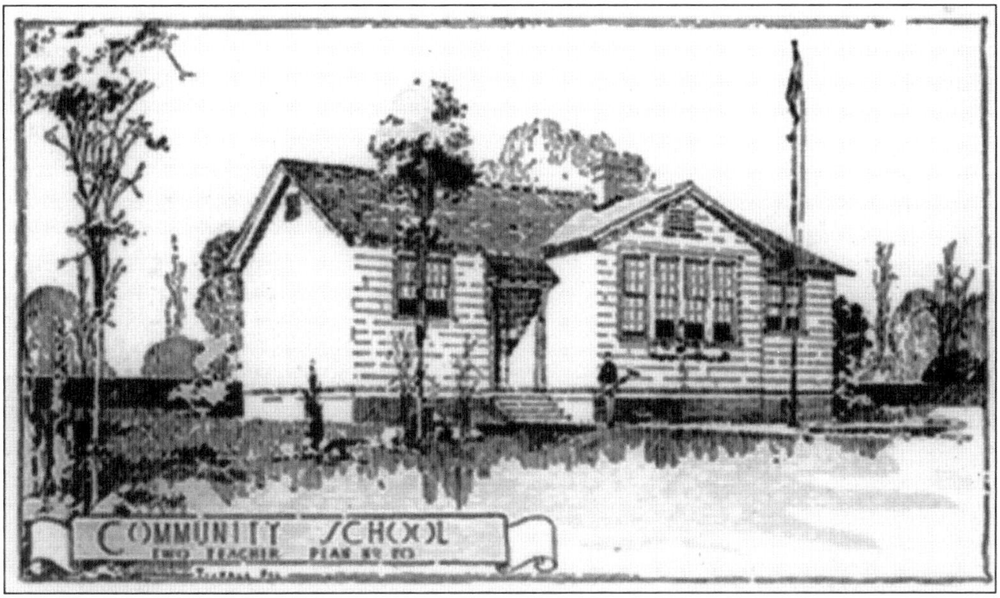

Chicago philanthropist Julius Rosenwald, chief executive officer of Sears, Roebuck, and Company, gave seed money to build 5,300 school buildings for African Americans in Southern states. In James City County, the National Register of Historic Places lists Chickahominy and Centerville as two-teacher schools. Another six-teacher Rosenwald School was built in Williamsburg. Many Rosenwald schools remained in operation until the 1960s, when the U.S. Supreme Court ruling against segregation was implemented. (Rosenwald School plans, National Register of Historic Places.)

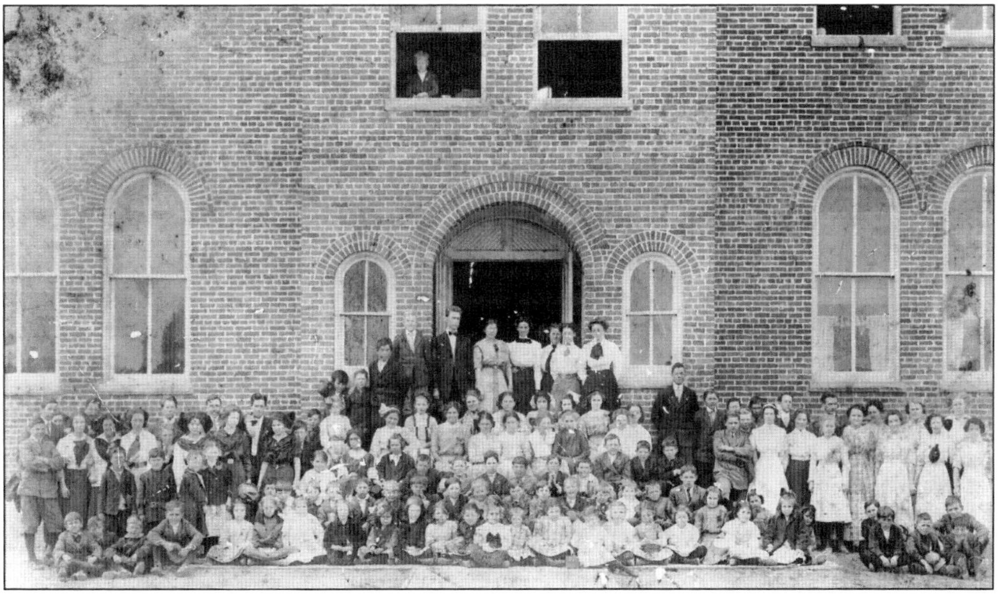

Toano School, built in 1908, was the only high school between Williamsburg and Richmond, attracting white students who lived west of Centerville Road in James City County's Powhatan and Stonehouse districts, as well as from Charles City and New Kent counties. Students traveled to school by boat, train, and horse-drawn school wagon. The first graduating class included two students: W. E. Hankins and Lou Geddy. This Toano School photograph was taken in 1912. (BG.)

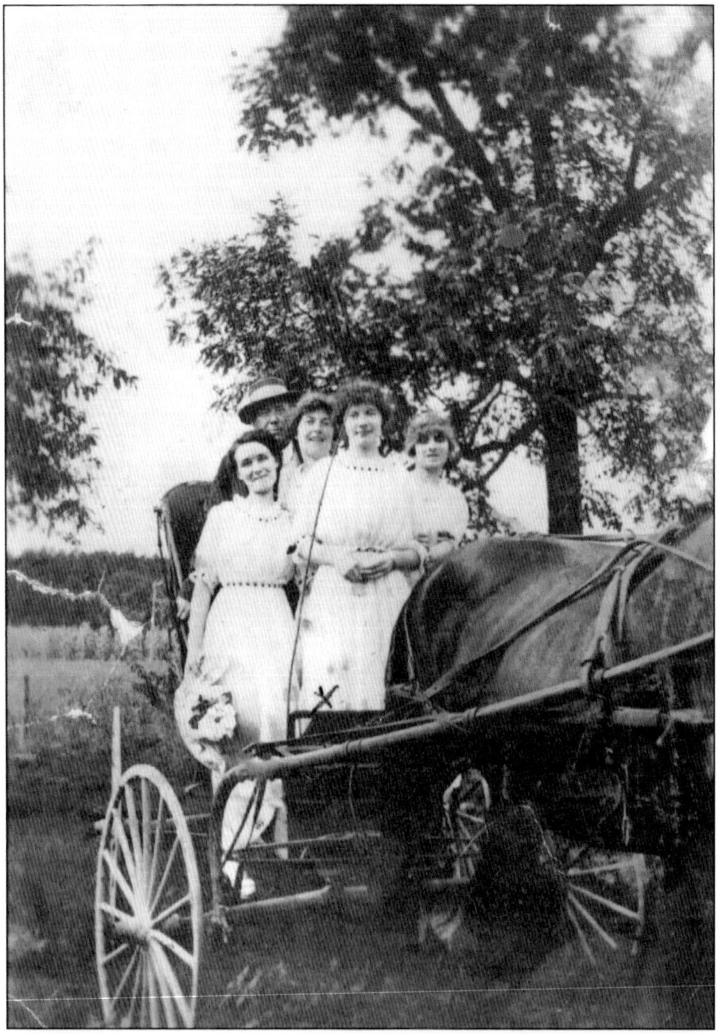

Liberty Baptist Church was located across Diascund Creek in New Kent County, but for white Baptists in the western portion of James City County, the church, which was founded in 1830, was the closest house of worship. The Slater sisters, seen in the early-1900s photograph at left, often wore matching dresses sewn by their mother and themselves. The buggy driver may be their brother. Seen below as it looks today, the wooden bridge that spans the creek was torn apart during the Civil War by Confederate soldiers who were pursued by Union troops. The Union soldiers later tore boards from Liberty Church to rebuild the bridge and continue the chase. (Above, GHD; below, SEL.)

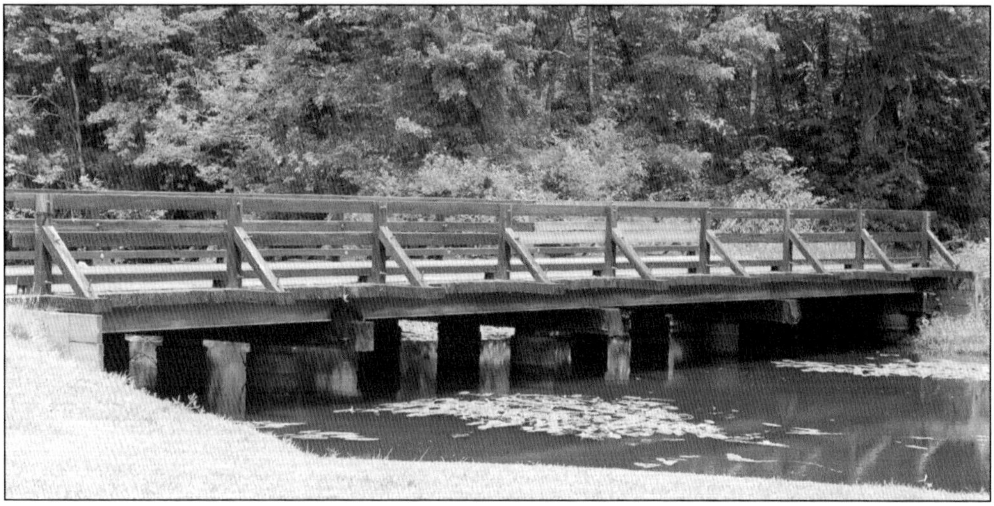

Five

Toano

An undated newspaper clipping titled "Toano in Bygone Days" states the following:

> Until 1881 there was no such place as Toano, this name being given by the C. & O. Railroad Company. . . . Until then . . . Toano, was known as Burnt Ordinary. Long years ago, before railroads were thought of . . . here and there at convenient stops were inns and post offices . . . known as ordinaries. This ordinary was burnt once and thereafter was always known as Burnt Ordinary. About a mile from Toano is a building known as Hickory Neck Academy. During the Revolutionary War it was used as a camp from time to time and later on many of our mothers and fathers received a part of their education there. Very recently it has been repaired and made into an attractive little Episcopal church.

Longtime residents remember that in the 1930s downtown Toano included the C&O depot, a blacksmith's shop, Piggott's Garage, Toano School, Green Shingle Inn, Banks Store, an Esso station, a barrel factory, Mount Vernon Methodist Church, Slater's Store, an ice plant, the county agent's office, Meanly's Store, a bank, a pool hall, a barbershop, a café, Martin's Store, a drugstore, the Felix Hotel, a town hall, Taylor's Garage, Wilkinson and Geddy Store, a post office, the Wayside Inn, two stables, a windmill, a well, a spring, and approximately 20 family homes. Two fires and highway construction destroyed many of these structures.

In 1977, a *Publick Observer* reporter wrote:

> Sheldon Lumber Co. anchors the east end of town. Barksdale's Drug Store, the Wayside Inn, Geddy & Wilkinson's Store, all are gone. But Mrs. Moseley's Diner has brought a measure of fame and popularity to Toano. . . . A good omen is the clear water flowing since July . . . as a result of the long-promised, finally-completed new well system. Local housewives had declared the water from their pipes unfit. . . . a good number of them had toted empty plastic jugs to the fire station to fill them at the only good well in town. In the nation's oldest county . . . progress still requires patience.

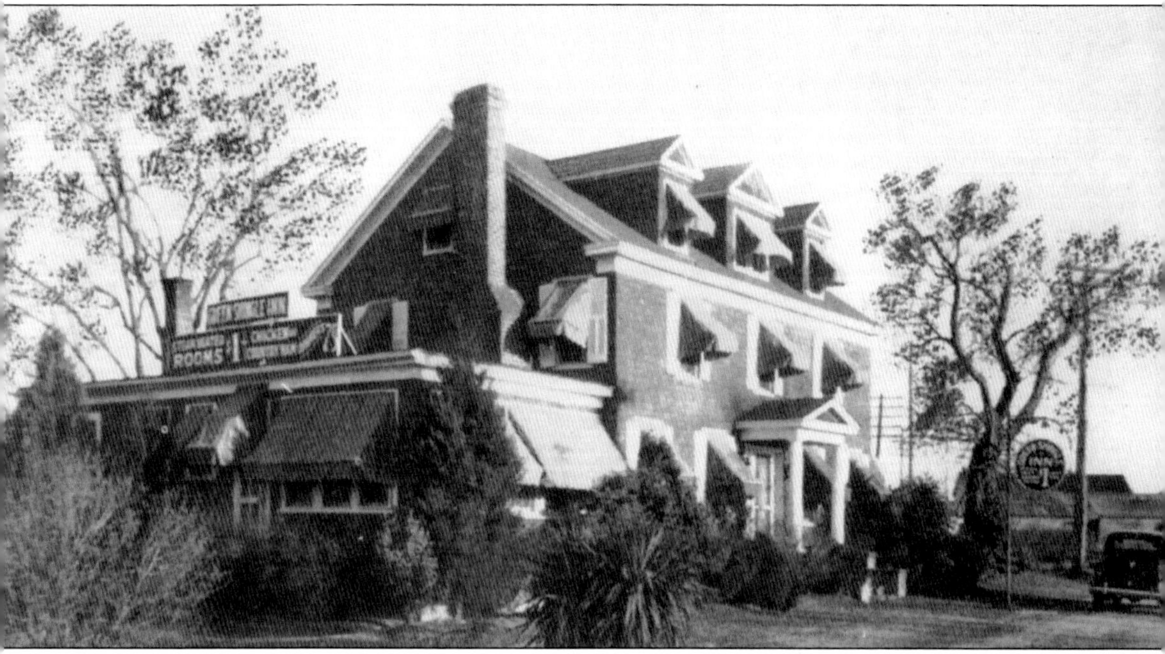

This postcard's caption states, "The Green Shingle Inn was built on the site of the Colonial Tavern which was burned by the British in 1781. Cornwallis passed here on his way to Williamsburg, June 27, 1781. McClellan's men camped on these grounds in 1862, using this house as his headquarters. Later it was used as a Hospital for the Northern Army. This property has been owned by the present family for the past 135 years. . . . After it was burned in 1781 it took the name of Burnt Ordinary and later the town was changed to Toano, an Indian name. In the heart of the most historical part of America, the Green Shingle Inn, which specializes in Virginia home cooked meals, is 8 miles from Williamsburg, Va., 12 from Jamestown, 18 from Yorktown, 38 from Newport News and 40 miles from Richmond." (BG.)

Pictured at right, Charles Smith and his Grandmother Smith enjoy the front porch of the Hotel Felix in Toano in 1929. In the 1898 *Directory and Handbook of the City of Williamsburg and County of James City*, Norvelle L. Henley, attorney and counselor at law with offices in the Peninsula Bank Building, advertised that he operated a branch office in Toano's Hotel Felix on Thursdays. Below, the Wayside Hotel was located on the east end of the village. The baby in the stroller on the hotel's sidewalk in this 1930s photograph is Jacqueline Moody (McSherry). The hotel was run by her relatives, uncle Plum and aunt Lil Jennings. Dances and other community gatherings were held at all three Toano establishments. (Right, CSM; below, BG.)

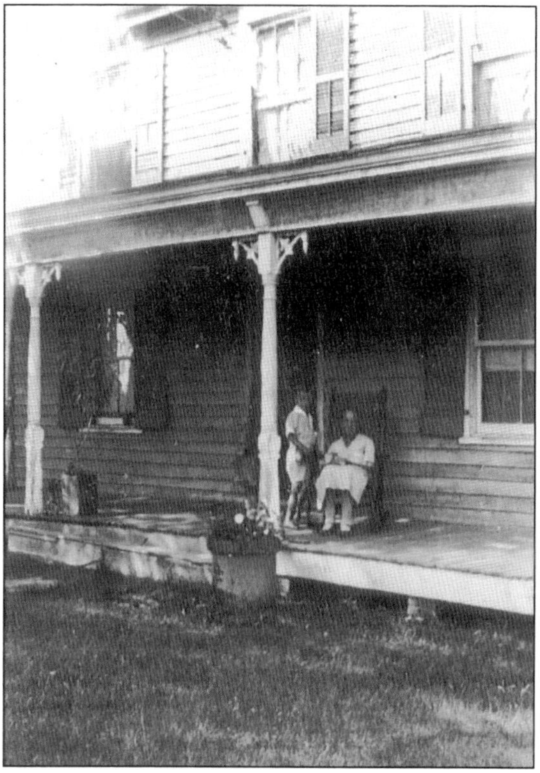

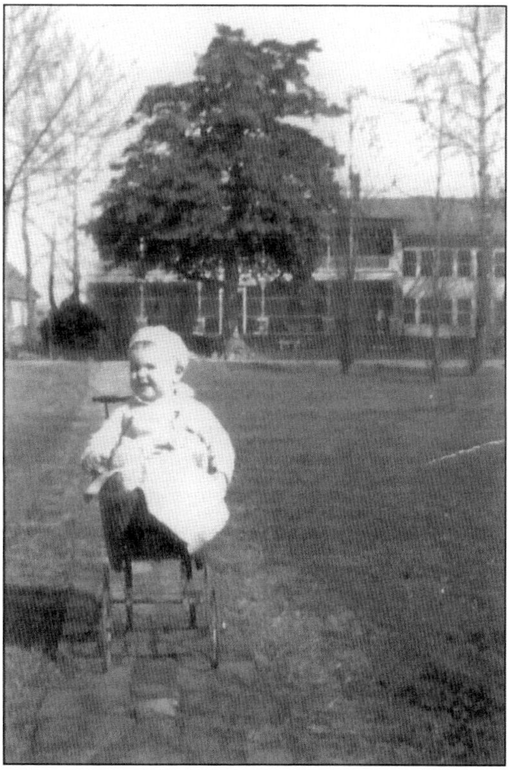

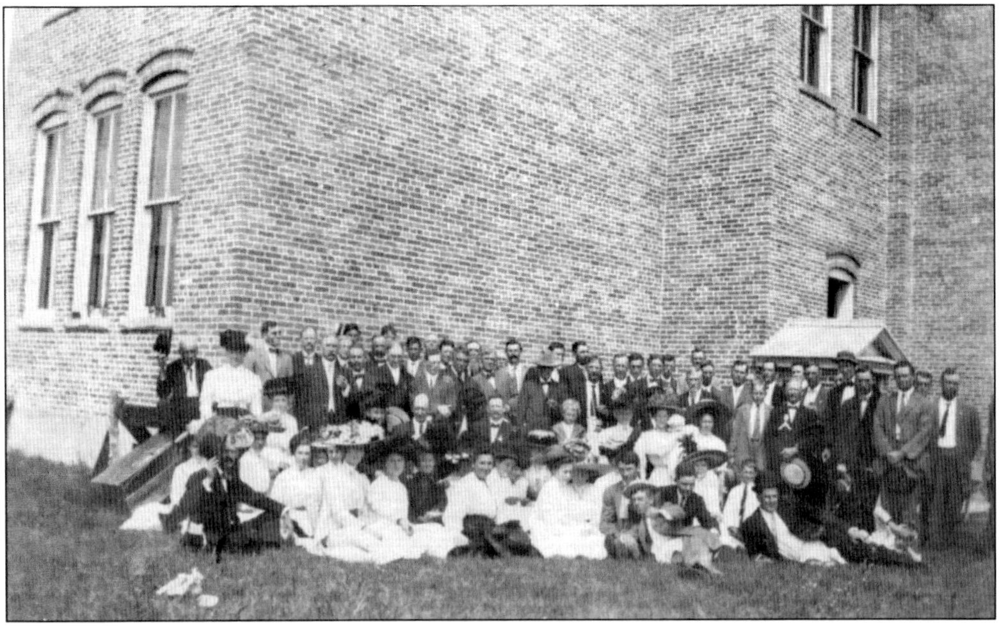

Community leaders gathered in 1910 for the dedication of the Masonic Hall, located across from Toano School. At the turn of the 20th century, most of James City County's leading businessmen, farmers, teachers, and families lived near the prosperous center of activity in Toano. (AB.)

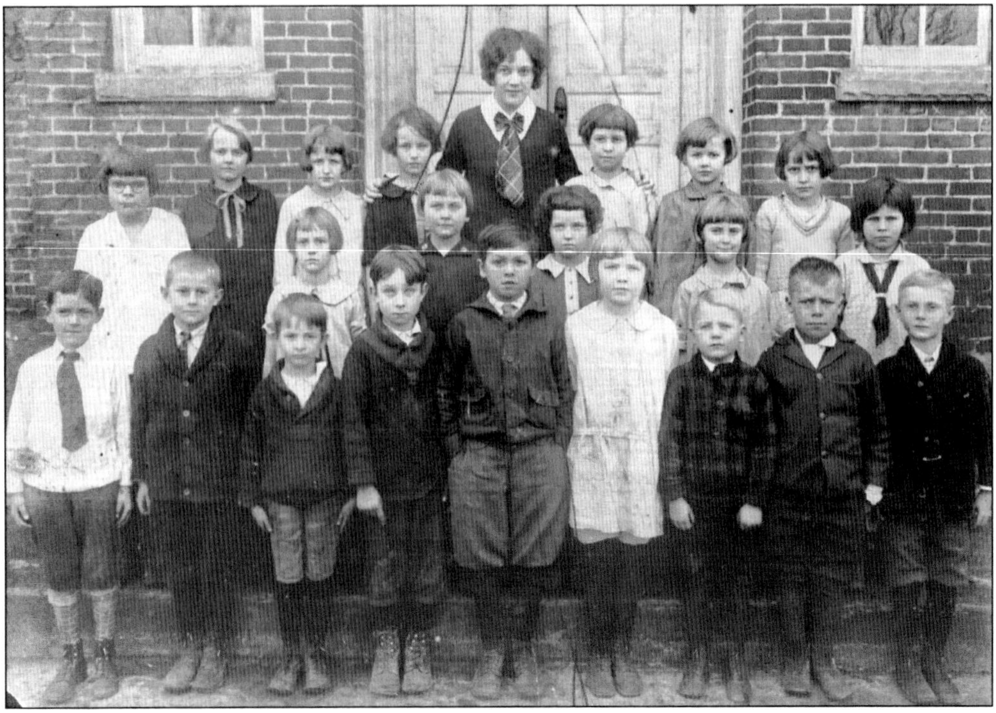

Toano School, which consolidated Hickory Neck, Croaker, and Old Forge Schools, was located where the James City–Bruton Volunteer Fire Department sits today. Student groups posed for photographs with their teachers on the steps of Toano School's elementary building. (WF.)

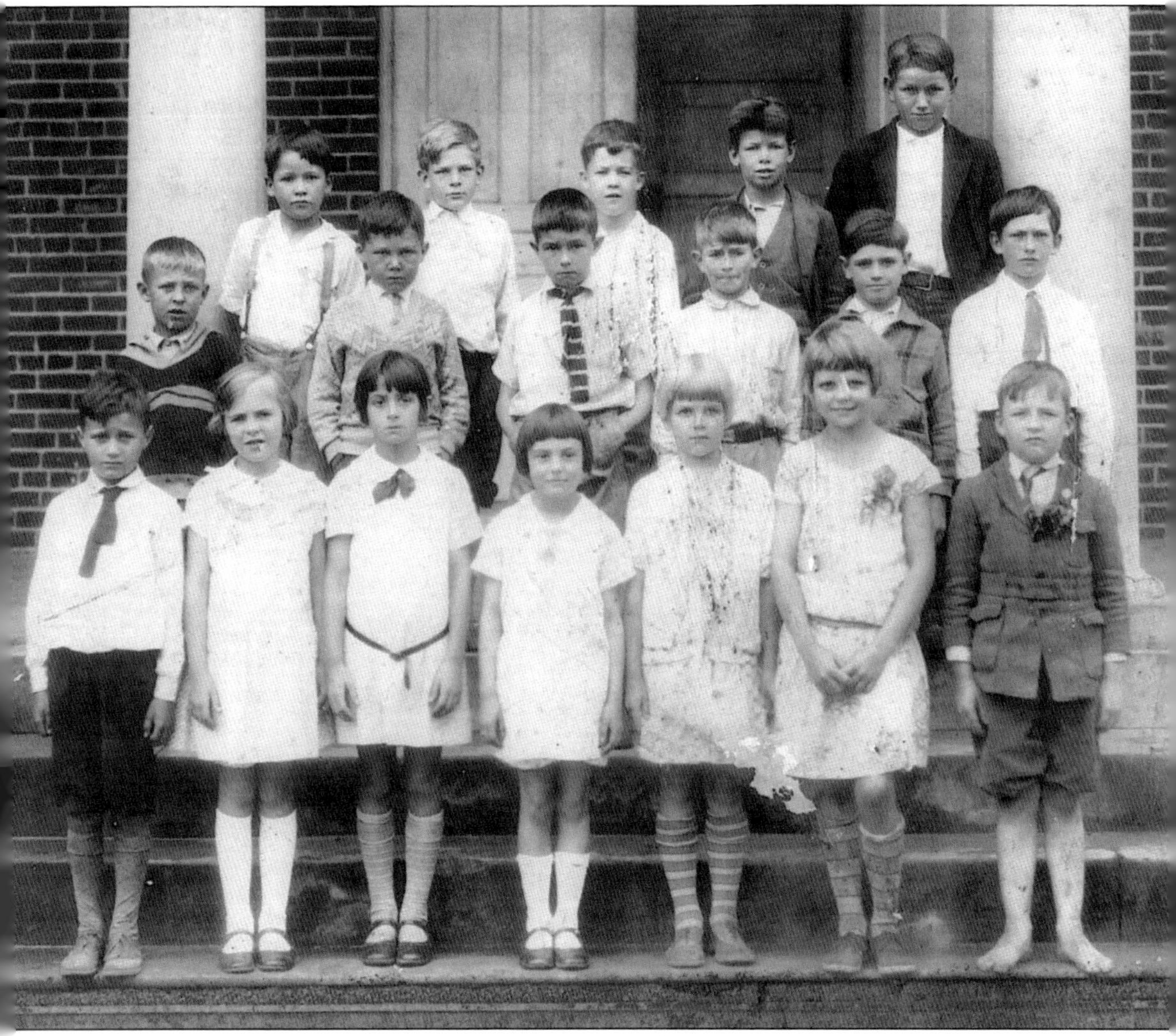

A 1926 class photograph was taken on the steps of the colonnaded high school building. Pictured from left to right are (first row) Edward Sanford, Nan Duer, June Showalter, Ruby Trice, Esther Tyssen, Madge Tyssen, and Lewis Peterson; (second row) Earl Downy, Linwood Apperson, John Woodward, Alvin Slater, William Yates, and Johnny Higgs; (third row) Nelson Farinholt, George Hockaday, Wesley Marston, Robert Garrett, and Arthur Richardson. Their teacher, not pictured, was Emma Geddy. (DTG.)

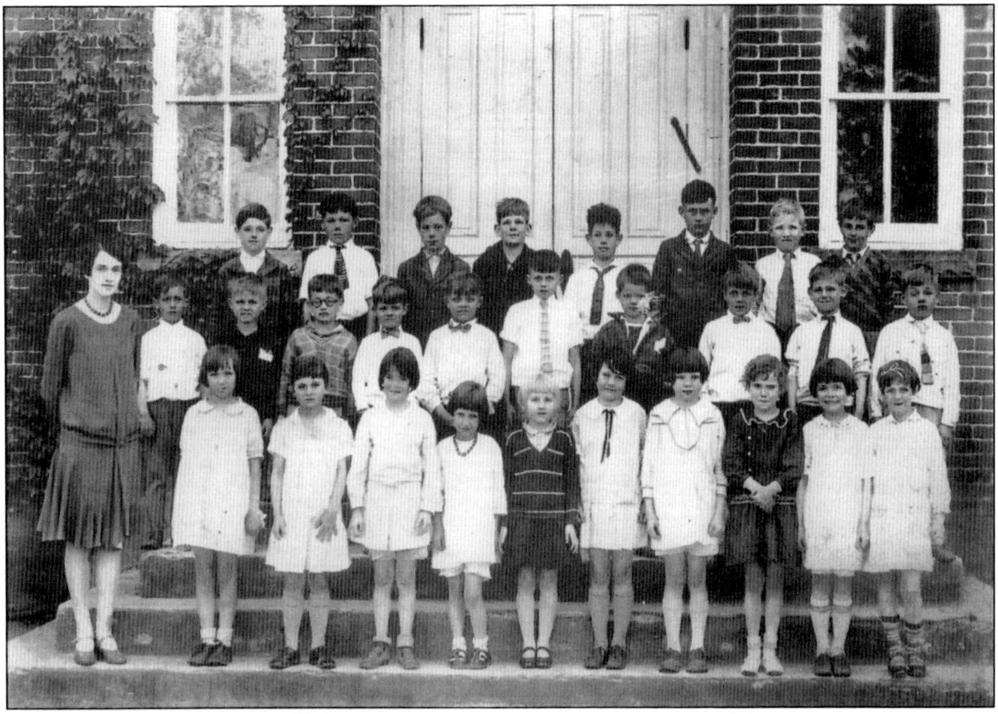

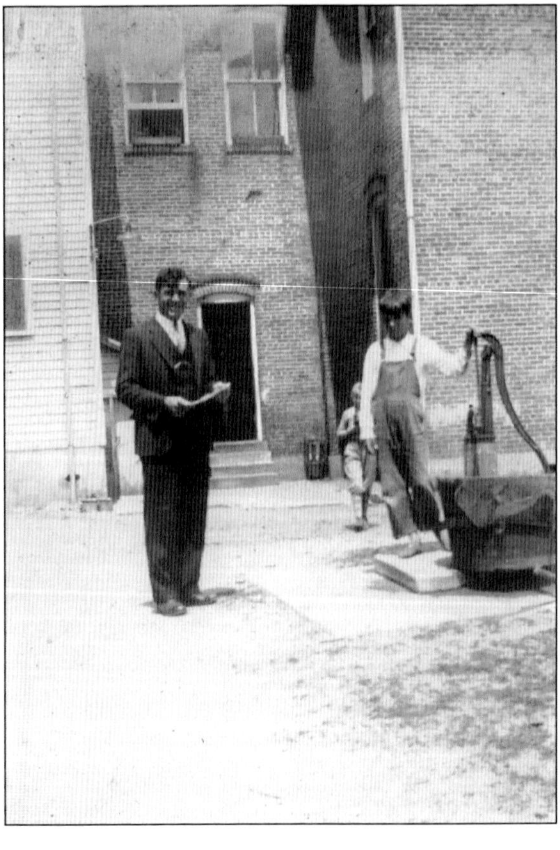

Mrs. Otis Geddy (Hattie Walton) taught students enrolled in Toano Elementary School when this photograph was taken in 1928. (RFW.)

R. M. Doub, school principal for many years, smiled for this 1937 photograph behind the school building with young Carl "Shorty" Meadows, who stands with a hand on the pump. The well was the source of drinking water for Toano students and faculty. (CSM.)

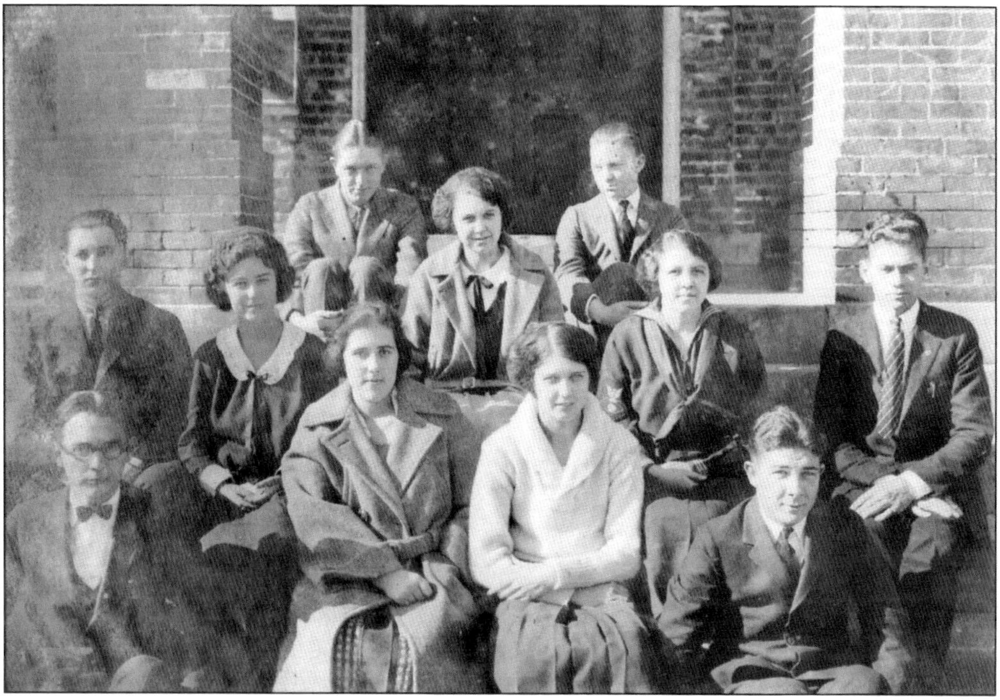

College of William and Mary students from the Toano community were members of the Toano Club. This group photograph was taken in 1922–1923. (BG.)

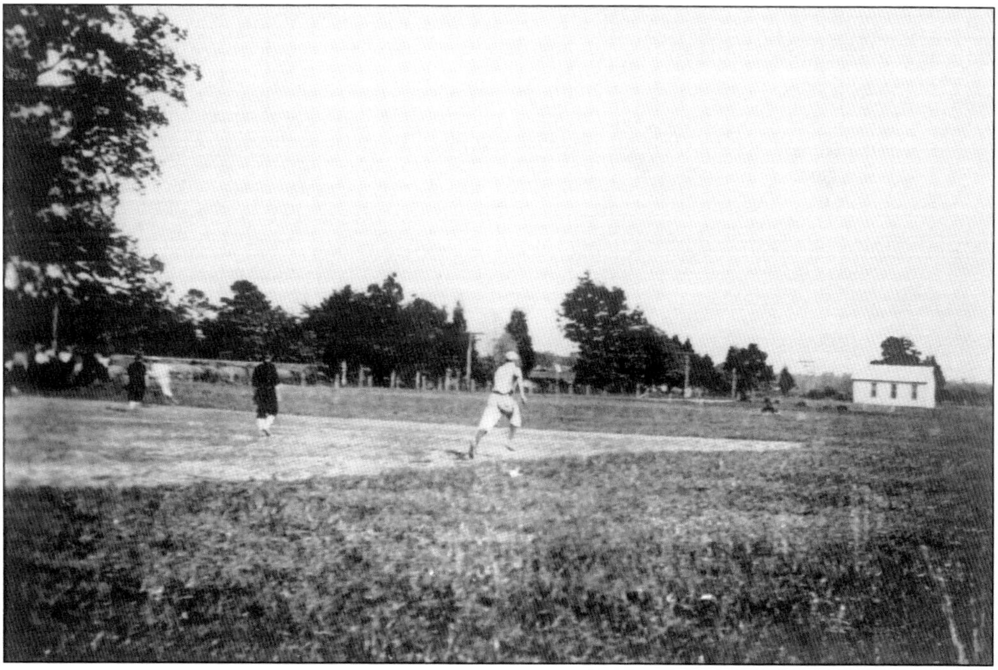

Norwegian resettlers built a school in 1904, but some were opposed to segregating the students and teaching the Norwegian language and culture. By 1912, older Norwegian students attended Toano High School, and the Norwegian School was closed shortly thereafter. In this photograph, students play baseball on Flatten Field near the Norwegian School. (Collection of Alfred Hove, DBW.)

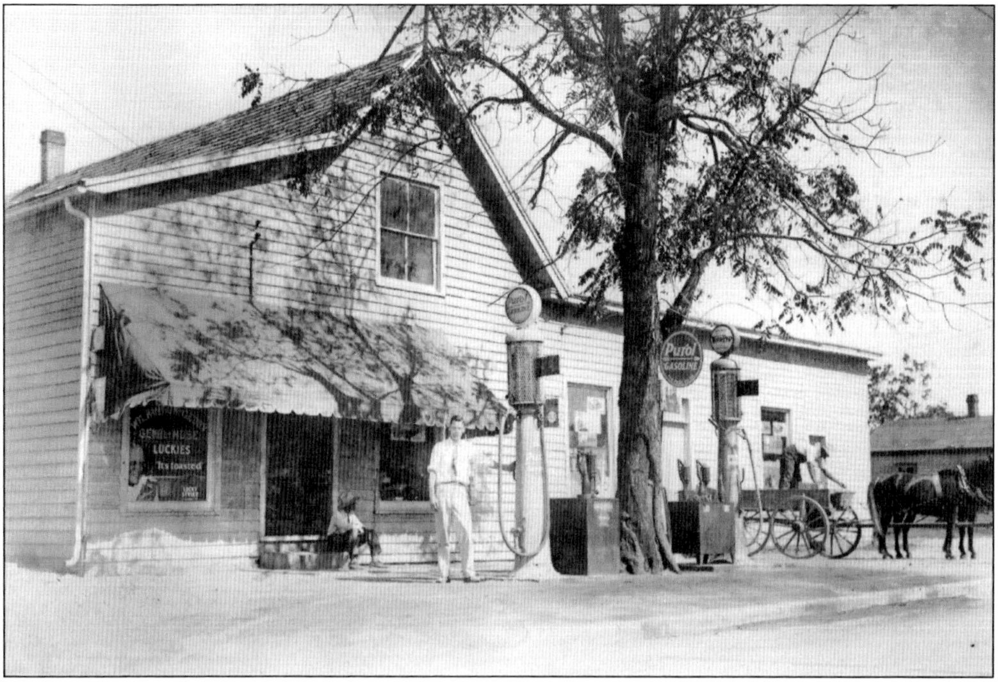

Above, Bert Geddy Sr. posed beside a gas pump at the Wilkinson and Geddy Store. The photograph below was taken in the late 1920s. The Wilkinson and Geddy Store was perhaps the busiest Toano store because of its large parking lot. Col. Richard F. Wilkinson remembers listening to a late-1920s conversation between Williamsburg mayor Vernon Geddy and his father, Roscoe Wilkinson. Geddy joked that he had come to Toano to look for $20 bills, which he could not find in Williamsburg. Business would soon gravitate to Williamsburg, however. In 1934, the public was told that John D. Rockefeller Jr. was the donor of funds for the restoration of Williamsburg to its Colonial-period appearance. (Above, BG; below, RFW.)

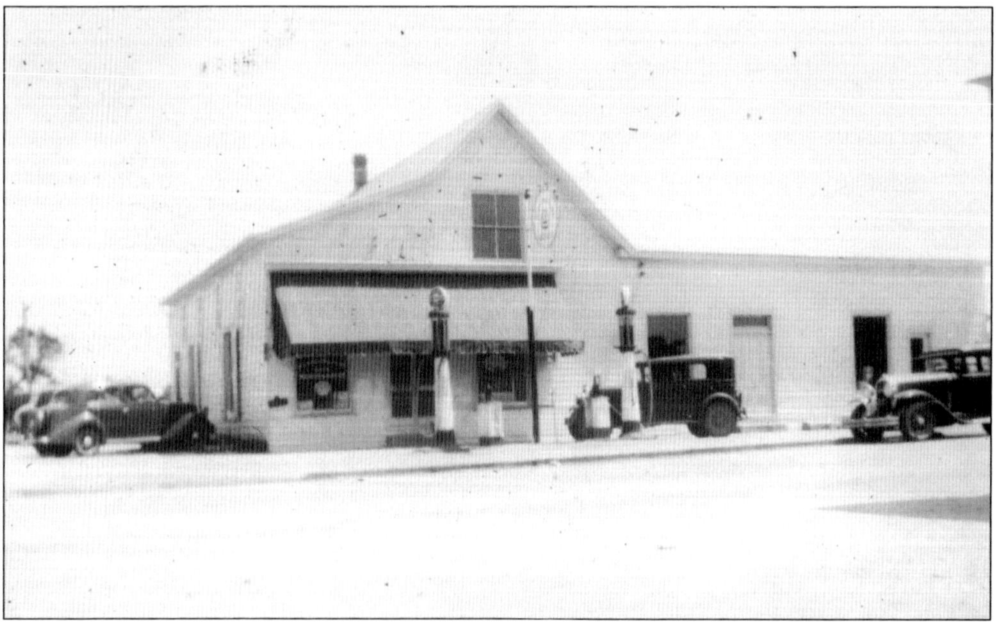

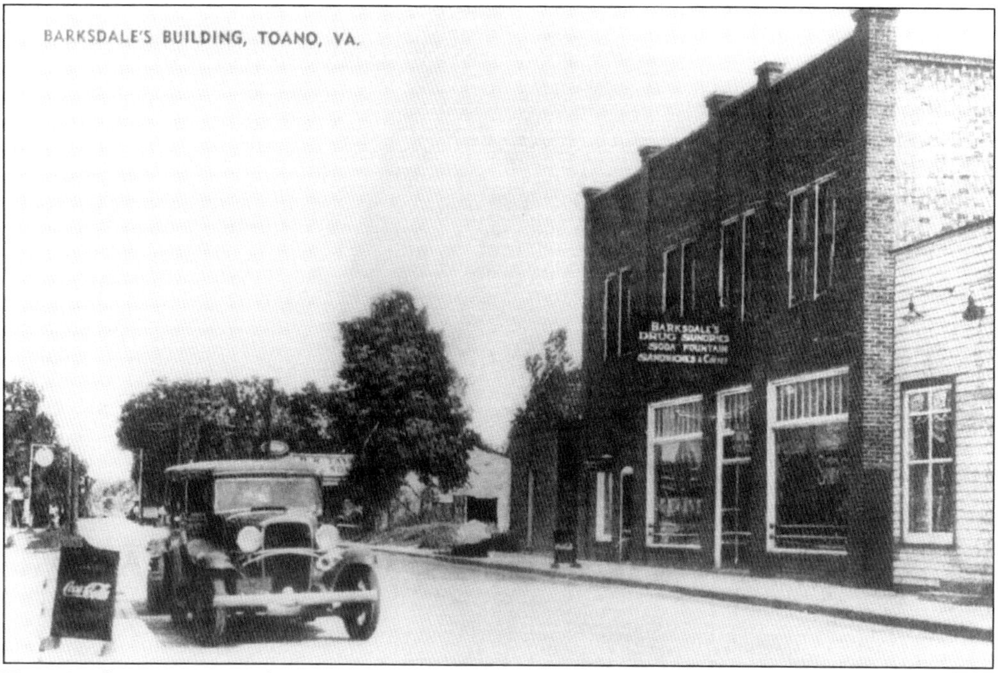

Toano's white townspeople enjoyed the soda fountain in the Barksdale's Drug store. This early view looks east during the period when automobiles came on the scene. They flew by in excess of 25 miles per hour and sent pedestrians scurrying to the sidewalks. The Barksdale building and others were destroyed in 1963 in preparation for the widening of Richmond Road. The four-lane road redefined the pedestrian-oriented life of the community. (WF.)

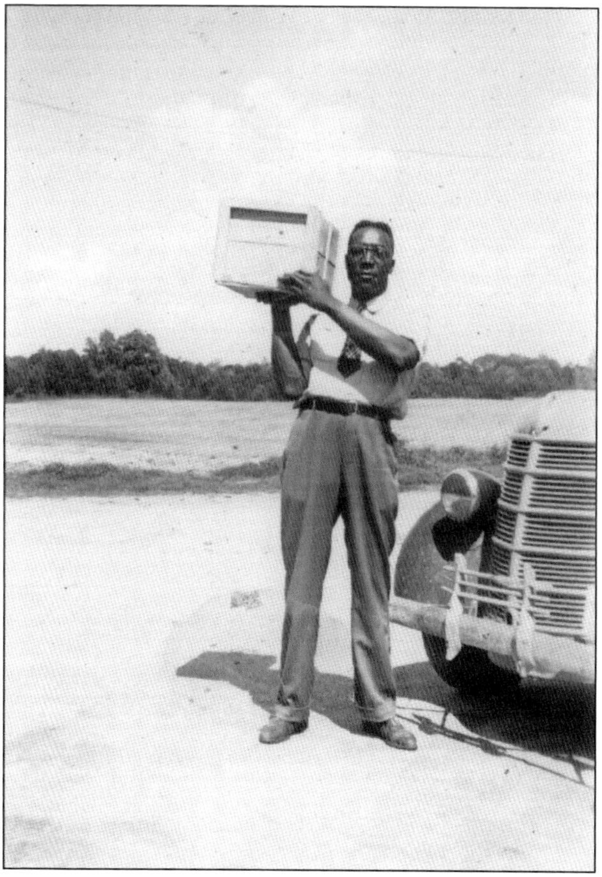

Before motor vehicles became the norm, Ed Taylor delivered groceries for the Wilkinson and Geddy Store. Customers sent their orders to the store to be picked, packed, and delivered. (RFW.)

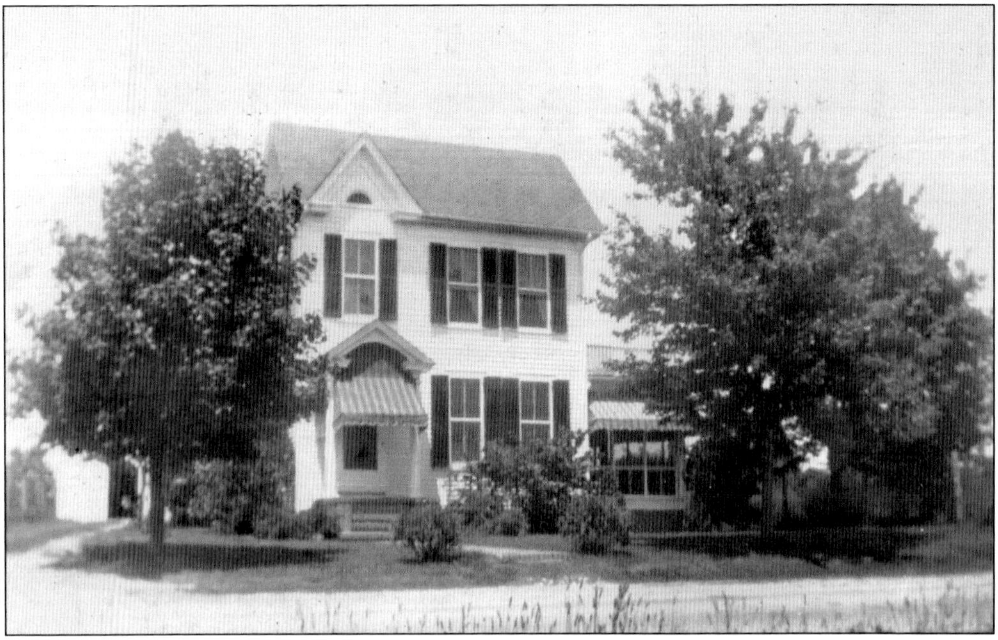

The Wilkinson home, located on the main thoroughfare near the family's store, was one of several that gave downtown Toano its charm. Richmond Road was the only paved road in the county until present-day Route 5 was paved in the 1930s. Today the front yard has been eliminated, and the house has been converted to use as a restaurant. (RFW.)

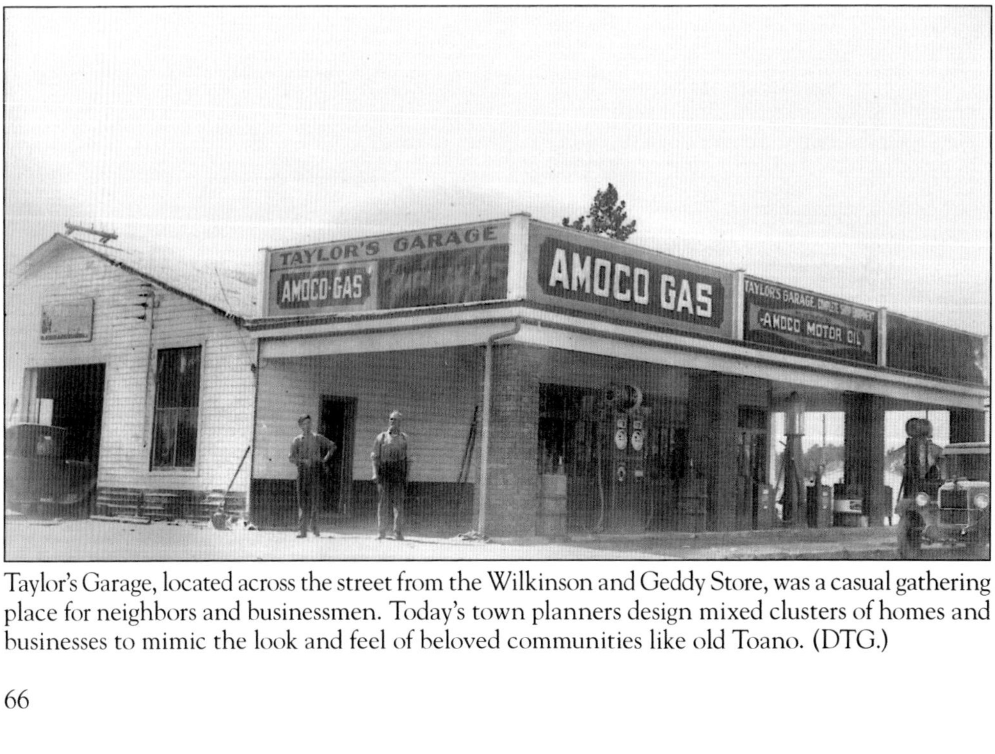

Taylor's Garage, located across the street from the Wilkinson and Geddy Store, was a casual gathering place for neighbors and businessmen. Today's town planners design mixed clusters of homes and businesses to mimic the look and feel of beloved communities like old Toano. (DTG.)

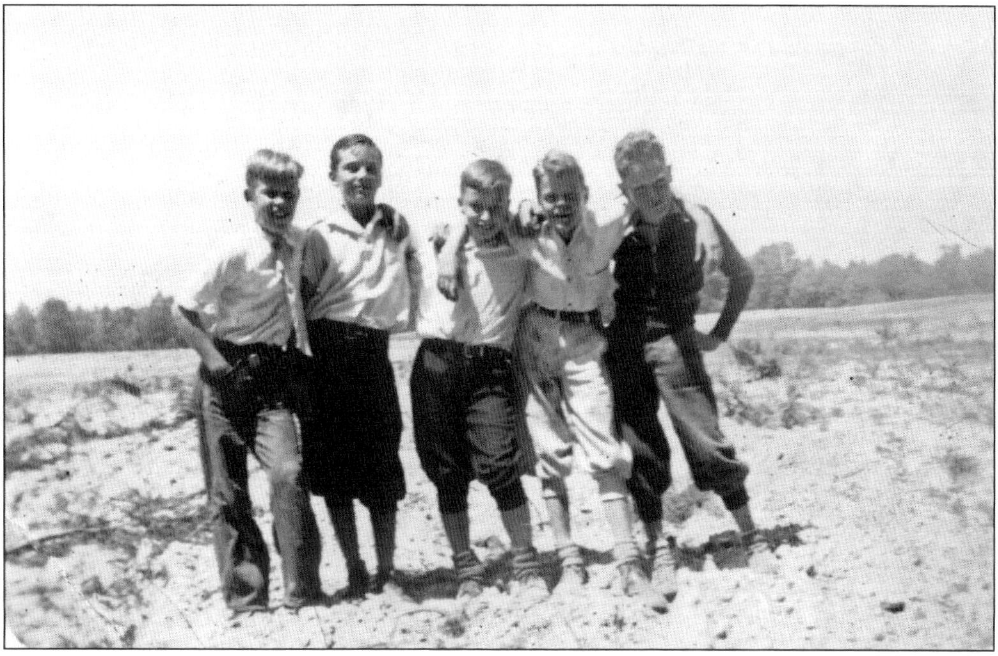

In June 1936, Toano friends (from left to right) Edmund Meanly, Homer Goddin, Robert Piggott, Preston Wilkinson, and Mahlon Cottrell posed for an after-school photograph. Community children who walked freely between school, home, work, and play grew up with a strong sense of personal responsibility. (RFW.)

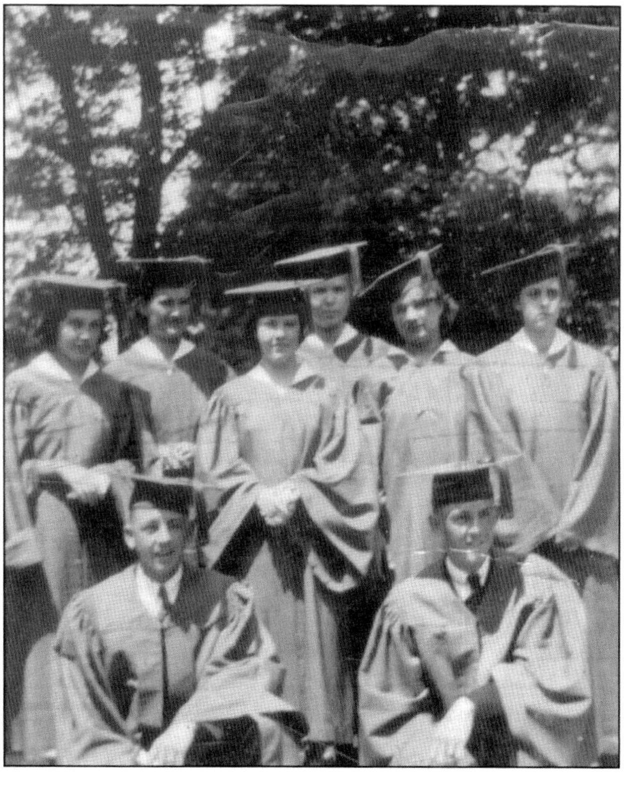

In 1935, some graduates of Toano School grouped around Glennis Hazelwood (center, standing with hands folded) included (order unknown) Edward Kilby, Neal Jenson, Laura Goddin, Bonnie Porter, Mary Hazelwood, Frances Cooke, Lorraine Benson, and Lilbourne Griffith. (GHD.)

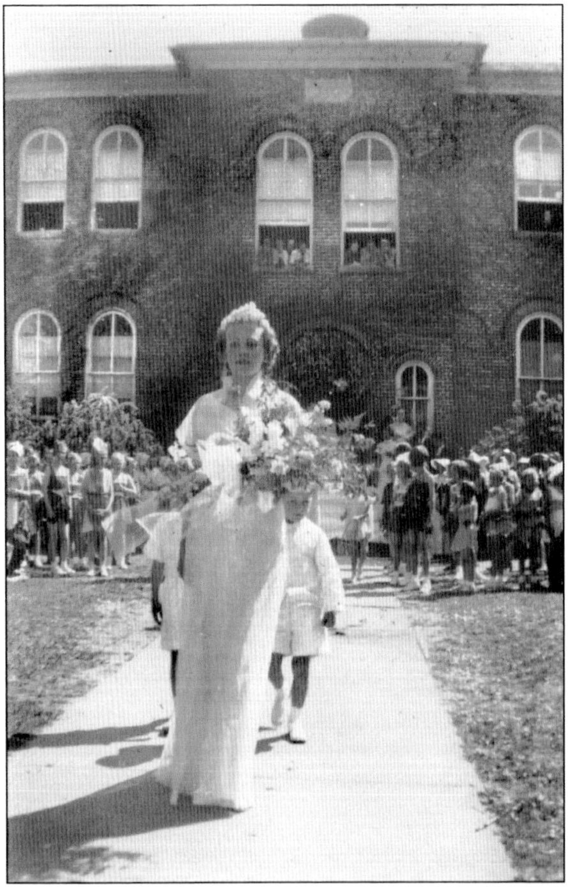

Photographs of Toano School May Days in the 1930s reveal that the annual celebration was a community highlight. The town turned out to admire the May Court and pageantry of costumed children in their supporting roles. May Day celebrations date to ancient times. In late-19th-century America, the celebration took on a political meaning as a commemoration of workers' rights. Shortly after the middle of the 20th century, the festivals were no longer held in public schools and were replaced by other spring carnivals, athletic field days, and Earth Day. (Left, RFW; below, DBW.)

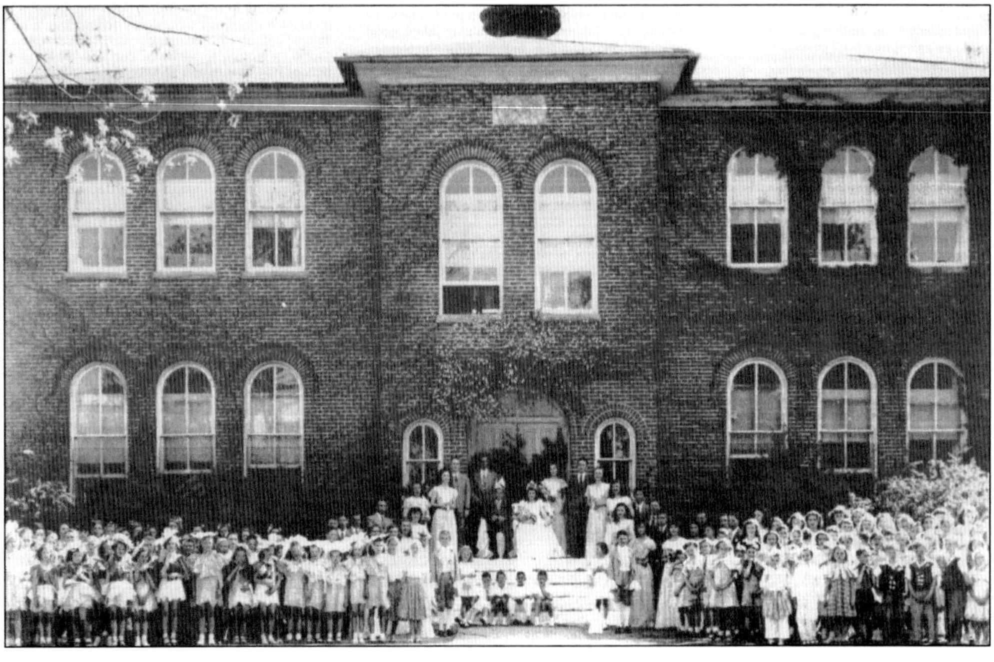

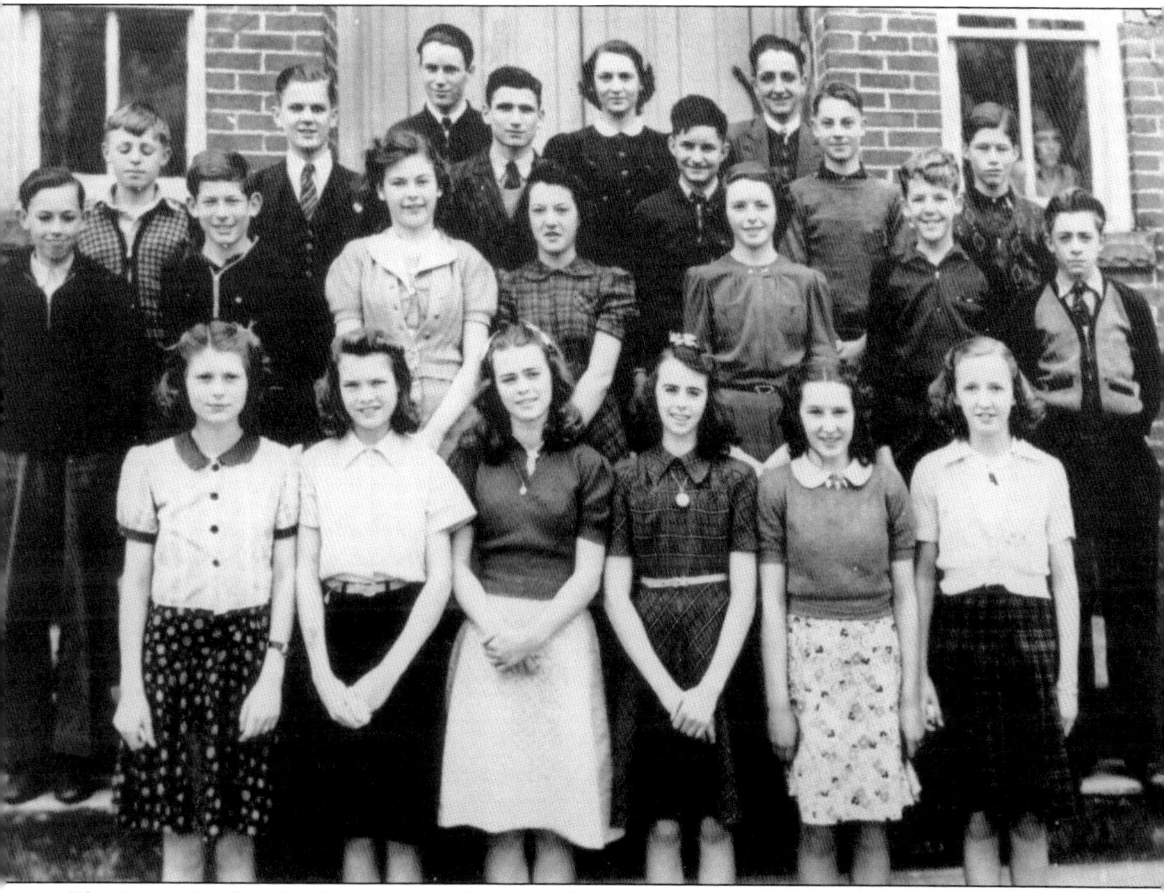

The Toano High School graduating class of 1943 included, from left to right, (first row) Doris Virginia Timberlake, Hattie Marie Smith, Marjorie Joanne Andrews, Mary Katherine McKown, Letha Elizabeth McGee, and Doris Virginia Benson; (second row) John Edwin Rogers, William Goodrich Rankin Jr., Shirley Porter, Della McGinley, Louise Josephine Wright, David Alfred Benson, and Harry Bangs; (third row) Curtis Hubert McSherry, Henry August Tyssen Jr., Louis Zuzma, Jesse Michael Wilson Jr., Louis Raymond Mustian, and George Moorman Hankins; (fourth row) Macon Sanford, Hilda Greenleaf, and William Earl Sweeney. Not pictured was John Hill Gardner. This photograph was taken of the class when they were freshmen. (DTG.)

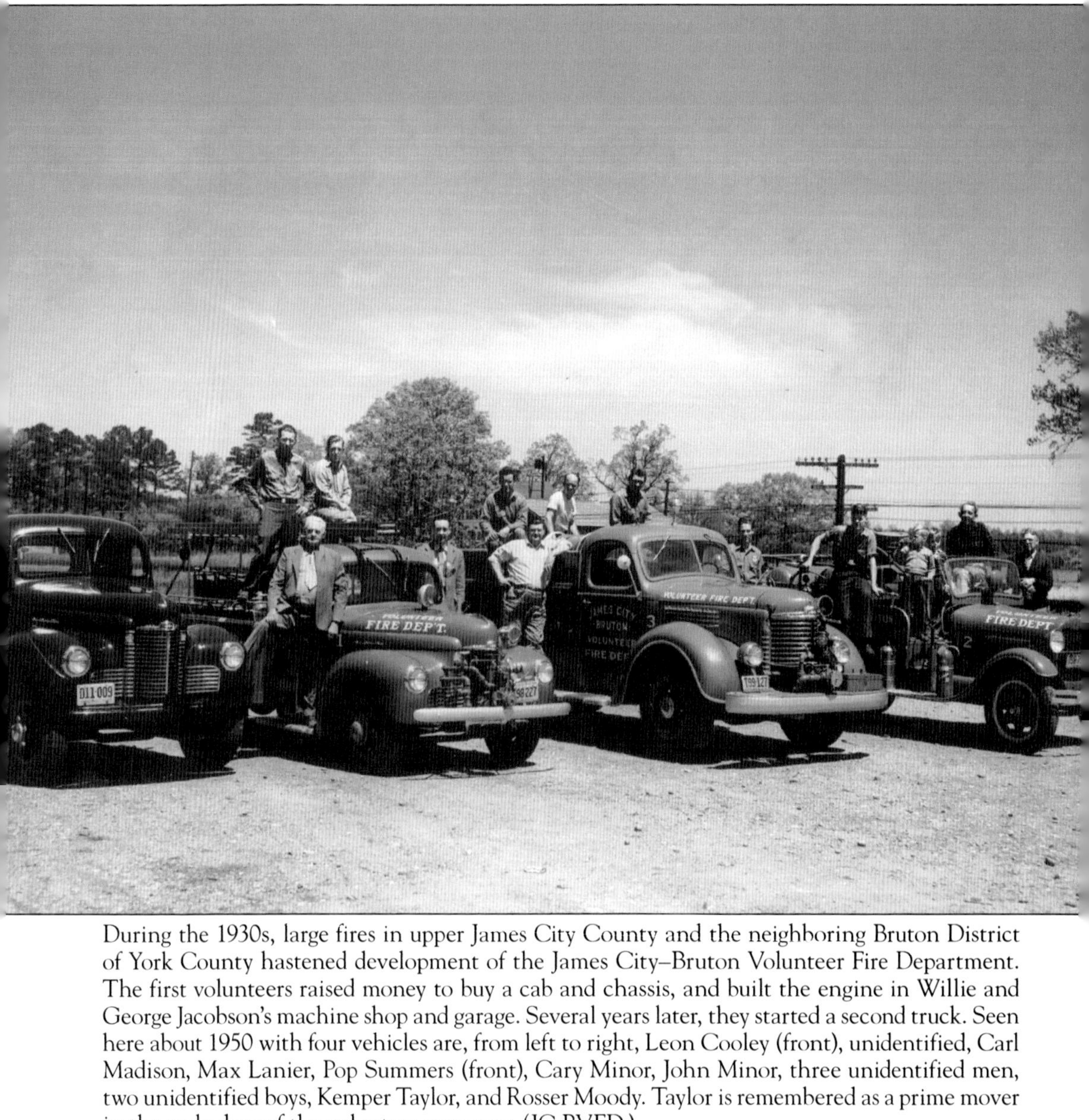

During the 1930s, large fires in upper James City County and the neighboring Bruton District of York County hastened development of the James City–Bruton Volunteer Fire Department. The first volunteers raised money to buy a cab and chassis, and built the engine in Willie and George Jacobson's machine shop and garage. Several years later, they started a second truck. Seen here about 1950 with four vehicles are, from left to right, Leon Cooley (front), unidentified, Carl Madison, Max Lanier, Pop Summers (front), Cary Minor, John Minor, three unidentified men, two unidentified boys, Kemper Taylor, and Rosser Moody. Taylor is remembered as a prime mover in the early days of the volunteer company. (JC-BVFD.)

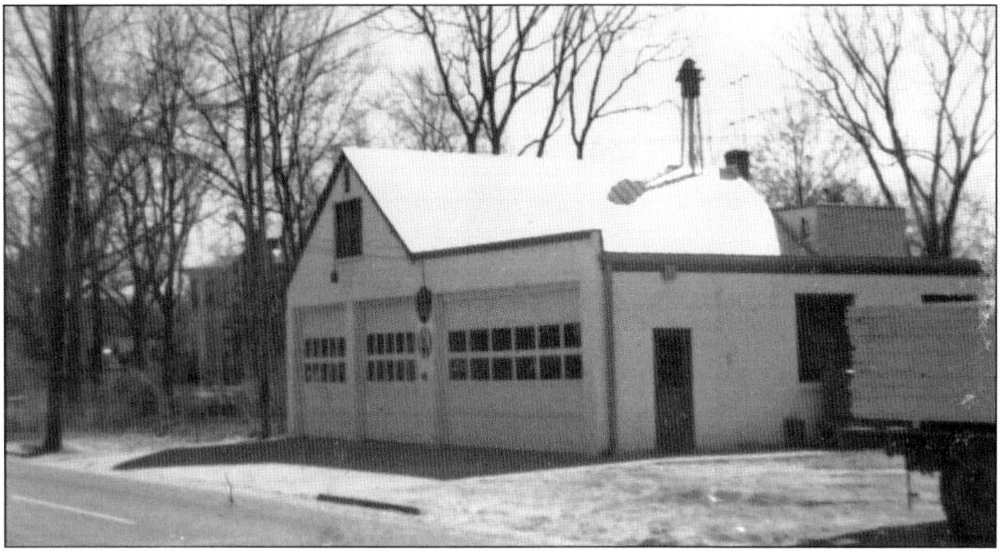

Founded in 1947, the volunteer fire department stationed companies in Toano, Ewell, Grove, Five Forks, and Norge. At first, one truck was stored in Pop Summers garage in Ewell, and a truck equipped with tank, pumps, and hoses was stored at a garage in Toano. Later the Ewell, Grove, and Five Forks companies merged with the Williamsburg Fire Department. The upper county department has remained a volunteer squad and serves the upper county and York's Bruton District; an early facility is pictured above. Pictured below from left to right, Bert Geddy, Woody Ellis, and M. E. Moseley roasted a pig for the Toano Volunteer Fire Department Shad Planking and Barbecue benefit in 1961. The annual fund-raiser is now the James City–Bruton Volunteer Fire Department and Rescue Squad Fish Fry. (Both, BG.)

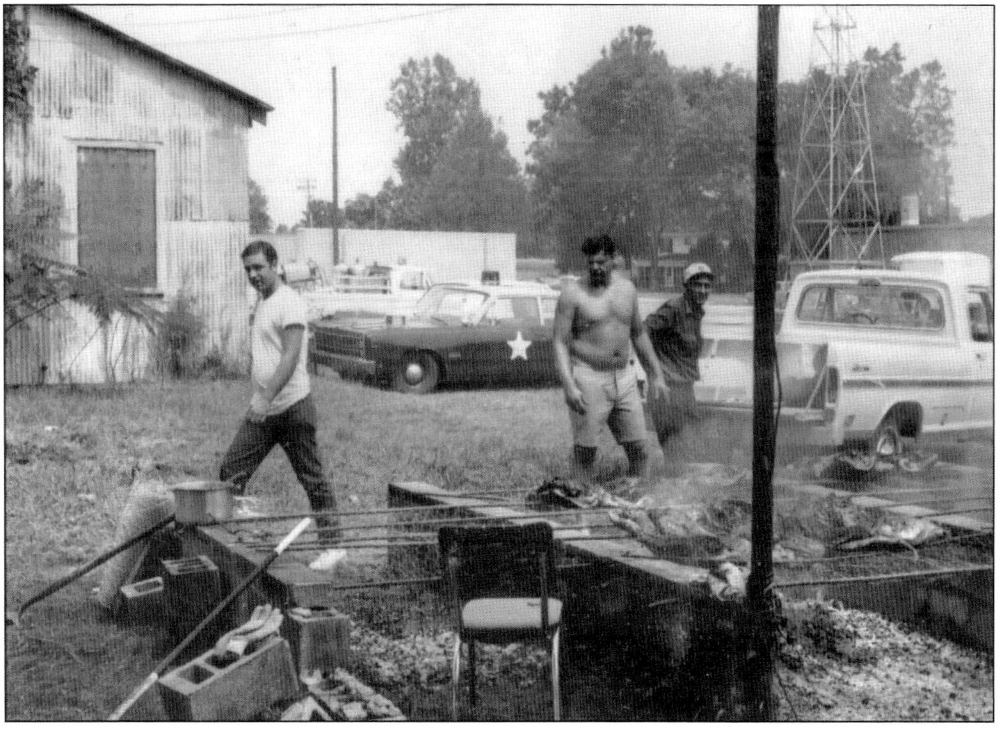

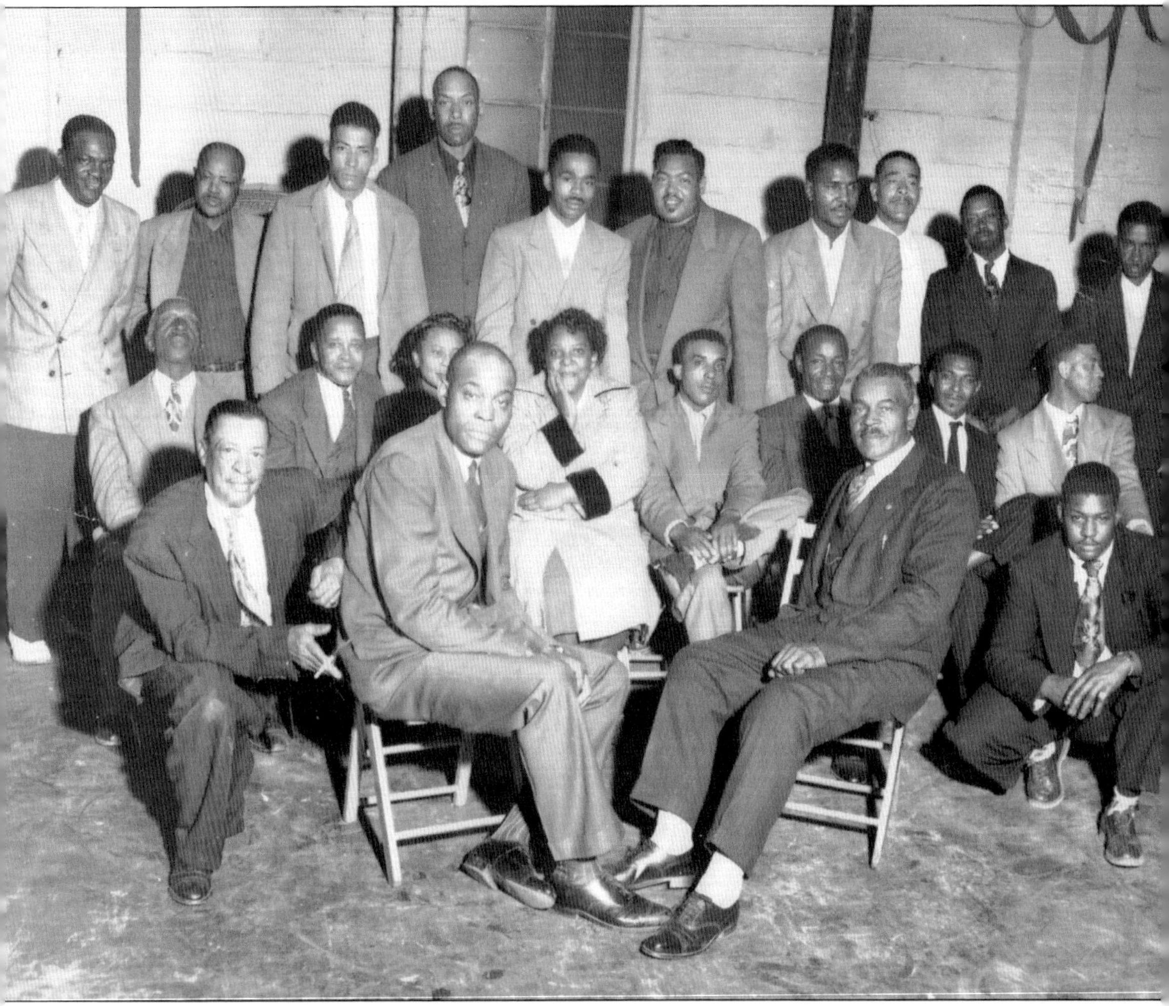

Hunt clubs in rural James City County provided an occasion for sport and socializing, as seen in this gathering at a Lightfoot restaurant. Members of this Toano hunt club included, from left to right, (first row) unidentified, Teddy Major, Andrew Jones, and June Ruttley; (second row) Will Shackelford, Alfred Simpson, Bessie ?, Eudora Robinson, William Cox, Ernest Taylor, Bud Simpson, and Early Hawkins; (third row) Bub Bartley, Garfield Robinson, George Crawley, Sam Meekins, Arthur Crump, Earl Tyler, Charles Travis, Ben Clark, Unis Ashlock, and Orlando Simpson. (Photograph by Albert Durant, OT.)

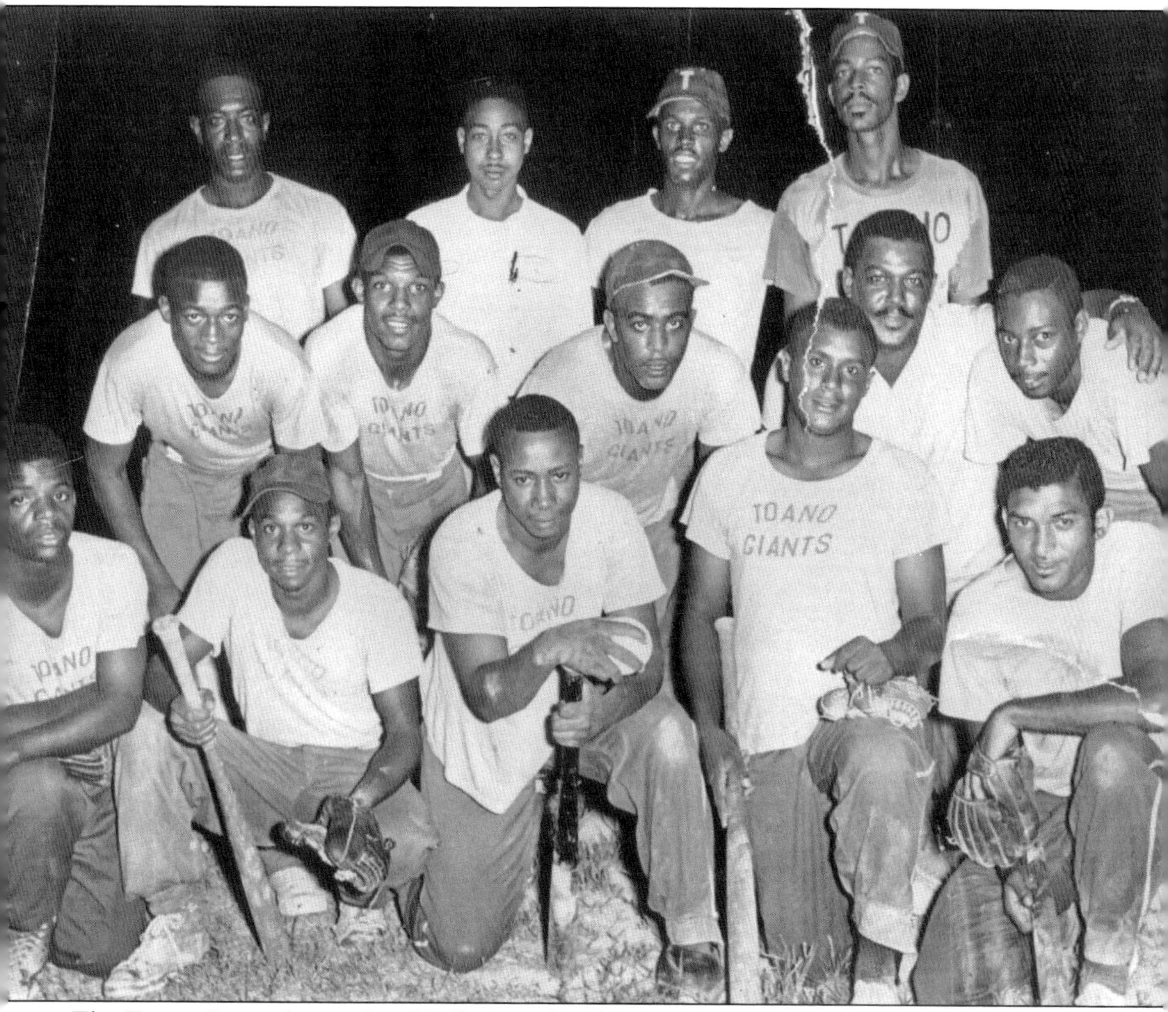

The Toano Giants fast-pitch softball team played community league ball at Bruton Heights School, which served the African American students of James City County, Williamsburg, and York County. The mid-1950s team included, from left to right, (first row) Daniel Wynne, Marshall Braxton, Nathaniel Baker, William Cox, and Lloyd Pierce; (second row) Howard Travis, William Braxton, James Cowles, Fred Christian, and Fred Wallace; (third row) Preston Owens, George Johnson, Preston Tabb, and Osborne Taylor Sr. (Photograph by Reginald Washington, OT.)

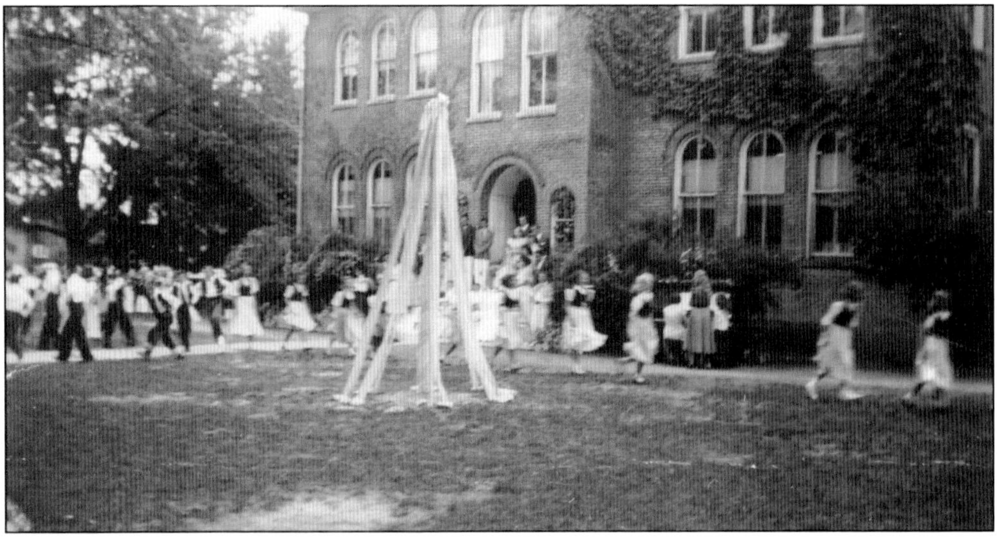

The 1950s ushered in the end of an era with the closing of Toano School. Above, the school's piano was brought outside for a final maypole dance. In 1954 (below), children participating in a Tom Thumb wedding included (in no particular order) Ann Taylor, Virginia Martin, Bert Geddy, Jim Crowl, Carolyn Taylor, Pam Meadows, Linda Goddin, Kay Hitchens, Betty Jo Cowles, and Wendy Tompson. The preacher's role was played by Tyree McKown. (Above, GHD; below, BG.)

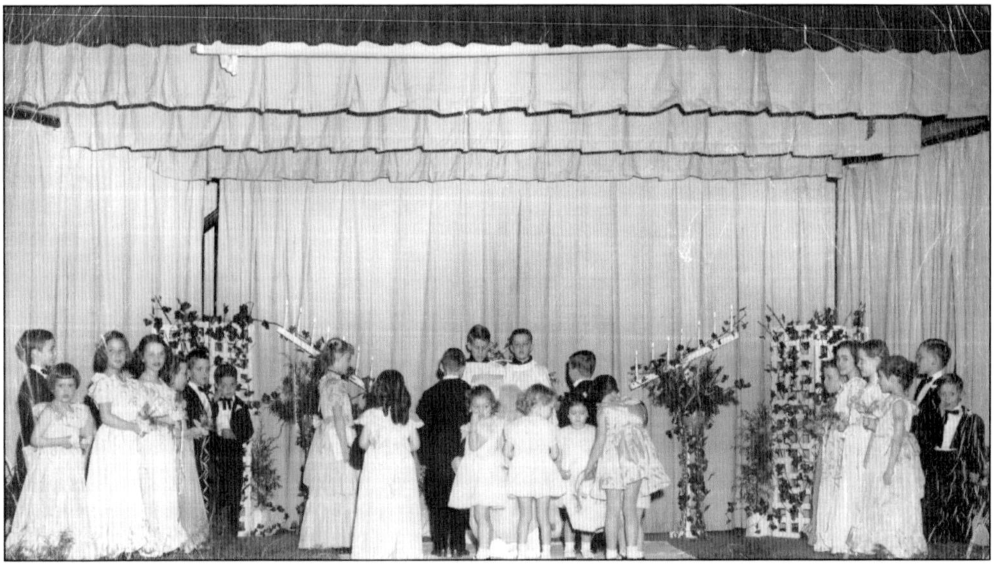

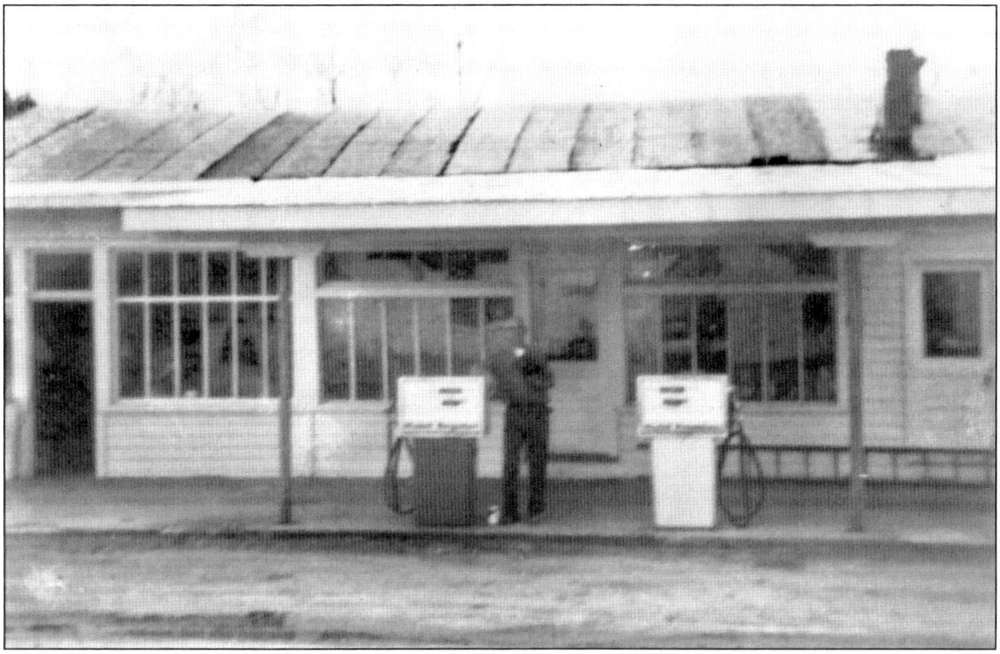

The 1960s widening of Richmond Road, increasing tourism, and faster automobiles brought an end to the slow pace of life that revolved around Toano. The gas tanks at Taylor's Garage had been updated by the time of the photograph above. Until it was demolished, it was the haunt of neighbors with stories to swap and tall tales to tell. Below, a final look at the south side of two-lane Richmond Road includes, from left to right, Bob and Eula Barksdale's drugstore, remembered for Eula Barksdale's thinly sliced ham sandwiches; Richardson's Store; and Anderson's lunch room. (Both, BG.)

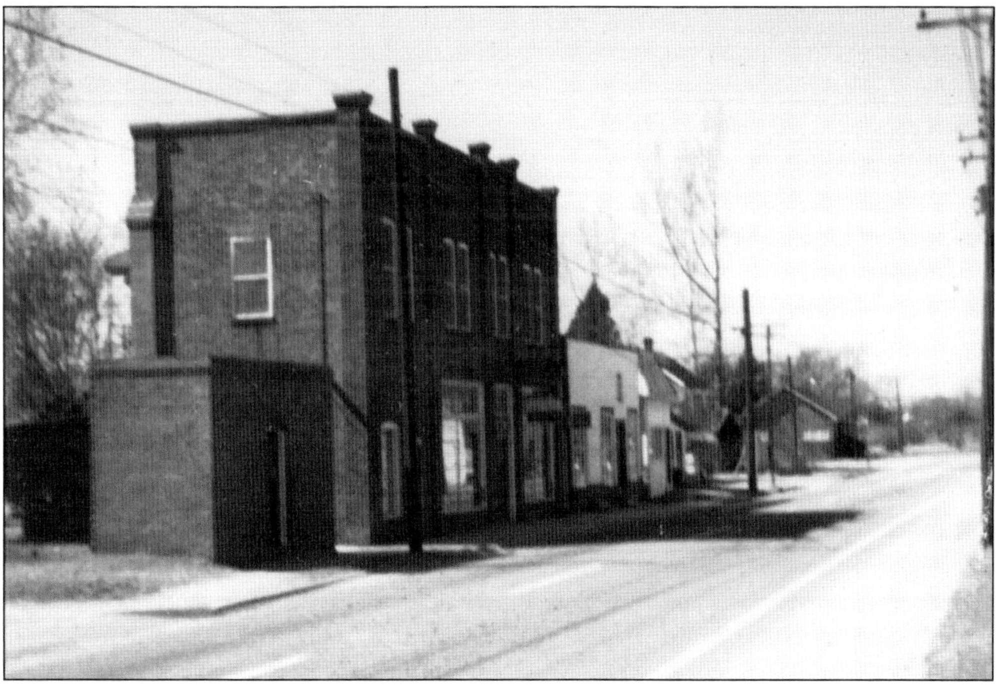

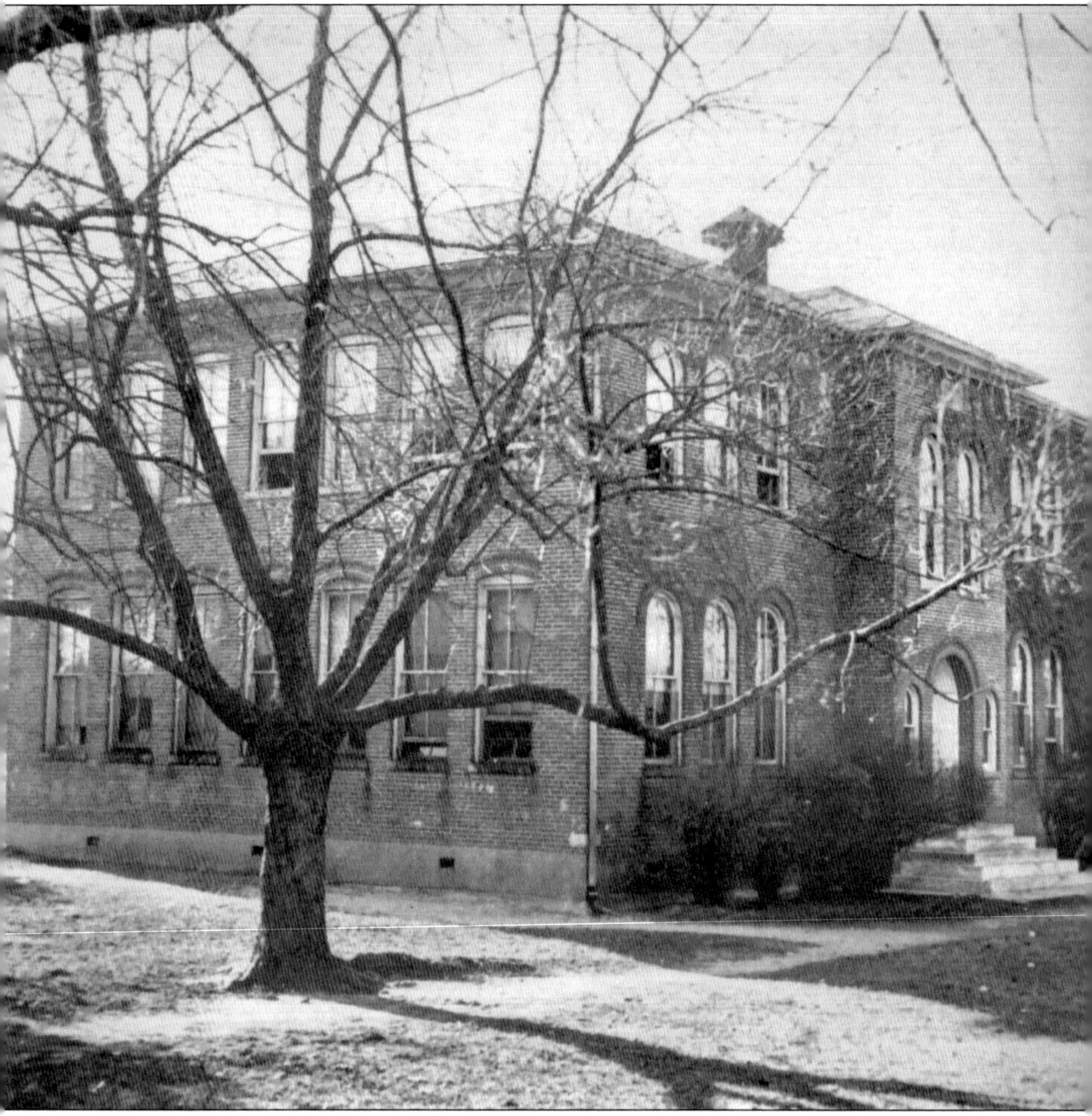

The 1954 Toano School yearbook, the *Chieftain*, included this dedication: "Here is our school just as it is today. Once it was beautiful and new, and stood as an example of the progress of public education. Soon it will be replaced for a new and better school. . . . The Senior Class of 1954 presents this annual with mixed feelings. We are proud to present it, because we believe it is a record of your high school days which you will cherish. We present it with sadness, also, for we realize that it is the last such record to be made of Toano High School. Take the CHIEFTAIN, then, as a beloved reminder of carefree days that can never be recalled." (W.F.)

Six

Rural Communities

Ruins and records of plantations on waterways inform James City County's Colonial accounts. The Richmond Road corridor from Lightfoot to Toano provides a focus for 19th- and 20th-century stories. But memories of scattered crossroad communities and farms county wide truly inform our understanding of day-to-day living. The sampling of photographs in this chapter helps color in the story of this rural James City County way of life. They help us imagine times when the surrounding waterways were busy with schooners and fishermen as well as ferries and steamboats at Grove, College Creek, Jamestown, Barretts, Cowles, Sycamore, and Croaker Landings. On the Chickahominy, the Hazelwood brothers' fish house at Hicks Island and the Menzel brothers' fish house near the old shipyard thrived by serving local and distant markets. As late as 1977, a *Publick Observer* article boasted, "If you are served turtle soup in Atlanta or catfish in Ft. Wayne, Ind., chances are good that the main ingredients came from the waters of the James or the Chickahominy." From Diascund in the west to Grove in the east, the county was linked by regular stops on the C&O Railroad line, convenient for shipping crops and receiving mail. Where roads crossed, stores supplied some needs. But rural families could be self-sufficient. They raised crops of white and sweet potatoes, and chickens laid eggs. Garden vegetables and orchard fruits ripened in turn. Fresh sliced tomatoes were delicious in summer, and apple pie combined its scent with fall air. By canning and butchering, food was saved for winter. A young boy could kill squirrels and rabbits for dinner. Every man could hunt and fish: Acres of land offered habitat for turkeys, deer, and quail. Rural people knew when shad would run and crabs would molt. Rural lives revolved around these things, as well as church and kin.

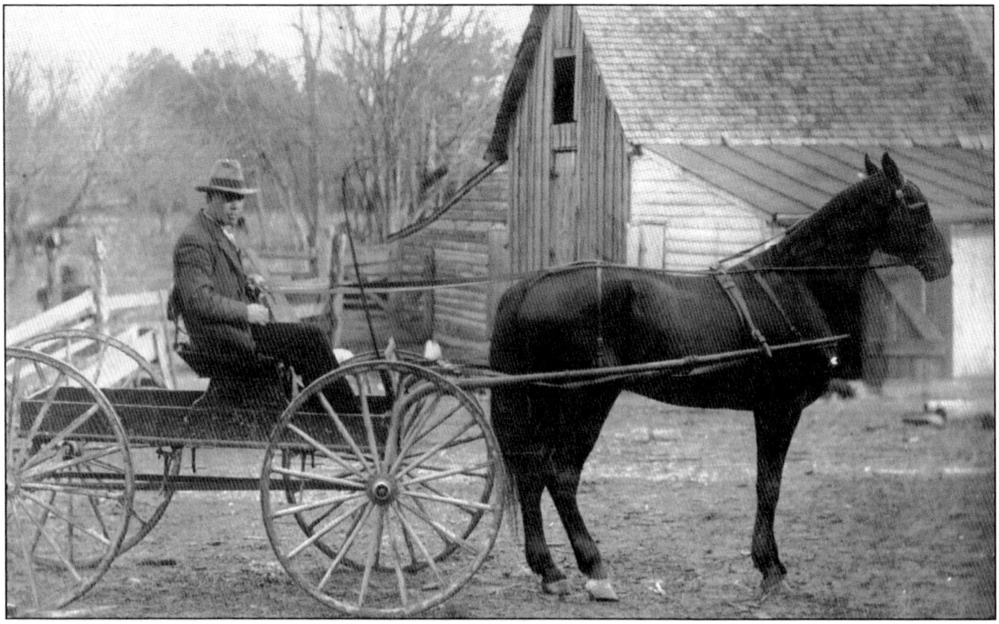

As a businessman, county deputy sheriff, and editor of a local newspaper, William Walker Ware traveled throughout the county and to Williamsburg from his home, Windsor, on Old Forge Road. When this photograph was taken in 1912, he rode in a wagon hitched to his horse, Dan Patch, named after the famous harness-racing horse that was the subject of popular books and movies. (WF.)

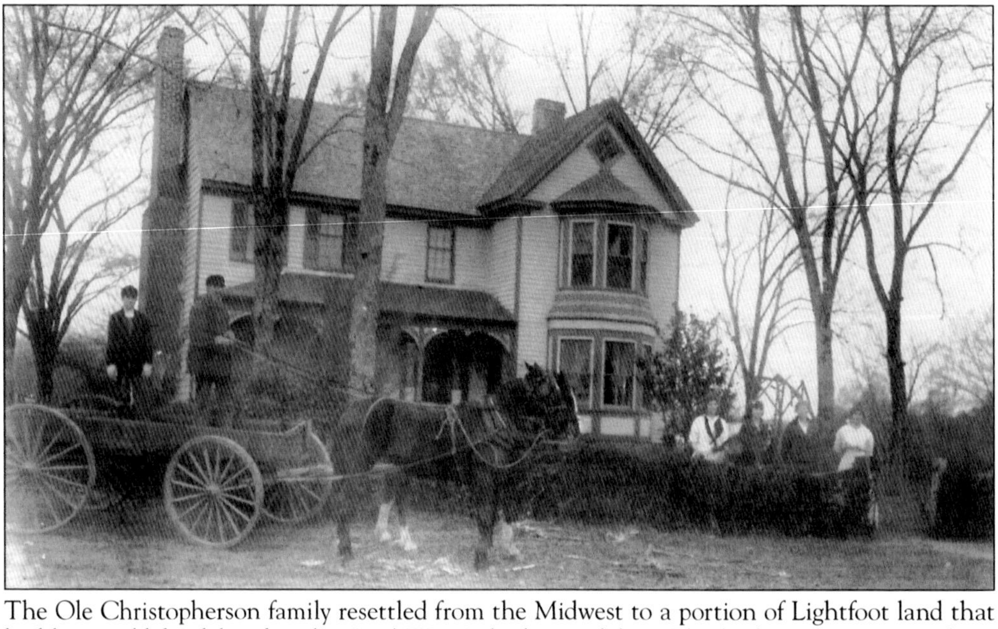

The Ole Christopherson family resettled from the Midwest to a portion of Lightfoot land that had been sold for debt after the Civil War. It had passed from Elizabeth Taylor to Humphrey Wynne Lee to Dr. Edward Camm Wynne. The Christophersons enlarged the house, and their farm was one of several in the area worked by Scandinavians. The earliest of these post-bellum newcomers were viewed with suspicion as "Northerners" or foreigners. (Collection of Christopherson descendant Gary Wilson, DBW.)

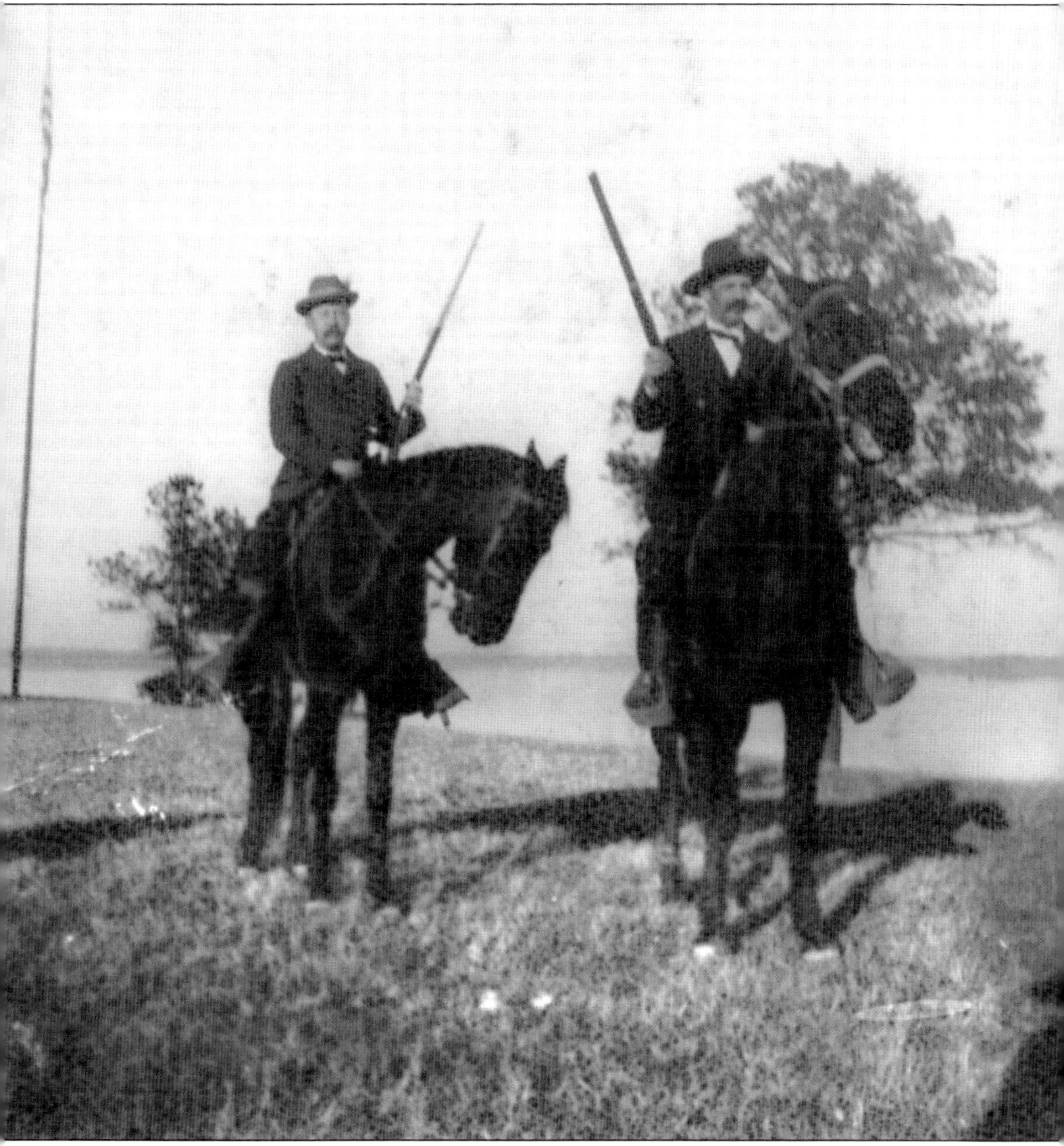

This photograph's inscription notes that S. S. Hankins and his friend, a Mr. Sweetser, were ready for a deer hunt at Taskinas [*sic*] on December 18, 1898. Taskinask Plantation on the York River in northern James City County was an early land patent of 900 acres that was enlarged by later owners. It was near Hankins's family plantations of Aspen Grove or Moss Side, Riverview, and Shellfield. The Hankins families were counted among the county's prosperous farmers. S. S. Hankins, a Confederate veteran, was a James City County commissioner of the revenue. He received his mail in Toano. Some other families listed in the 1898 *Directory and Handbook of the City of Williamsburg and County of James City* with a Toano address included Martin (7 families); Hazelwood (5 families); Geddy, Marston, Taylor, and Wilkinson (4 families each); and Branch, Cowles, Garrett, Slater, and Warren (3 families each). (SW.)

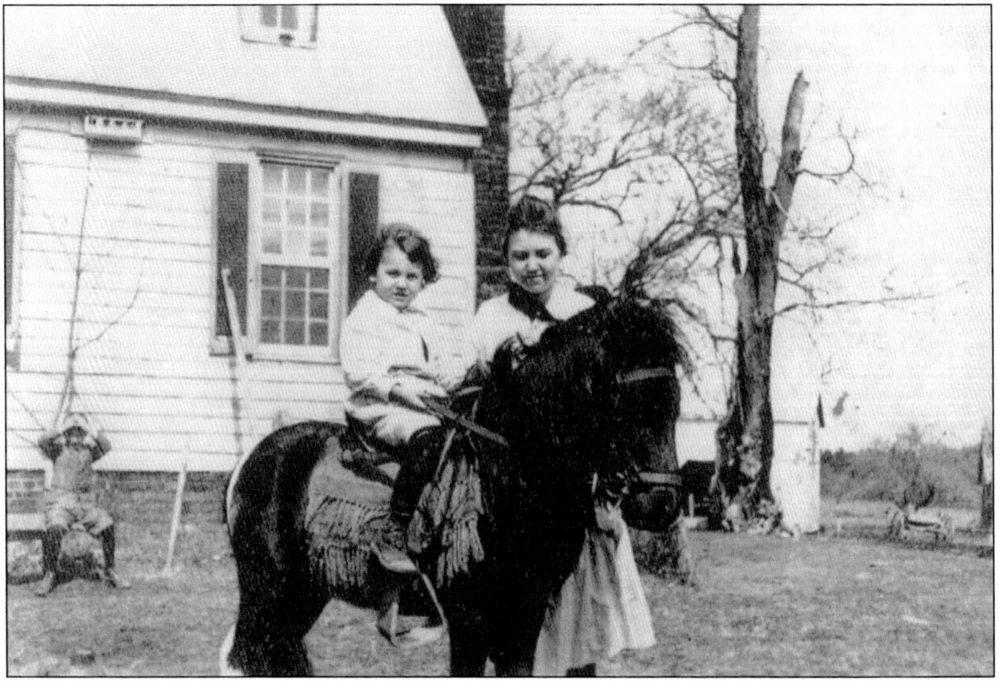

Above, at Windsor in the 1910s, the Ware children learned to ride a pony when they were quite young. Below, in about 1930, Dick Wilkinson was also an equestrian, although by this time cars were widely used. However, if a family's car broke down, they could count on a horse to get them where they needed to go. Early James City County records indicate that a great deal of effort was expended to keep the county's roads in good repair. Horses and horse-drawn wagons were often more convenient for travel because most roads were not paved and were frequently too rutted and muddy for motor vehicle travel. (Above, DW; below, RFW.)

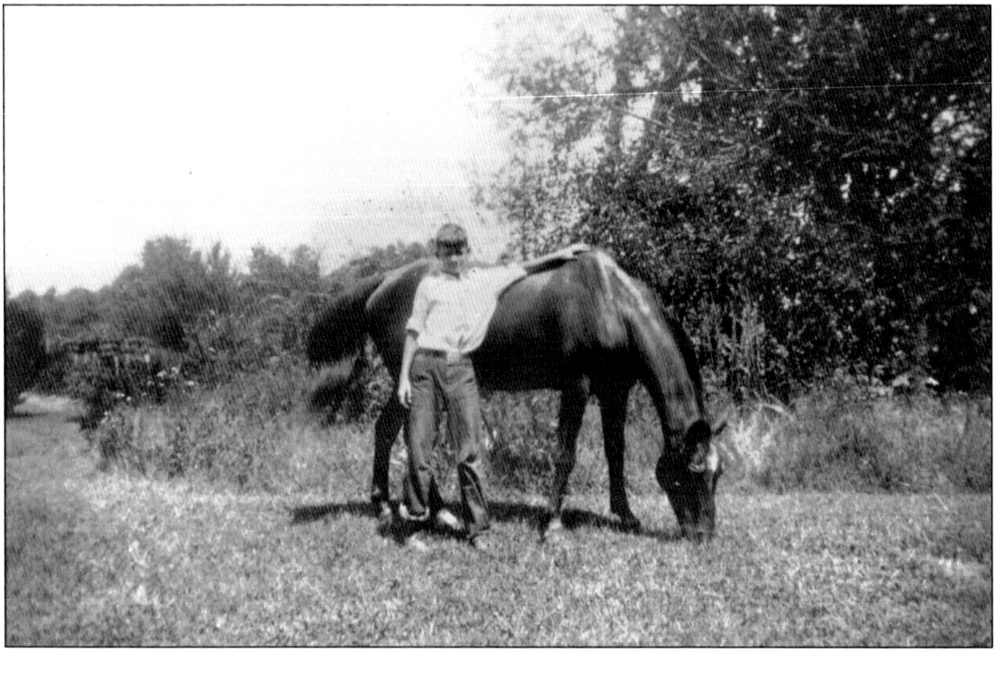

Kent and Carl Meadows posed on mules for this early-1930s photograph. Large farmers like C. C. Branch brought in railroad cars full of mules to help gather potatoes at his farm. The number of horses and mules in use as draft animals and for transportation reached a peak in Virginia in the mid-1920s. As motor vehicles became more popular, horse numbers declined. According to the Virginia Transportation Research Council, in 1920, there were 312,465 horses and ponies on 133,570 Virginia farms; by 1950, there were 132,894 on 67,743 farms. (CSM.)

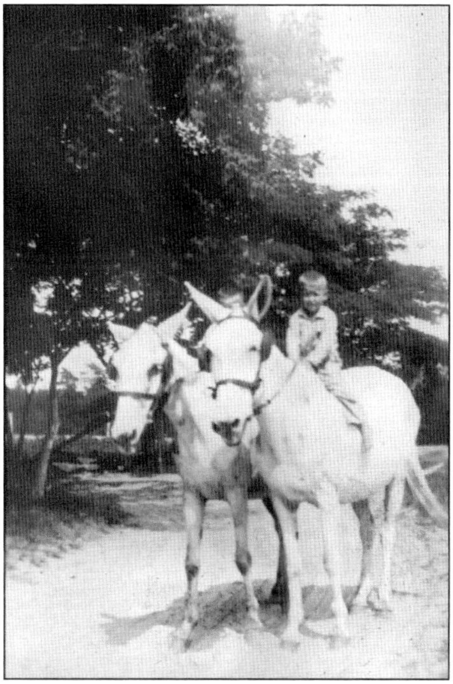

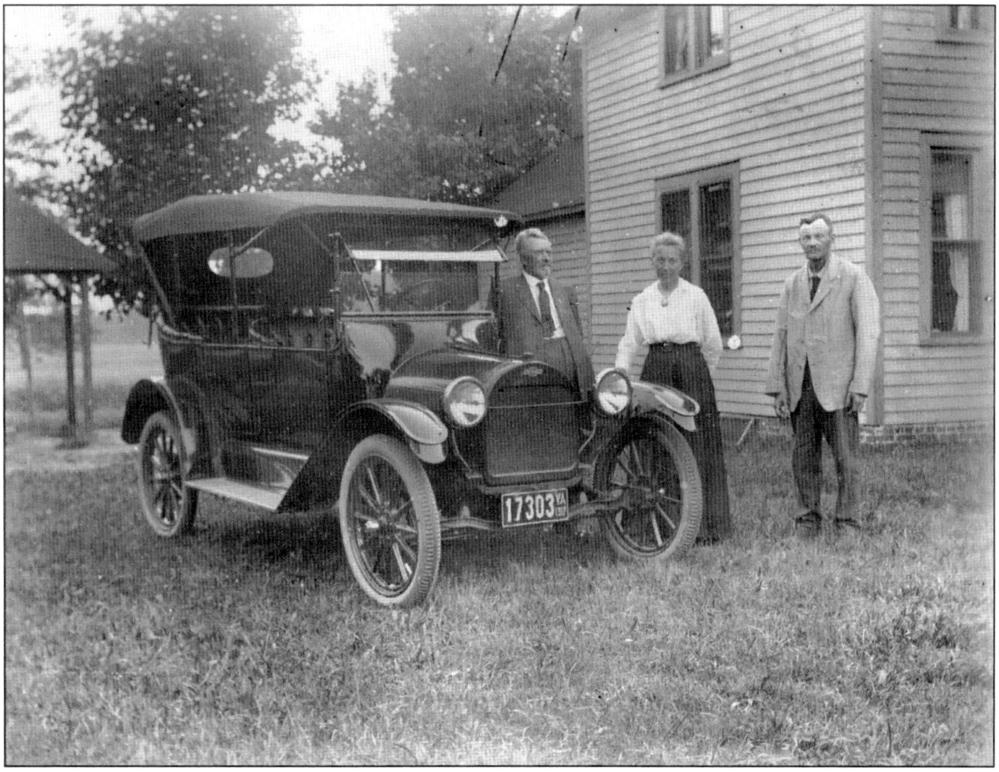

The automobile's license plate identifies the year 1917 as the date when Mr. and Mrs. John O. Larsen (right) posed with a brother. He leaned close to the central subject of the photograph, the car. (Collection of Chrissie Hughes, DBW.)

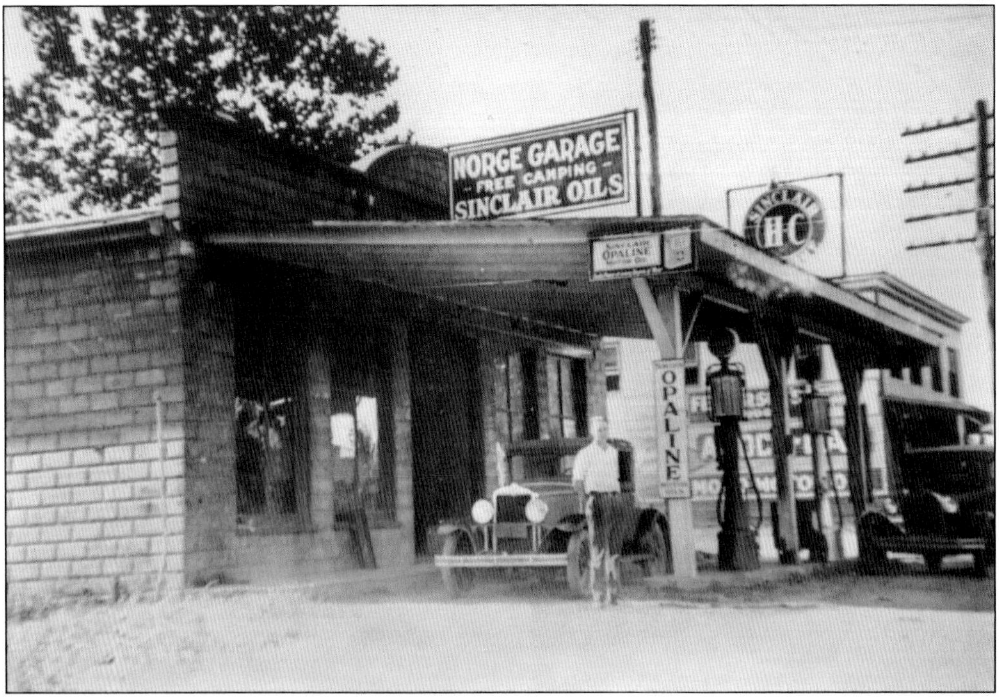

Changes came to Richmond Road as more people acquired automobiles. Milliard Brenegan ran the Norge Garage. The old Kinde Store (see page 44) seen in the background was one of the few c. 1900 structures that remain along the modern highway. (Collection of Joan Brenegan Miller, DBW.)

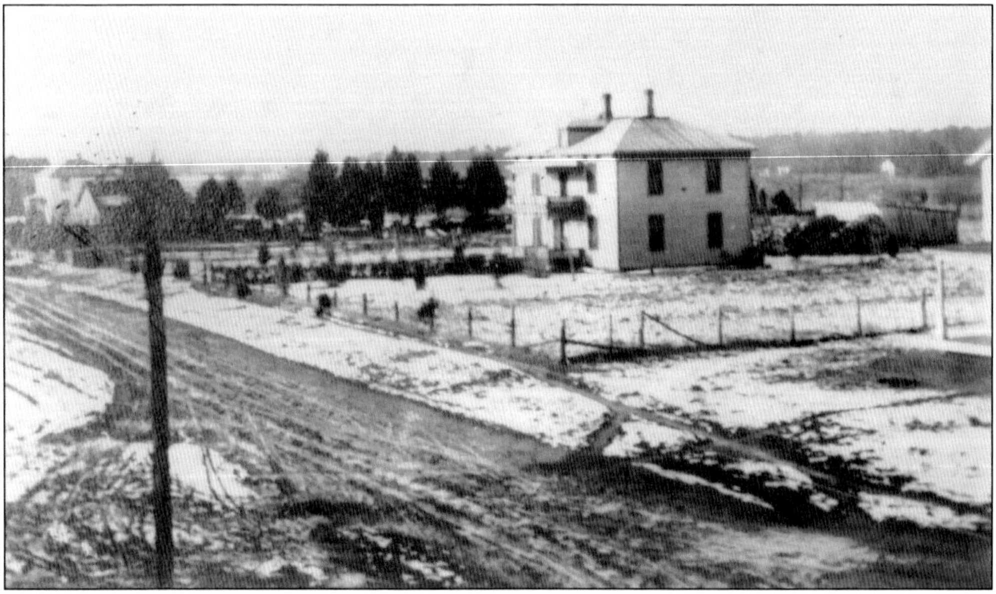

This view of the Hans Kinde house, which burned in the 1920s, shows the condition of Richmond Road one might expect if traveling from Williamsburg to Toano in the early 20th century. A horse-drawn wagon would have been more reliable than a car on the day after a snowfall like the one pictured here. The road was paved in 1923. (Collection of Frances Hamilton, DBW.)

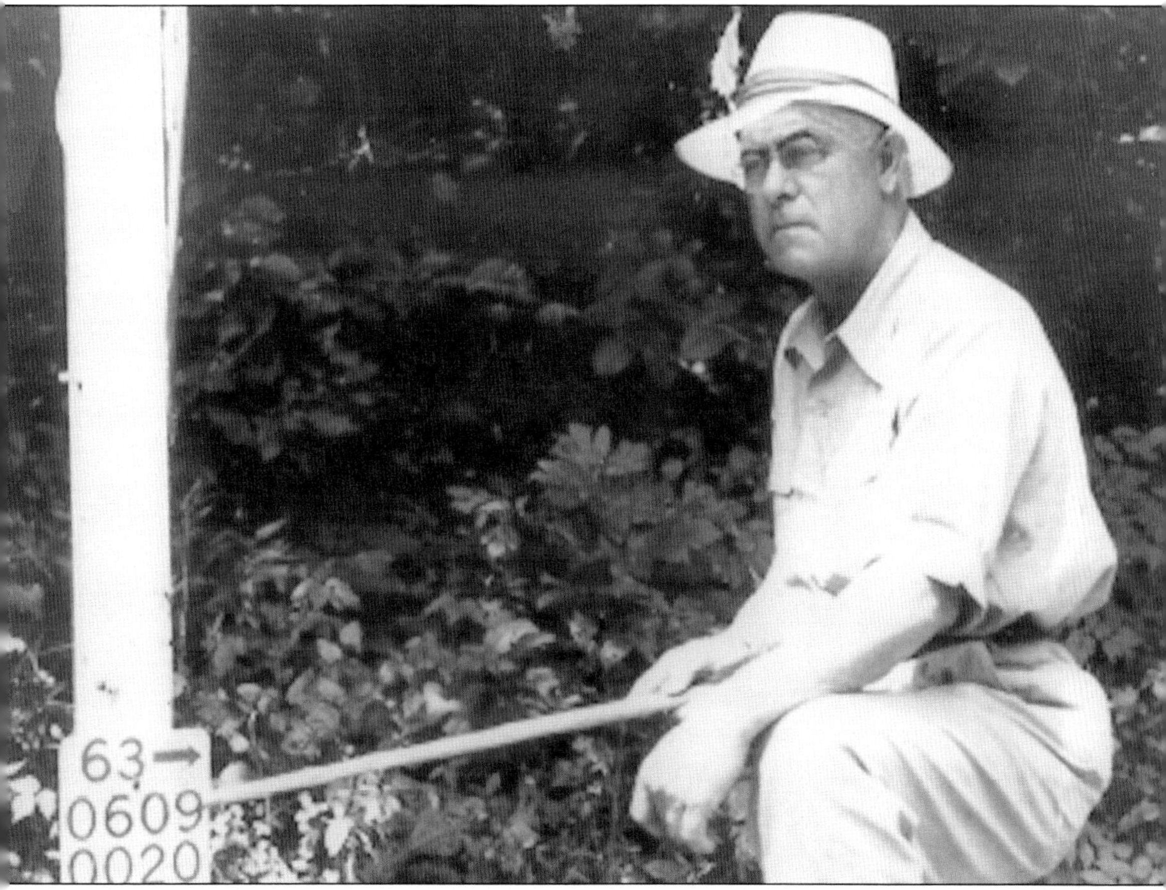

Charles Clifton Hazelwood (1893–1961) was a Virginia Department of Transportation maintenance supervisor. He oversaw road projects in eastern Charles City, New Kent, and western James City County from his Holdcroft office. Some early work was accomplished with laborers provided by the Civilian Conservation Corps, a Depression-era work relief program. *A History of Roads in Virginia: The Most Convenient Wayes* provides an overview of Virginia highway development. (GHD.)

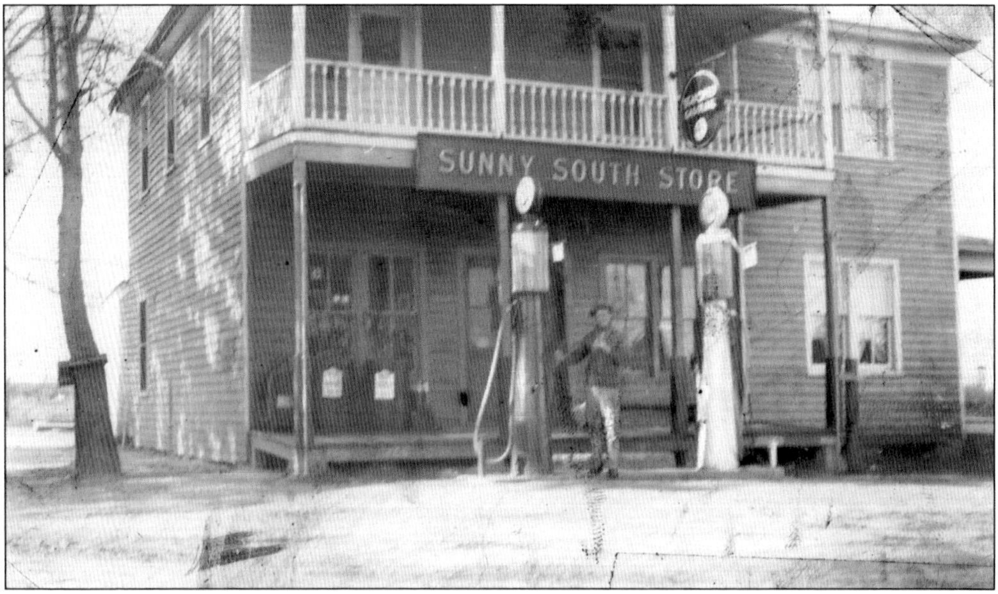

The Sunny South Store was at the crossroads of Croaker, Riverview, and Ware Creek Roads. J. E. "Pete" Madsen (1898–1951), who worked for a Newport News wholesaler, bought the store from Benny Garrett. He sold gasoline, dry goods, and groceries. Madsen's father, Pedar Madsen, emigrated from Denmark to New York and resettled in the county. He farmed, peddled eggs, and built the county's first sweet potato curing house. (GDMM.)

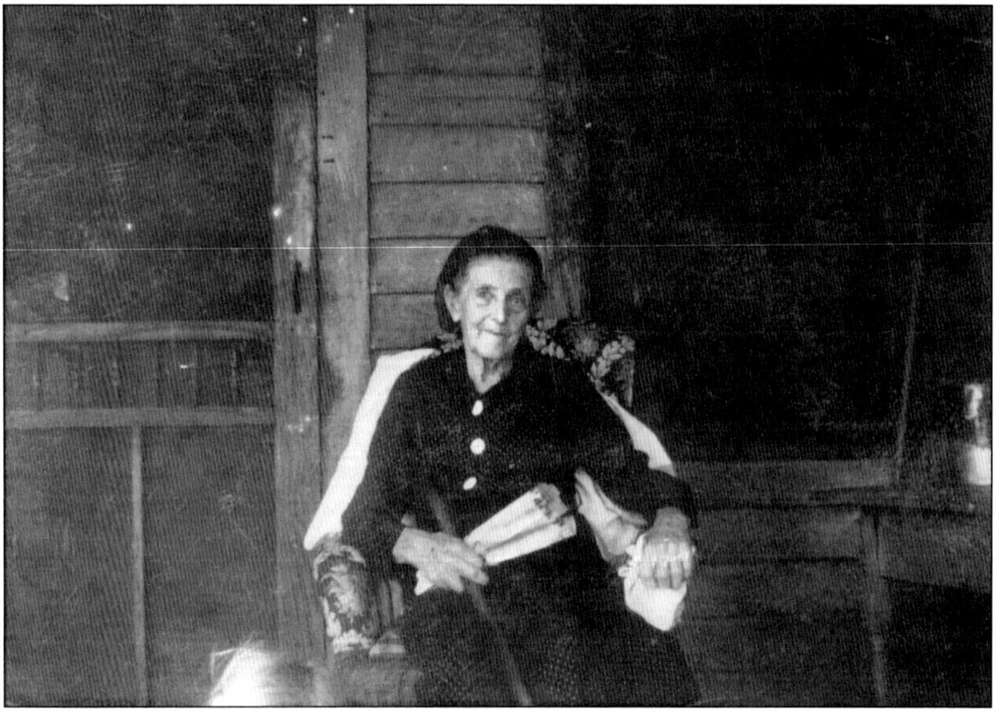

Emma Christensen posed for this photograph on her front porch. The Christensen family name became associated with the corner where the road from Lightfoot ended at Riverview Road. (SW.)

Bus service was a common mode of transportation before car ownership was widespread and affordable. Pictured at right, Greyhound Bus driver George Hitchens made a regular stop in Toano, where he met and married a local girl, Eva Meadows. The Hitchenses owned Powhatan Motor Court in Norge. Below, buses were still the most frequently used mode of transportation among James City County's rural population in the mid-20th century. Ralph Washington of Washington's Bus Service is pictured on the left. (Right, CSM; below, collection of Craig James, SW.)

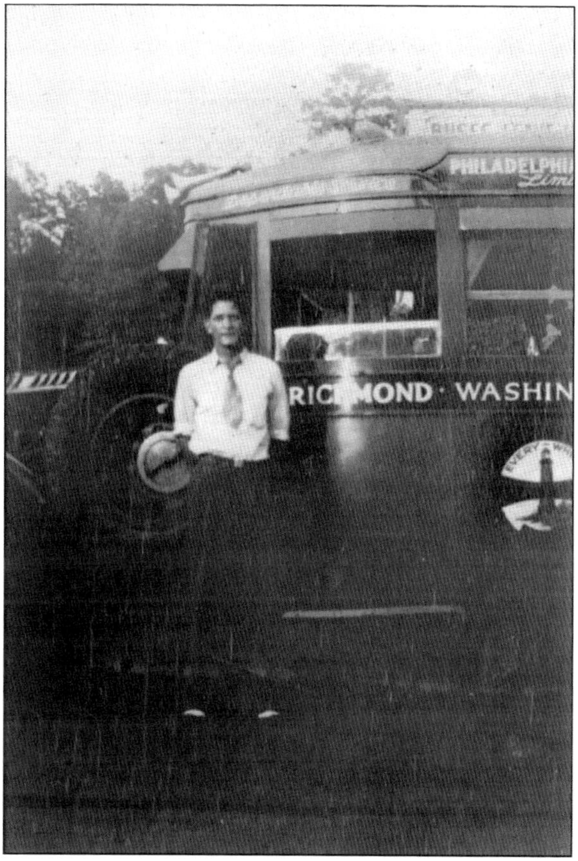

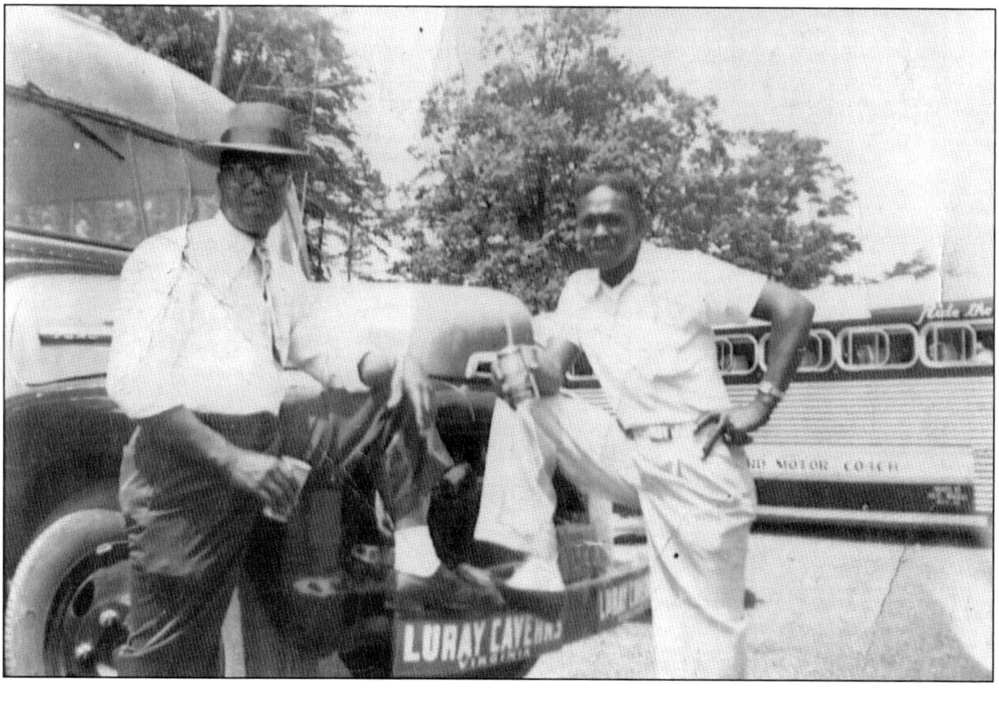

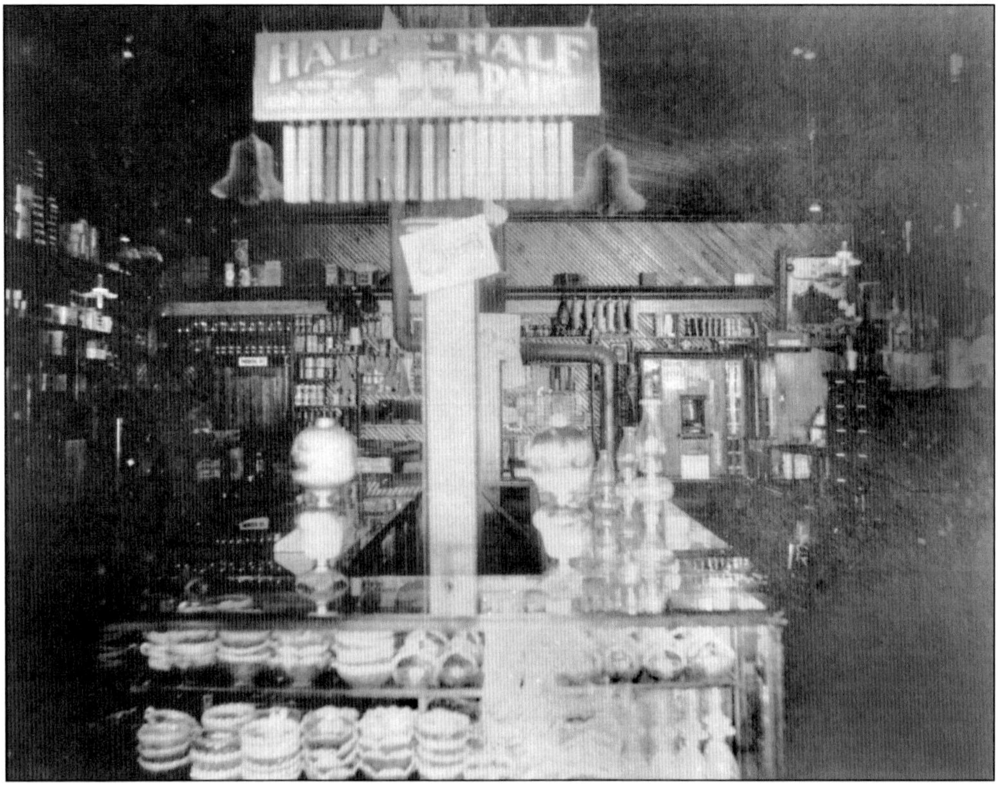

Early-20th-century stores like Kinde's in Norge (pictured above) sold oil lamps, dishes, and canned goods. "Pete" Madsen sold canned goods at his store in Croaker (pictured below), but he also sold Ball canning jars and lids. Other brand-name goods visible on the shelves include Duz and Tide laundry soap, Sir Walter Raleigh tobacco, and BC headache powders. He also sold shoes. (Above, collection of the Kinde family, DBW; below, GDMM.)

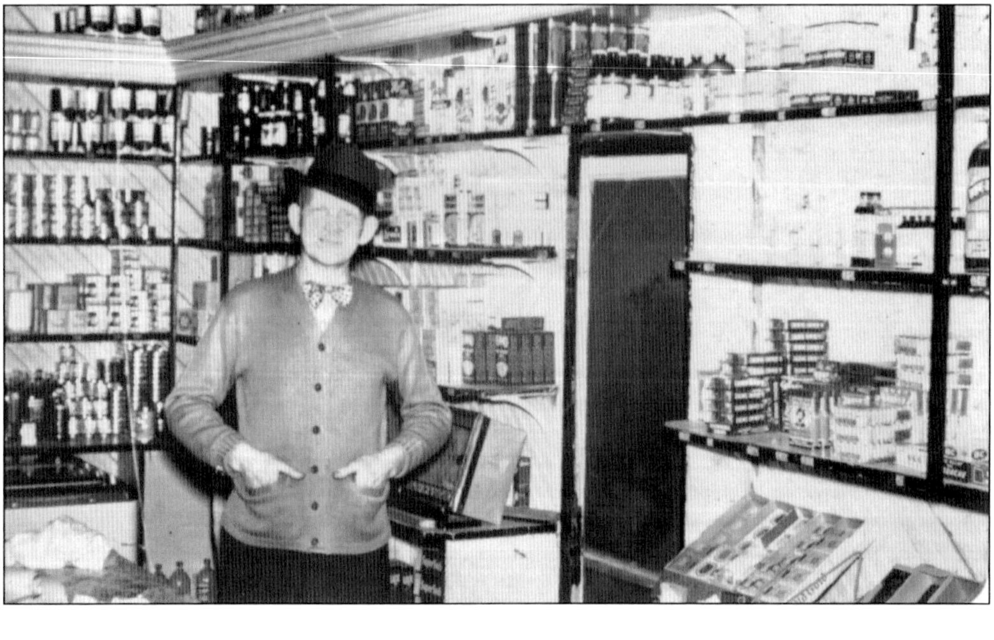

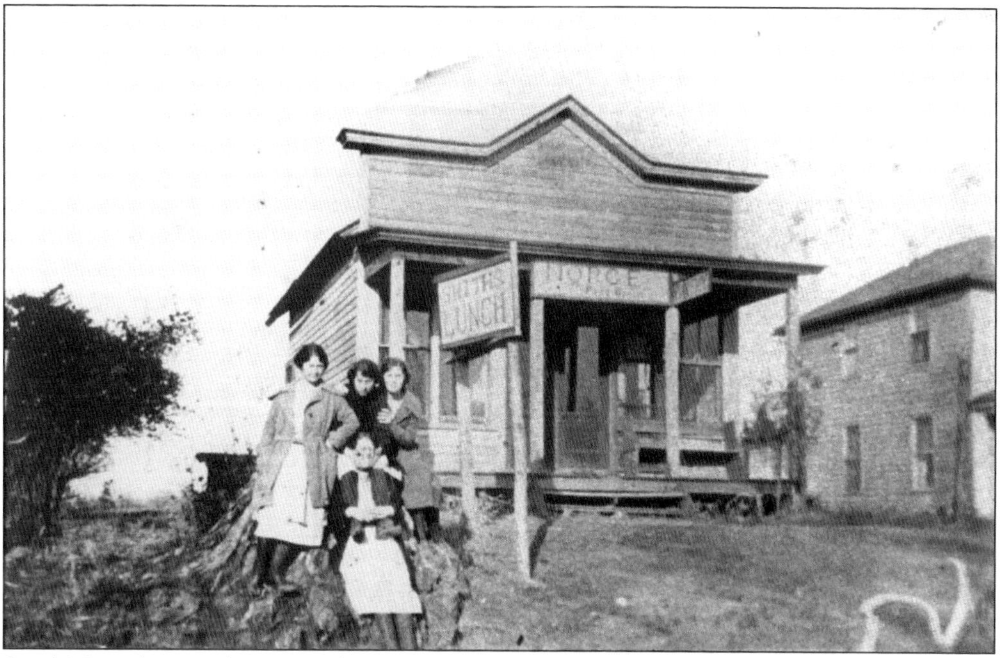

Smith's Lunch was a favorite gathering spot known to generations of rural families, including Cora Hughes and her friends, seen here. Arthur Smith's ice cream was made with local cream, and a neighborly tall tale involved knowing when the dairy cows had eaten wild onions in the pasture. (Collection of Frances Huckstep Hamilton, DBW.)

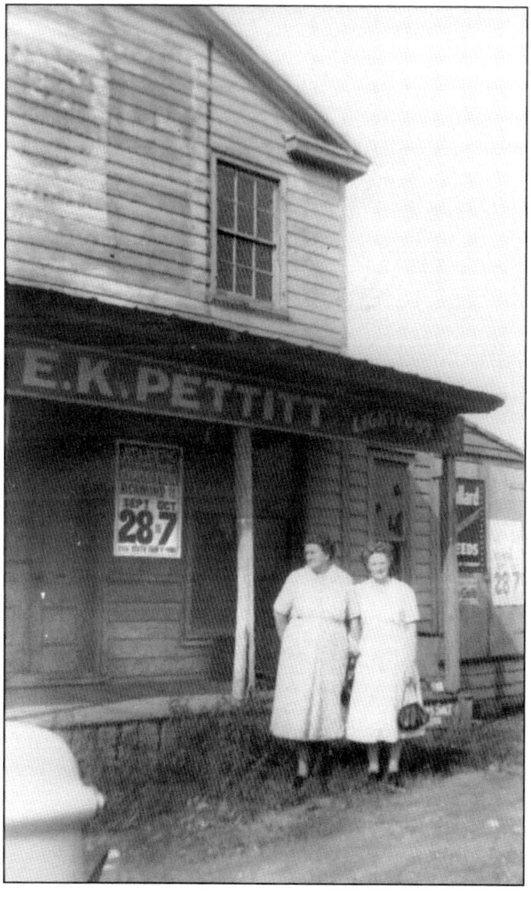

Valborg Christopherson Benson, left, and her sister Mabel Christopherson Dukleth posed in front of E. K. Pettitt's store on Richmond Road when they came from the West Coast to visit family. Pettitt also owned a grocery store across the street at the corner of Lightfoot and Richmond Roads that was partially in James City County and partially in York County. (Courtesy of Lorraine Benson Rodgers and DBW.)

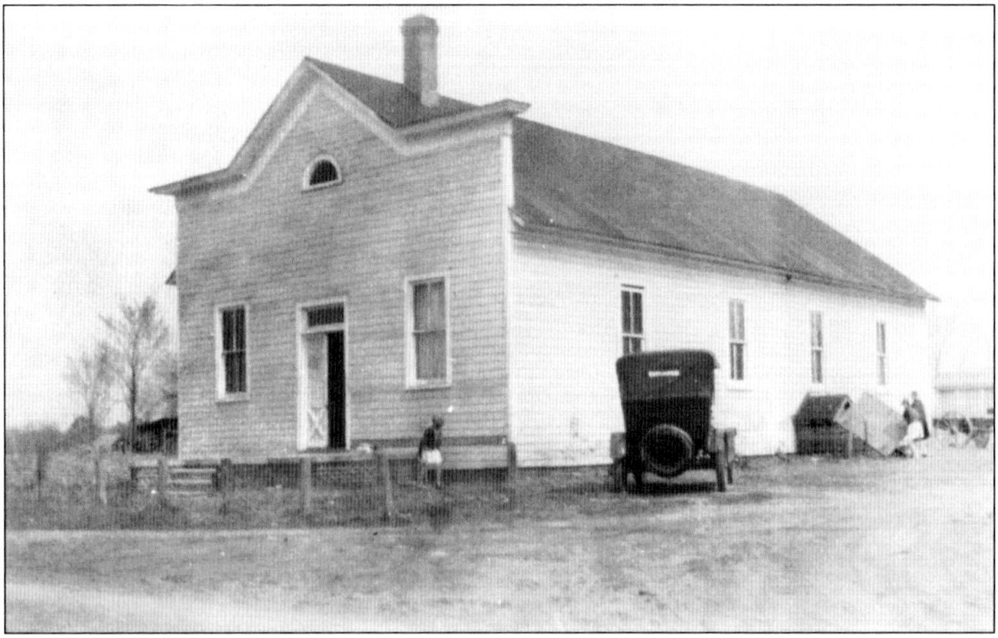

Norge Hall was built especially for neighborhood social gatherings by young men of the community, who called themselves the Vikings. Popular dances of the day included the waltz, two-step, square dance, schottische, and hop waltz, and music was played on the piano, guitar, and violin. Called Viking Hall until 1920, the community center was a Norwegian institution transplanted to the South. The 100th anniversary of Norge Hall was celebrated in 2007. (Original photograph in Toano EOC building, DBW.)

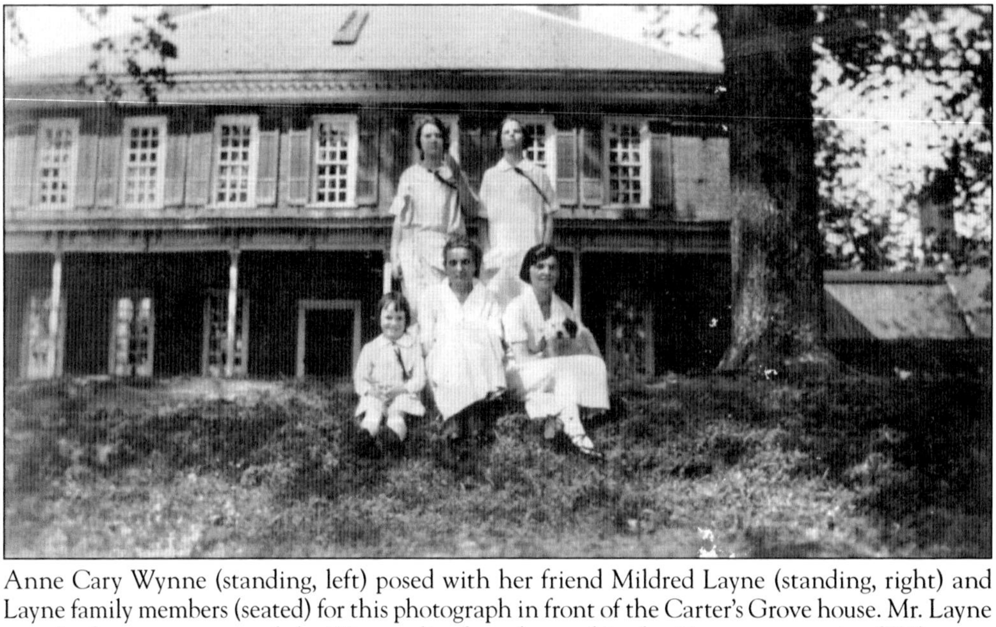

Anne Cary Wynne (standing, left) posed with her friend Mildred Layne (standing, right) and Layne family members (seated) for this photograph in front of the Carter's Grove house. Mr. Layne was the farm manager, and the Wynnes lived up the road in the Grove community. (FB.)

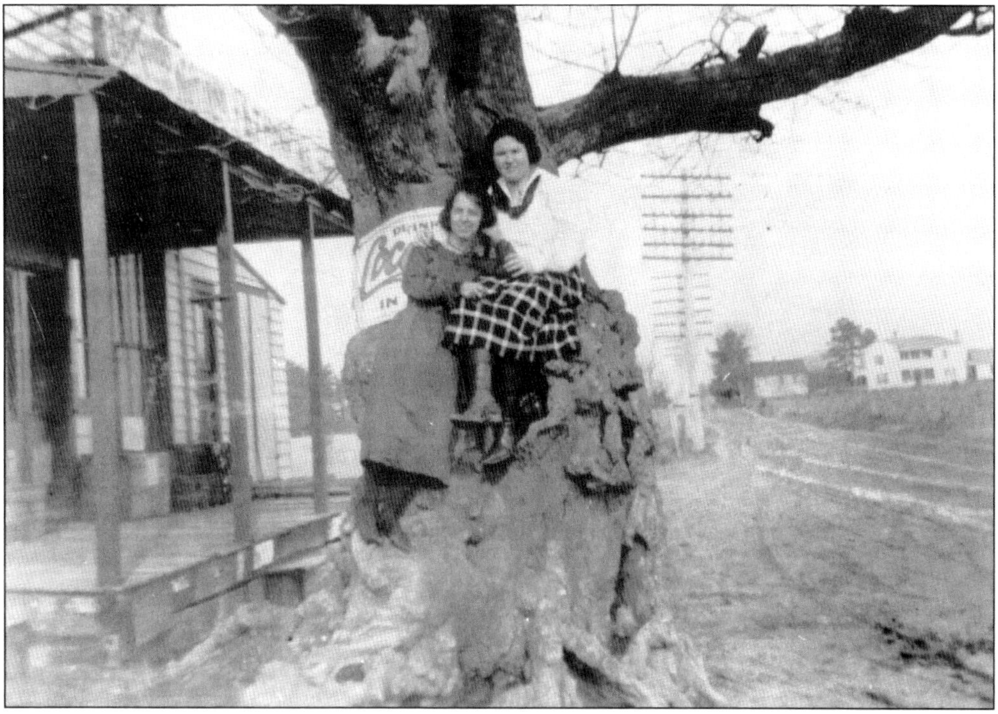

Alice Brand (left) and Emma Drummond sat in the large tree in front of Hankins Store to gossip. The store was located at Lightfoot where today's Williamsburg Outlet Mall is sited. Behind them and west on Richmond Road, the Lightfoot Post Office and the Benson home can be seen. The trees in front of the post office are still growing in the Richmond Road median as this publication goes to press. (Collection of Walter Dutton, DBW.)

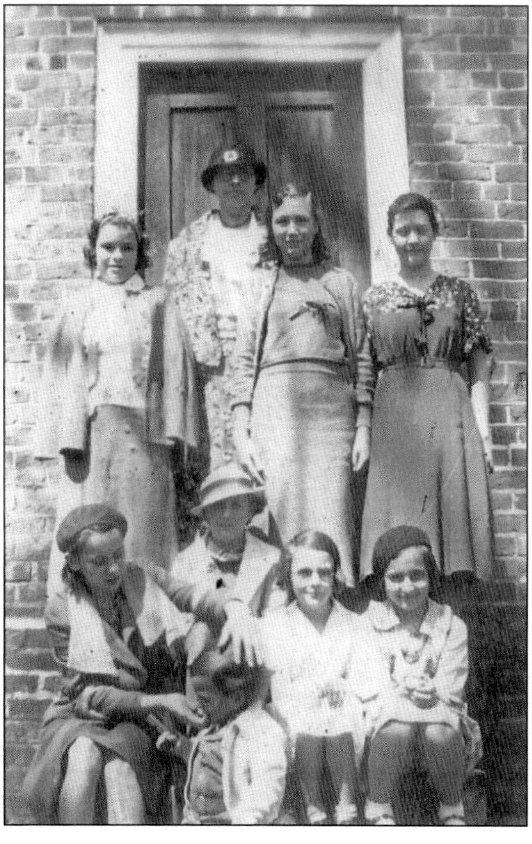

A Sunday school class from Olive Branch Christian Church included, from left to right, (first row) Lois Showalter (Plunkett), unidentified child, Josephine Showalter (behind child, wearing hat), Nancy Smith (Bradshaw), and Genevieve Eley (Drewery); (second row) Wanda Cooke (Calhoon), Mrs. Robert (Evelyn) Eley (Sunday school teacher, wearing hat), Eileen Otey (Waltrip), and Evelyn Hoar (Anderson). (Collection of Robert Eley, DBW.)

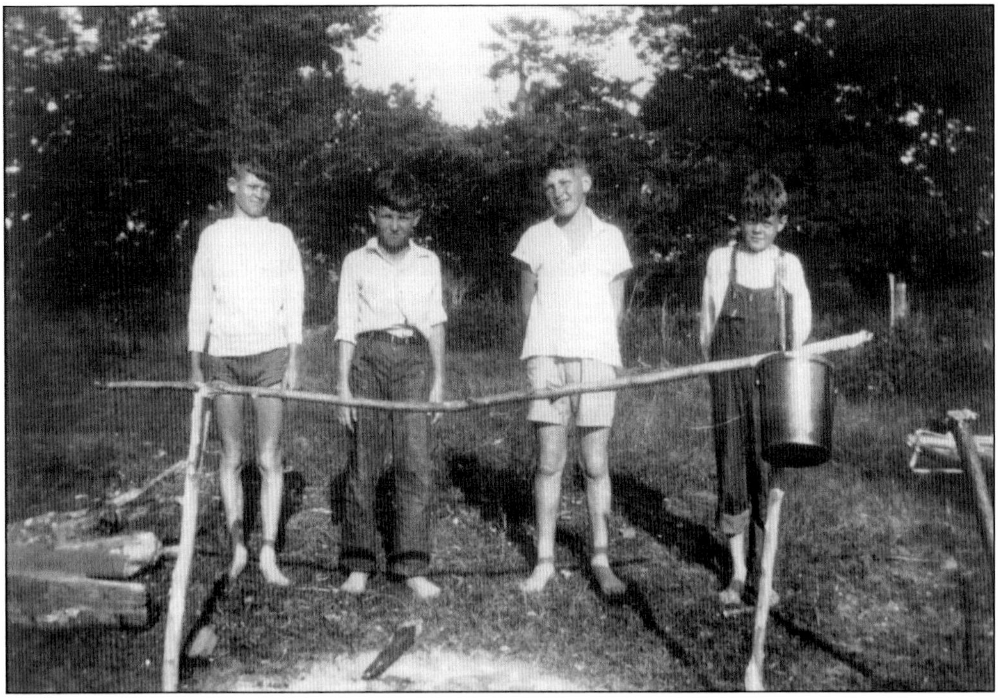

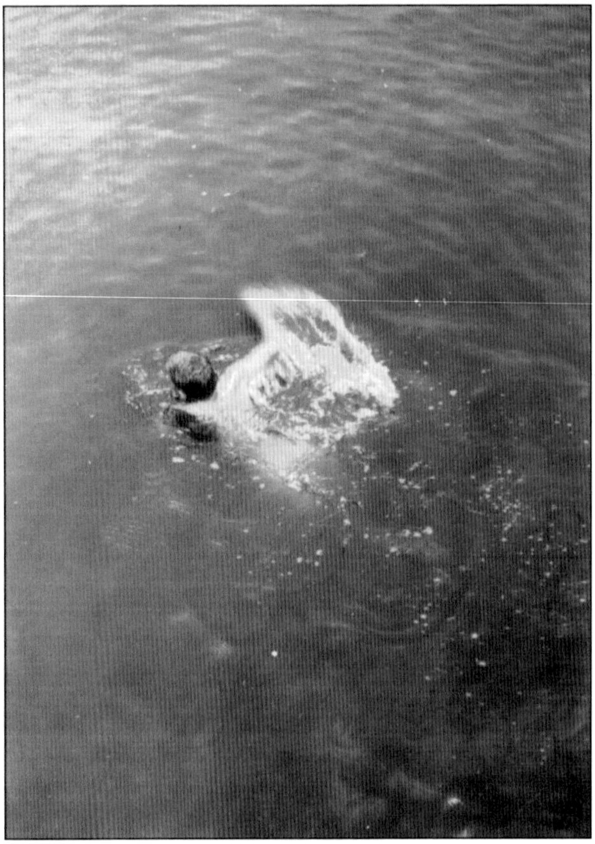

In the years between the World Wars, Toano boys Walter ("Ju Ju") Martin Jr., Tom Martin, Preston Wilkinson, and Richard Wilkinson (pictured above from left to right) would spend a month swimming and camping on the banks of the Chickahominy River at property owned by the Martin family (today's Chickahominy Haven). A Civil War–era map includes the name Daniel Jones near this location. The Ware family, who also remember the journey to the Chickahominy to cool off in the summertime, owned the farm known as "Jones." In the early 20th century, there were no homes nearby, and the closest building was the Hog Neck Landing brickyard run by the Booth family. The boys pitched tents beside the river and were accompanied by the Wilkinsons' dog, Sport. Pictured at left, the older boys taught the younger ones to swim, and they sometimes swam across the river and back. (Both, RFW.)

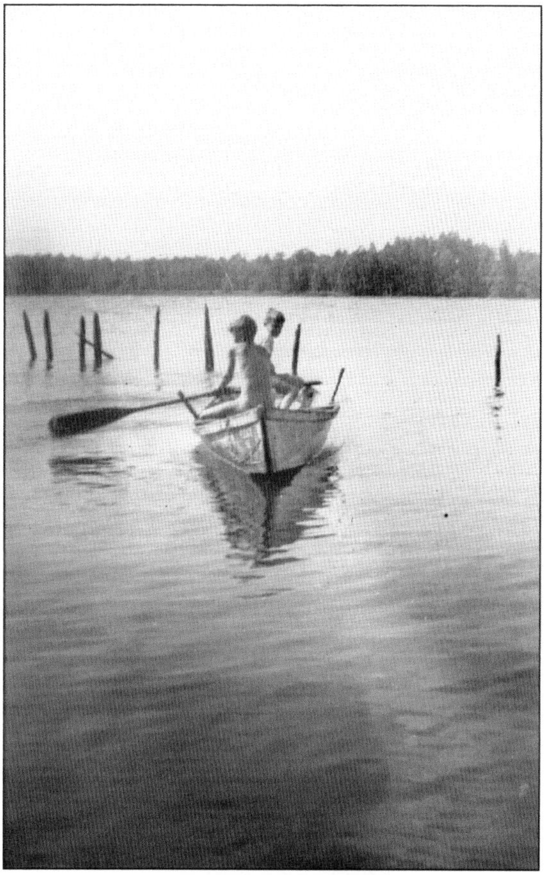

In a 1997 memoir, Tom Martin recalled, "We had some kind of tent, and also that there was a wooden row boat there which we used one day, going with the tide, to go to Lanexa (about 5 miles by water). We tied up the boat at the public wharf, and walked over to Grandmother Martin's House. . . . she took us out into her garden and gave us a nice cantaloupe, which we took back to our camp." In a memoir written in 2002, Marilynn Vaiden Ware Johnson recalled, "There was an old farmhouse near where we went to swim. Aunt Trittie said when she was growing up, in the hot summertime (no electricity/no fans) the whole family (and hired help) would pack up and move to the house at Joneses where they would catch the river breezes." (Both, RFW.)

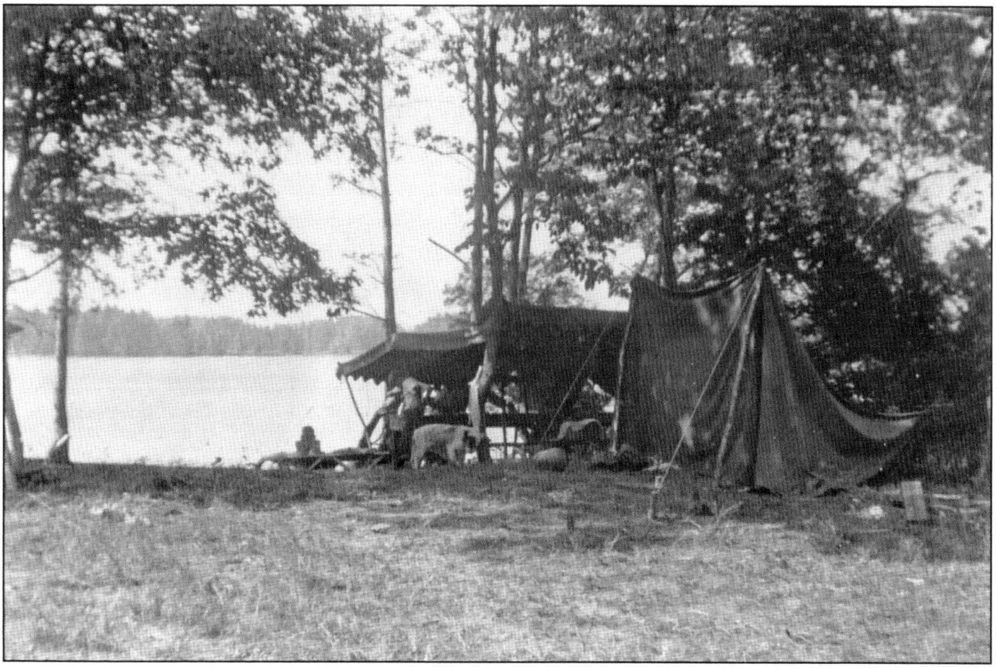

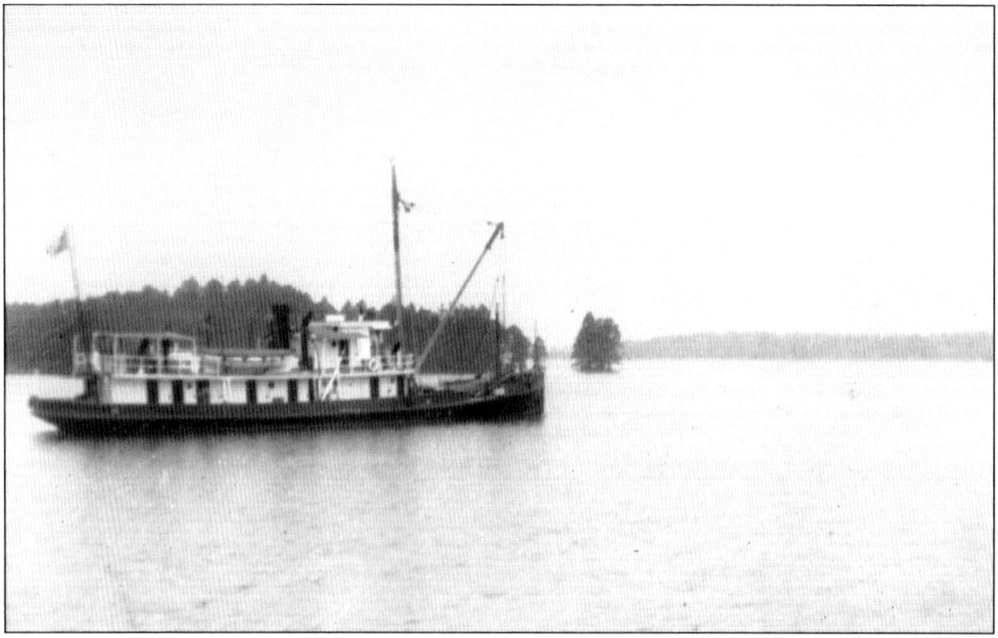

Barge traffic was a regular sight when the Martin and Wilkinson boys camped at Joneses. Shallow-bottomed barges, also called lighters, hauled freight from larger ships on the Chesapeake Bay or rivers to inland piers. Bricks from the Chickahominy brickyard were hauled by vessels to other locations on the bay. The Davises of Mobjack in Mathews County received bricks barged from the Chickahominy and resold them from their pier. At Jamestown (pictured below), the *Captain John Smith* ferry carried cars and passengers to Scotland Wharf in Surry. (Above, RFW; below, WSG.)

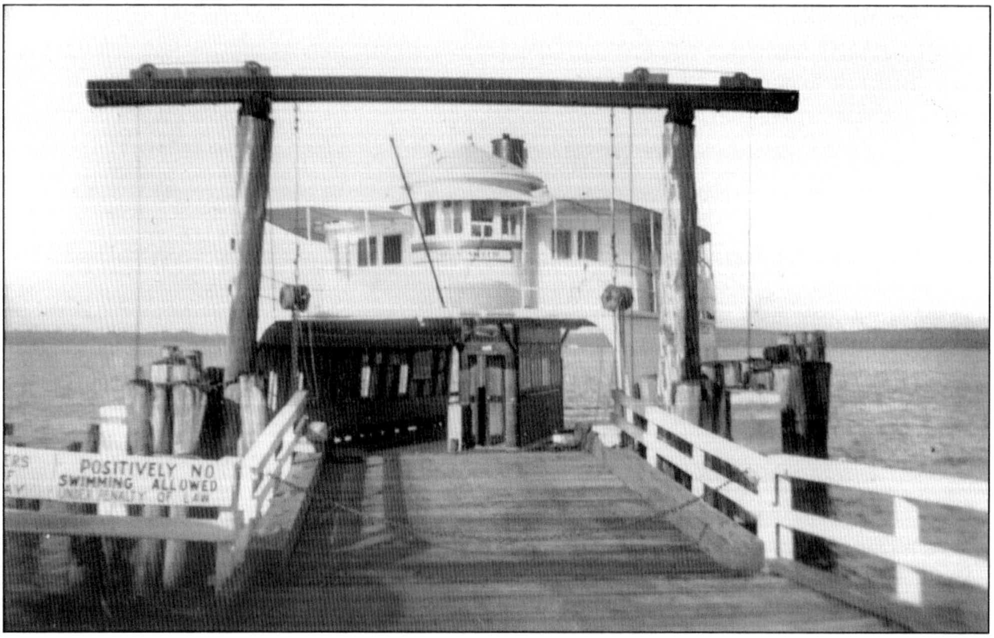

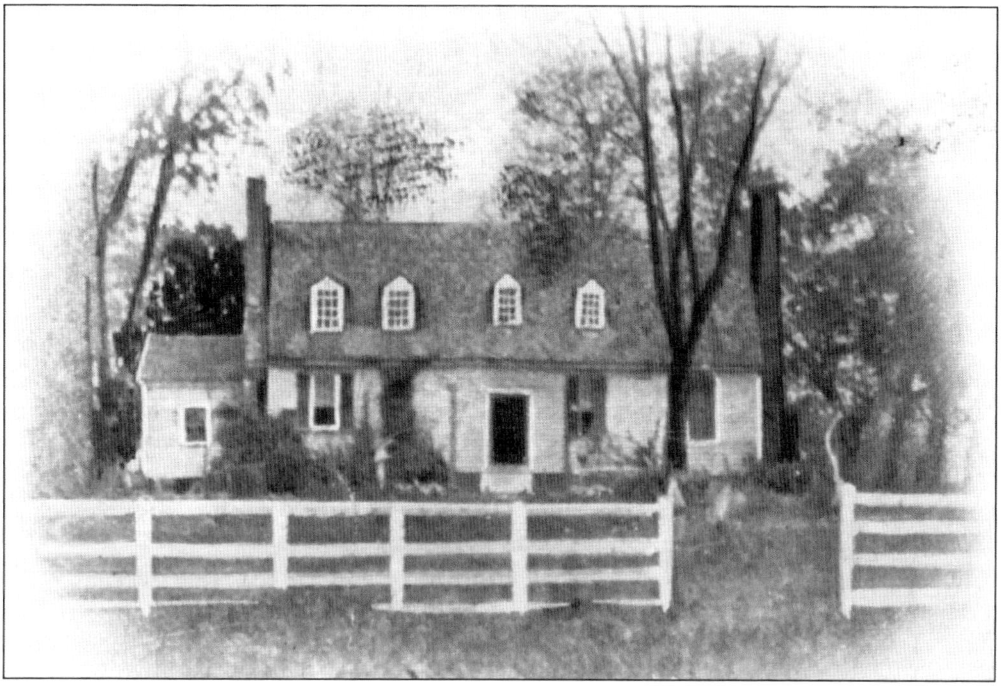

An undated postcard, possibly from before 1900, advertised Windsor as a hunting lodge where visitors to the Chamberlain Hotel in Hampton could travel for hunting. (WF.)

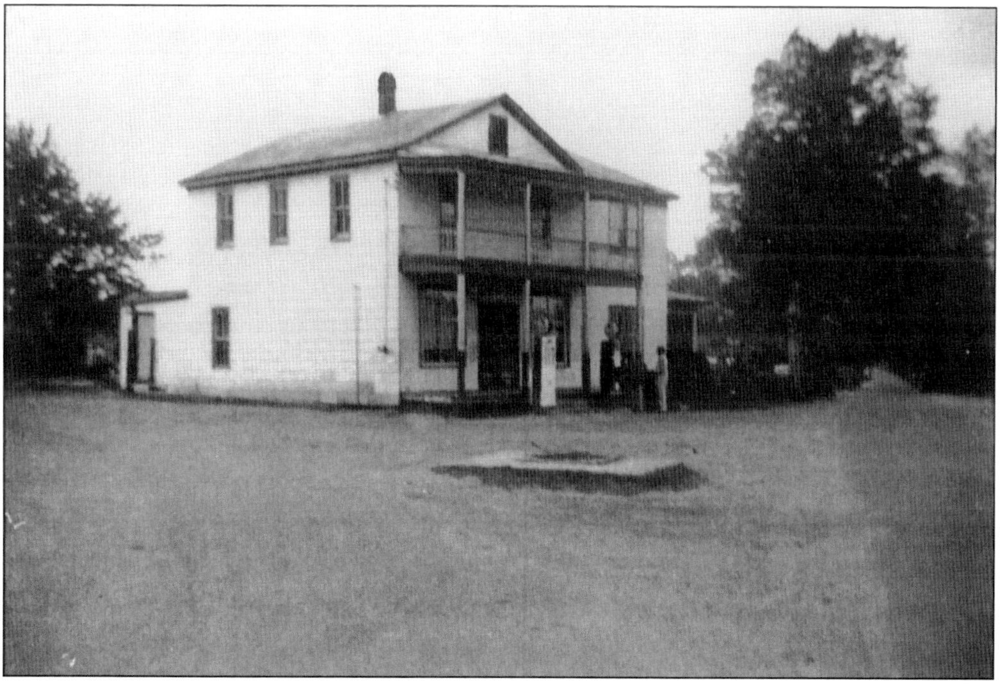

The community well can be seen in the foreground of this photograph of Ford's Store at Croaker, also seen on page 84. In the 20th century, the James City County Board of Supervisors paid for the cleaning of public wells. There was concern at that time about the spread of disease like the pandemic flu that had swept around the world during and after World War I. (SW.)

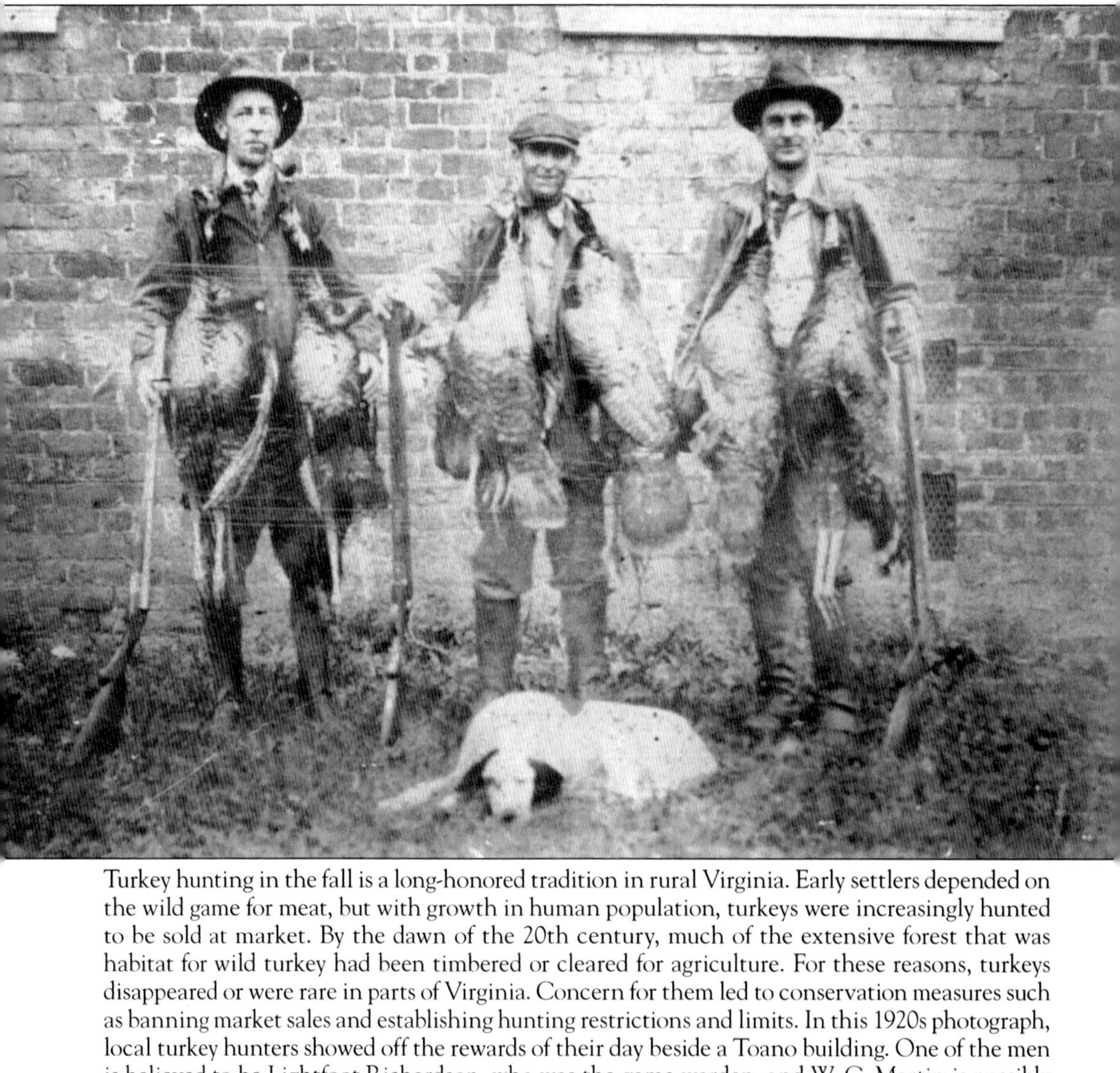

Turkey hunting in the fall is a long-honored tradition in rural Virginia. Early settlers depended on the wild game for meat, but with growth in human population, turkeys were increasingly hunted to be sold at market. By the dawn of the 20th century, much of the extensive forest that was habitat for wild turkey had been timbered or cleared for agriculture. For these reasons, turkeys disappeared or were rare in parts of Virginia. Concern for them led to conservation measures such as banning market sales and establishing hunting restrictions and limits. In this 1920s photograph, local turkey hunters showed off the rewards of their day beside a Toano building. One of the men is believed to be Lightfoot Richardson, who was the game warden, and W. C. Martin is possibly the hunter in the center. (BG.)

Seven

The World Wars

In 1914, war broke out in Europe. The United States got involved in 1917 after several merchant ships were sunk. An area on the York River was used for the development of mines. Housing developments were created for civilian workers and soldiers. Local citizens were asked to make sacrifices to preserve food and materials needed for the war effort. World War I ended in 1918. Afterward, modernization continued apace. The American Red Cross and youth clubs promoted hygiene, civic responsibility, and agricultural productivity. Perhaps the most significant local event was the return to the area of Dr. W. A. R. Goodwin, for whom the modernization of historic buildings in Williamsburg came as a shock. Goodwin inspired a noteworthy future for the area. At meetings with John D. Rockefeller Jr. in the early 1920s, Goodwin revealed his idea to restore the Colonial town. An appreciation for the idea grew in the philanthropist. He secretly purchased buildings until the Williamsburg Restoration was announced in 1934. Tourism developed. County citizens took jobs with the Restoration and the College of William and Mary, which grew concurrently. During the World War period, the National Park Service was founded, the Colonial National Monument at Jamestown was created, and a scenic motorway connecting Jamestown, Williamsburg, and Yorktown was begun. The City of Williamsburg annexed portions of surrounding counties and enacted preservation ordinances. Sewer, water, and electricity came to Williamsburg. By the time World War II broke out, the Scandinavian community had begun to be absorbed by the larger community. The same was not true for African Americans, who had been the majority population at the end of the 19th century. Segregation and Jim Crow laws incited many to move to Richmond and cities farther north and west. Families who lived on land acquired by the government were resettled. The military buildup brought temporary and permanent residents to James City County. A building boom in Newport News required the Chickahominy to be dammed; water was piped to the growing city on James City County's southeastern edge.

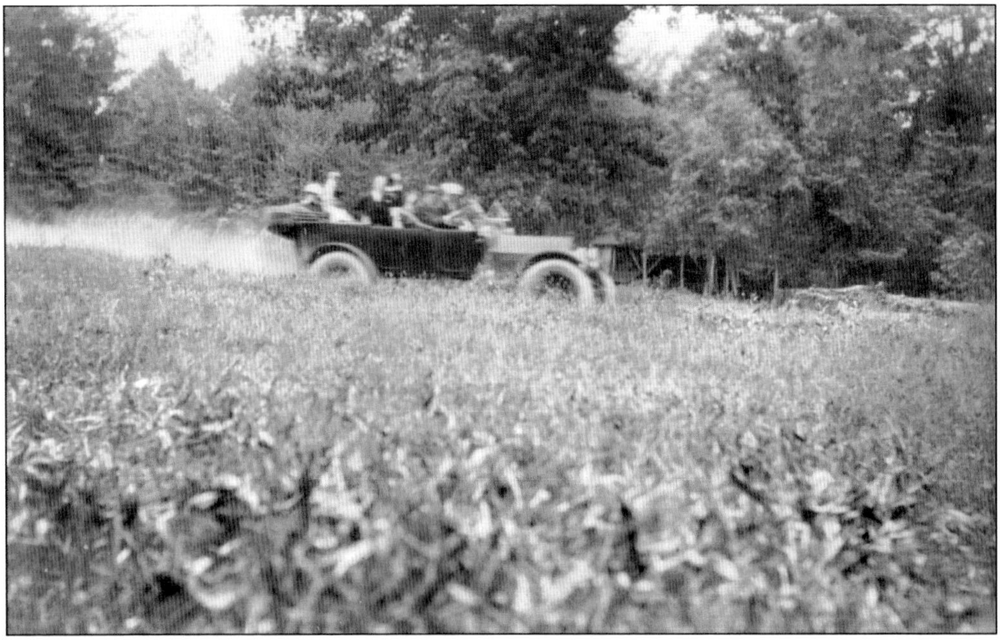

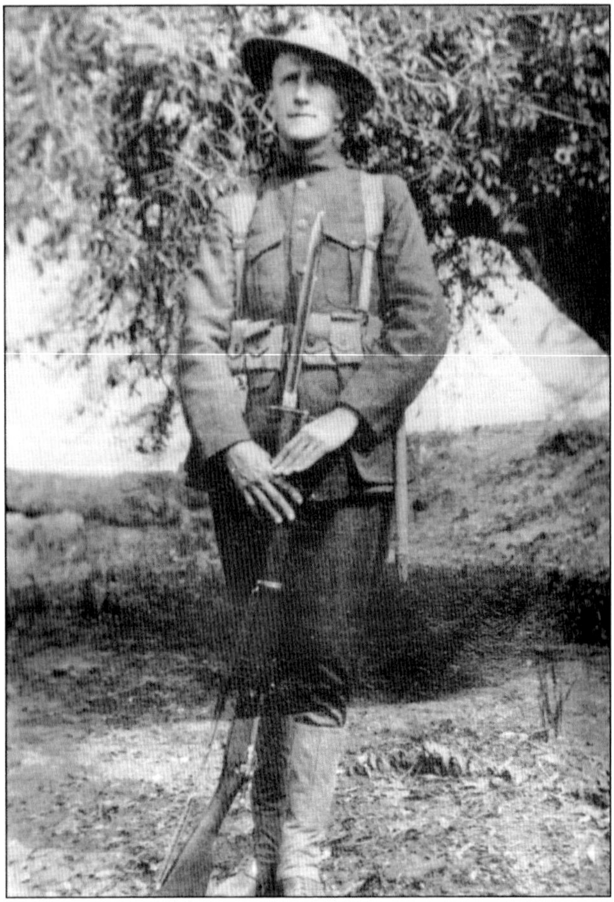

Virginian Woodrow Wilson served as the 28th president of the United States from 1913 to 1921. In 1916, he signed the Organic Act into law, which created the National Park Service to manage the country's national parks. On a trip to the area, Wilson took a boat from Washington to Jamestown Island and motored along the road from Jamestown (today's Neck O' Land Road) to Williamsburg. Willard Gilley waited on his front porch and was able to capture the historic moment with a box camera. President Wilson waved as he passed Gatehouse Farm, the Gilleys' dairy operation. (WSG.)

George Clopton of Peach Park on Old Forge Road in Toano died while serving in World War I. His parents worked at Eastern State Hospital in Williamsburg. (WF.)

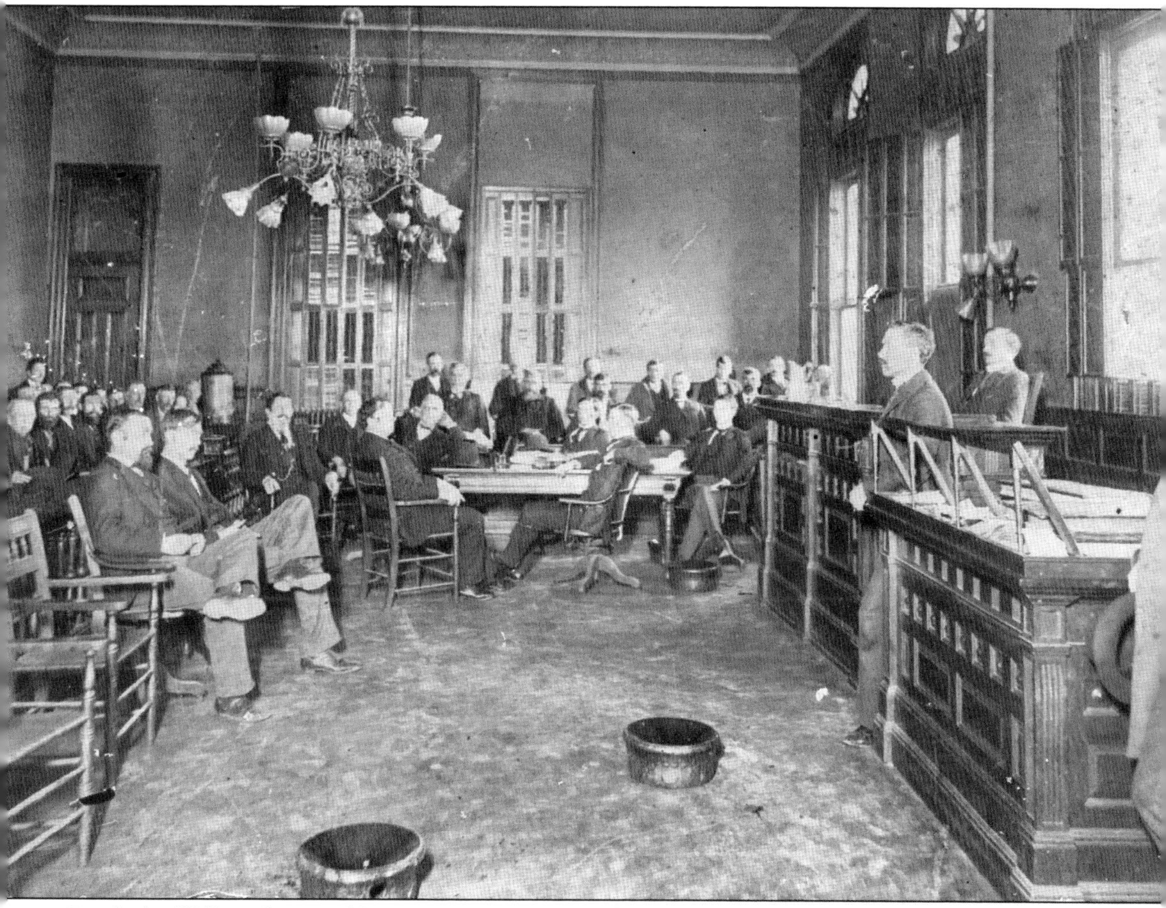

Inside the Williamsburg and James City County Courthouse on Duke of Gloucester Street, William Walker Ware of Toano can be partially seen leaning on the judge's bench on the far right. Ware was the county's deputy sheriff in 1898 and sheriff from 1904 to 1916. The 1898 *Directory and Handbook of the City of Williamsburg and County of James City* said, "This quaint brick building which is owned jointly by the city and county . . . was built in 1769. Before its door and within its walls have been enacted scenes that are now history." The building would be purchased by John D. Rockefeller Jr. for Williamsburg Restoration, Inc., and a new courthouse would be constructed on Francis Street. Another courthouse would be built within the city limits in the mid-20th century. The current shared courthouse for the municipalities was built at the start of the 21st century in James City County at a second "New Town" (see page 12). The planned development is a mix of offices, stores, and homes intended to bring to mind the slower pace of pre–World War communities like Toano. (WF.)

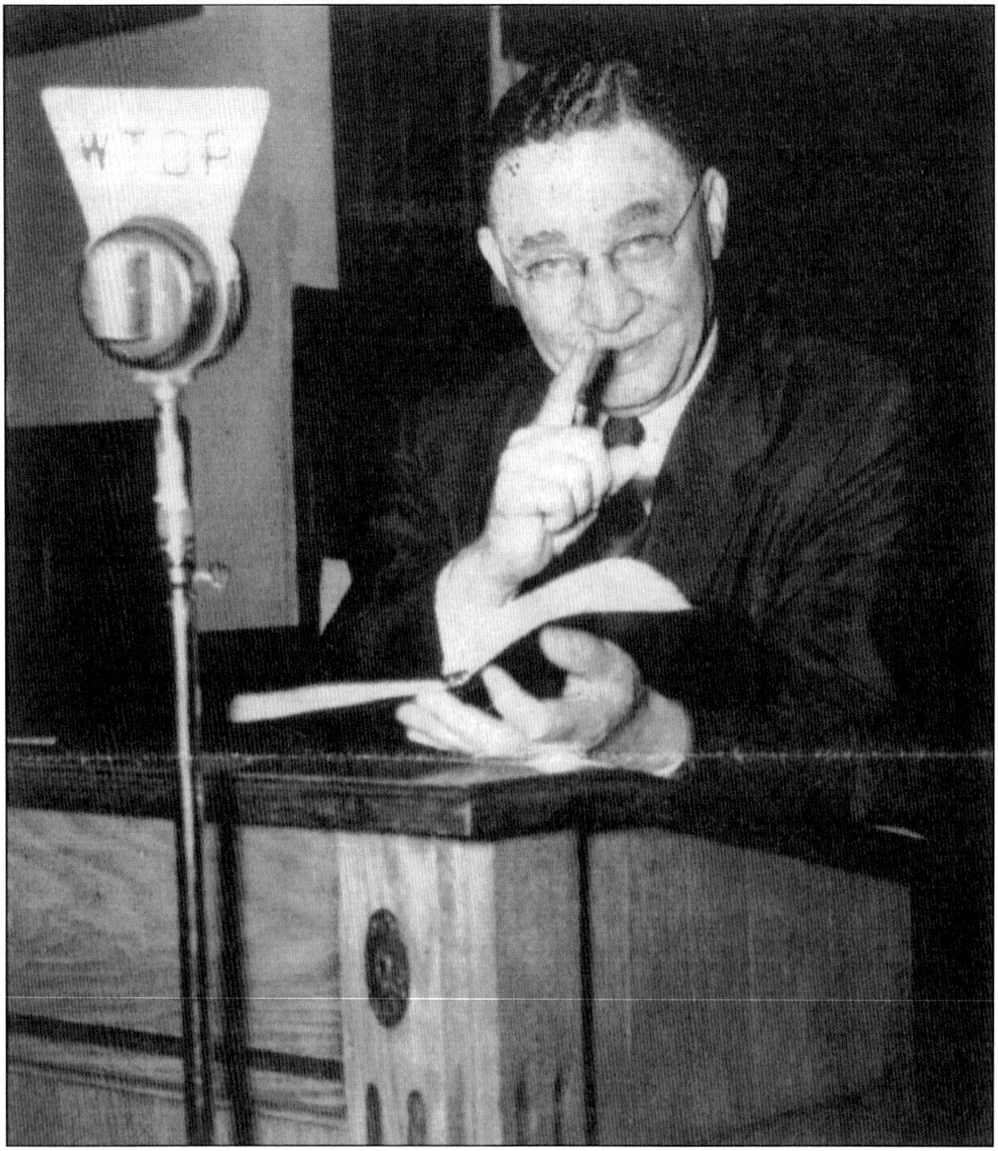

Elder Lightfoot Solomon Michaux founded 10 Gospel Spreading Church of God locations in the United States. He preached on radio and television, and wrote a newsletter. He was active in the civil rights movement, owned restaurants, and spearheaded housing developments. His dream was to establish a farm and a "National Memorial to the Progress of African Americans." Toward that end, he purchased a large parcel of land along the James River between College and Mill Creeks. On October 20, 1992, a memorial marker dedicated to his life's work was unveiled on the road to the property where his followers commemorated the delivery of the last slaves to America. (*Daily Press* file photograph reprinted on February 29, 2008.)

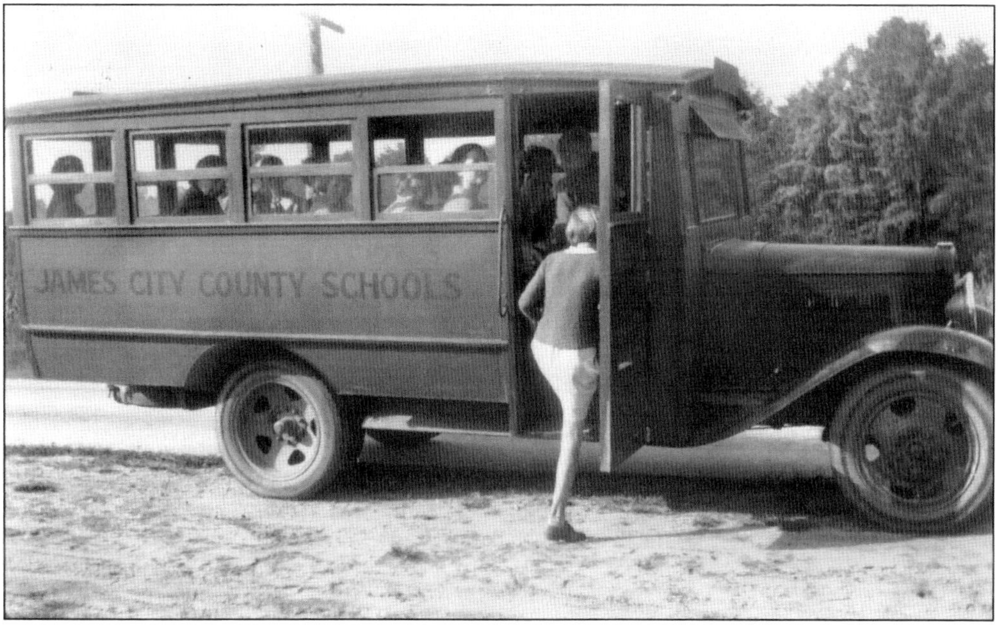

In 1933, when these photographs were taken, white high school students in two of James City County's three magisterial districts, Powhatan and Stonehouse, attended Toano School while children from the Jamestown district attended Williamsburg High School. African American children attended the James City County Training School. Above, Pearle Benson is pictured boarding the bus, which she caught with her three younger siblings, (below, from left to right) Melvin, David, and Doris, in front of their home on Richmond Road in Lightfoot. (Both, DBW.)

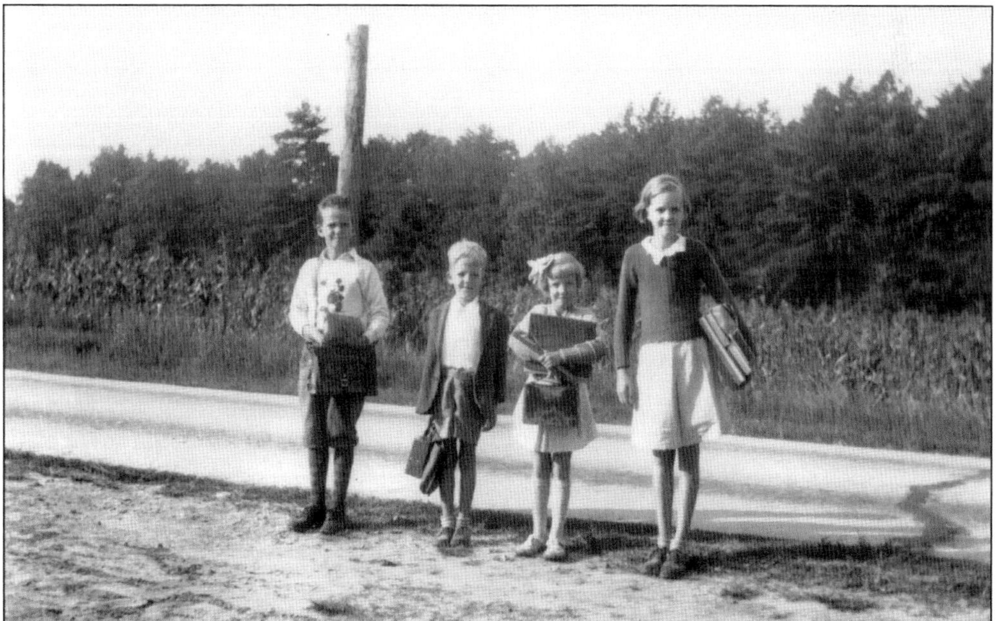

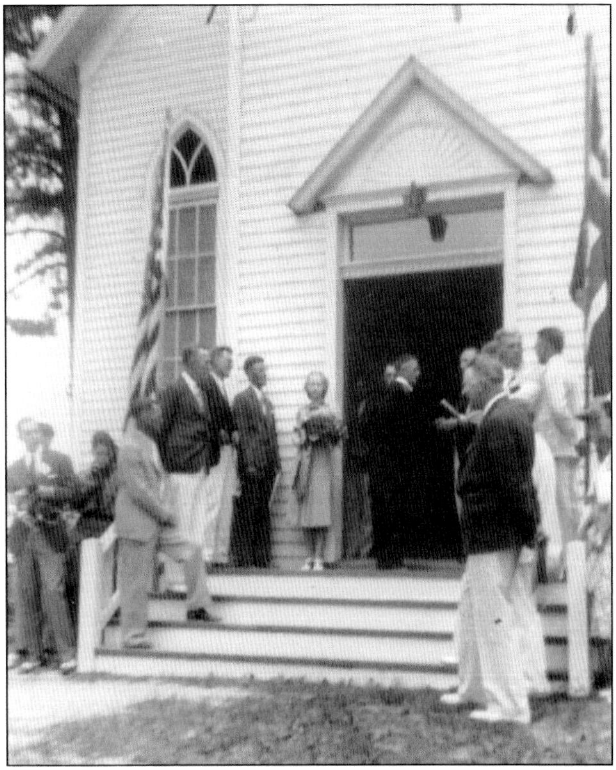

On June 27, 1939, Norwegian monarchs Crown Prince Olav and Crown Princess Martha visited Our Saviour's Lutheran Church in Norge to honor early emigrants. Norma Rolfsen is seen here waiting outside the doorway with a large bouquet to present to the couple. (GDMM.)

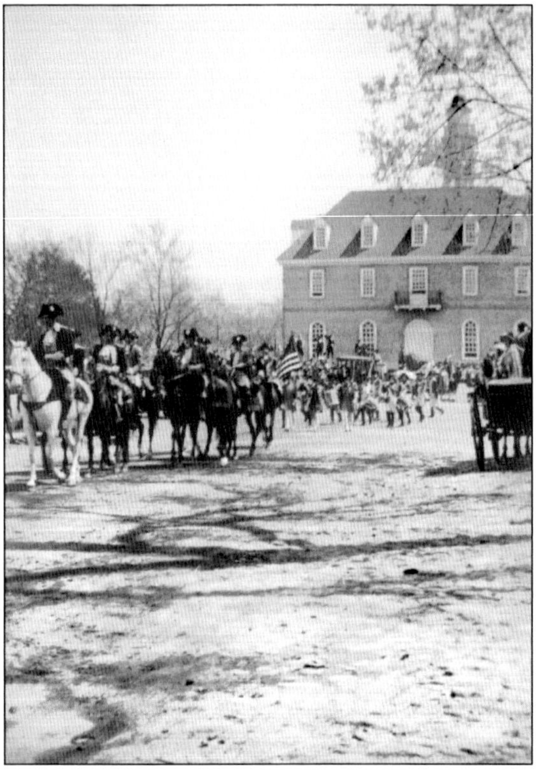

The Howards of Virginia (1940), filmed in part in Williamsburg and at Carter's Grove, provided excitement for local citizens, who snapped photographs of movie stars Cary Grant and Martha Scott. The scene played out here reveals George Washington, played by George Houston, leading Grant and other patriots to war. (WSG.)

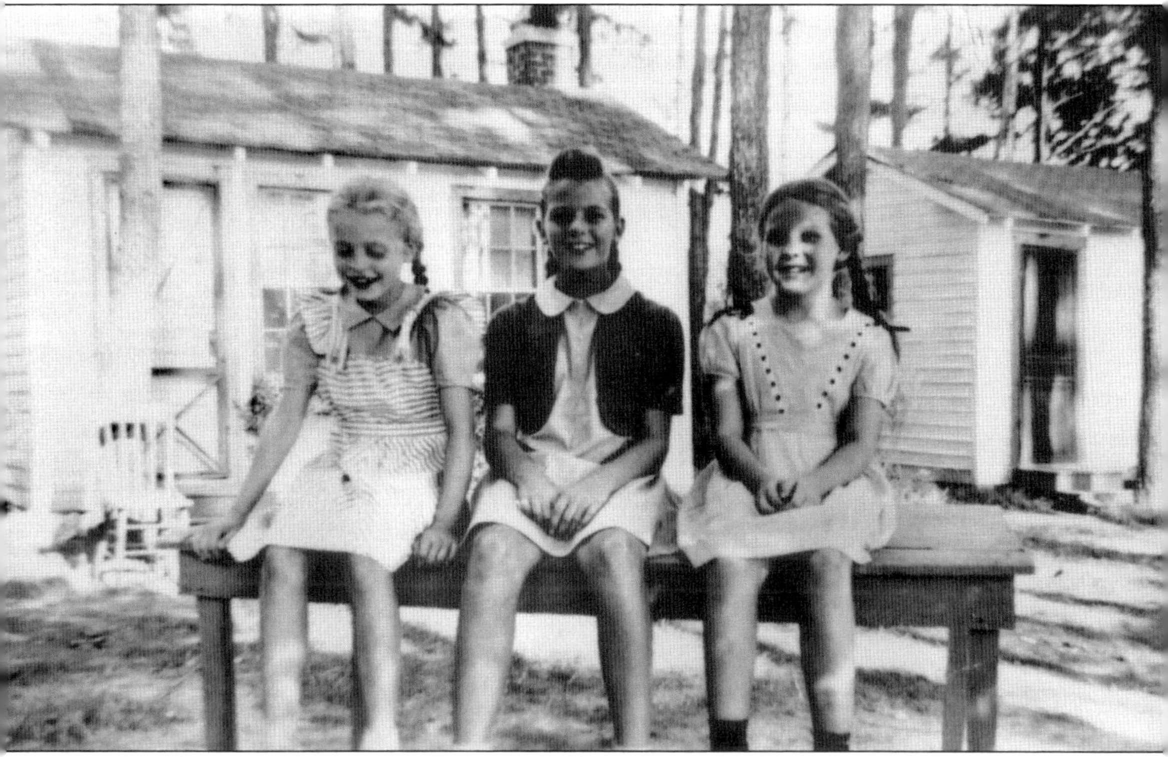

Between the World Wars, military personnel and civilian workers took up residence temporarily or permanently in James City County, especially as part of operations at Camp Peary, Cheatham Annex, the Naval Weapons Station in York County, and the U.S. Army transportation facility at Fort Eustis in Newport News. Residents who had lived on the land near the towns of Magruder and Penniman were moved to other locations, such as Highland Park and Wales in Williamsburg and Grove in James City County. At Lightfoot, Olson Cottages (in the background) was one of several businesses established to offer families temporary housing. Vivian Olson (left) and Janice Opheim (right) talked with a young girl from Texas who lived in a cottage. (Collection of Vivian Olson Matthews, DBW.)

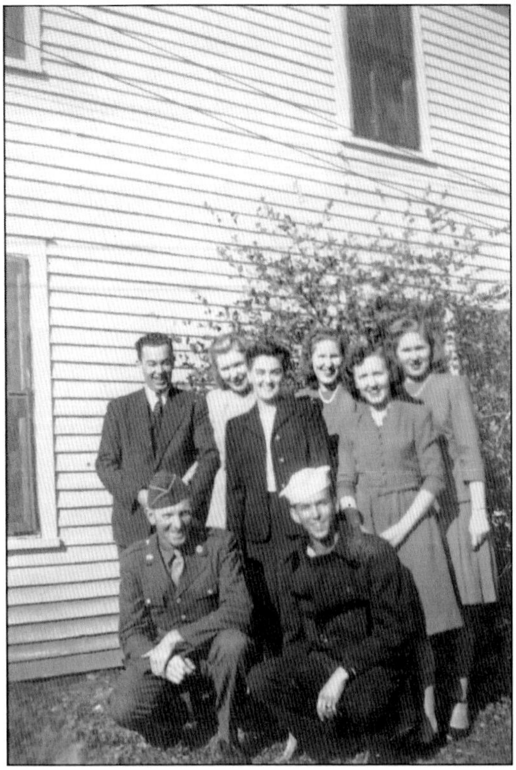

Elmer (left) and Melvin Benson were drafted into the army and navy, respectively. They gathered with family members before shipping out. (DBW.)

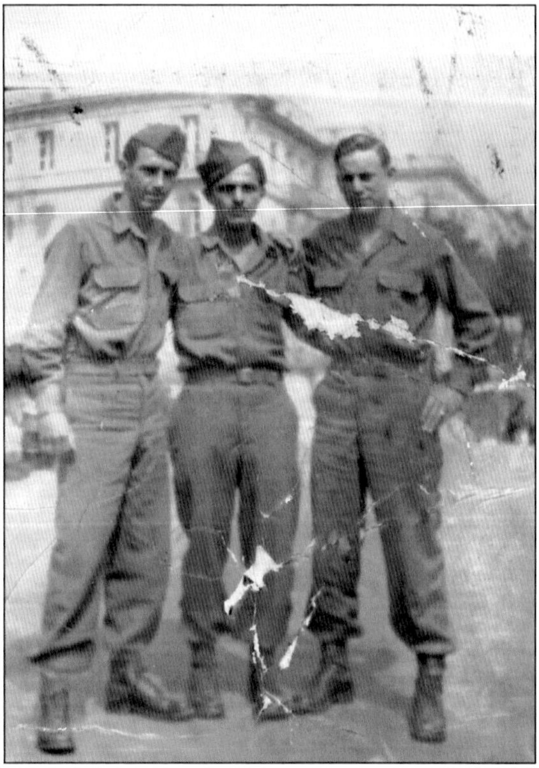

Charles Waverly Hazelwood (right) sent this photograph to his family from Europe. He is pictured with George DeLullo (left) and Joe Langa, possibly men from his unit. The photograph is dated April 1944. (GHD.)

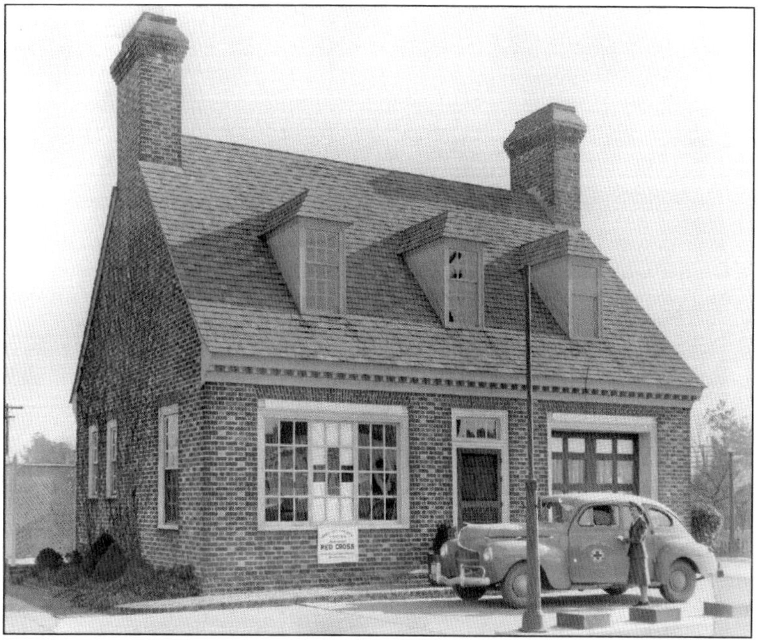

The American Red Cross was an important means for the local community to contribute to the war effort. The organization's office was located on Richmond Road at its intersection with Scotland Street. This area would be annexed from James City County by the City of Williamsburg. (CVC-ARC.)

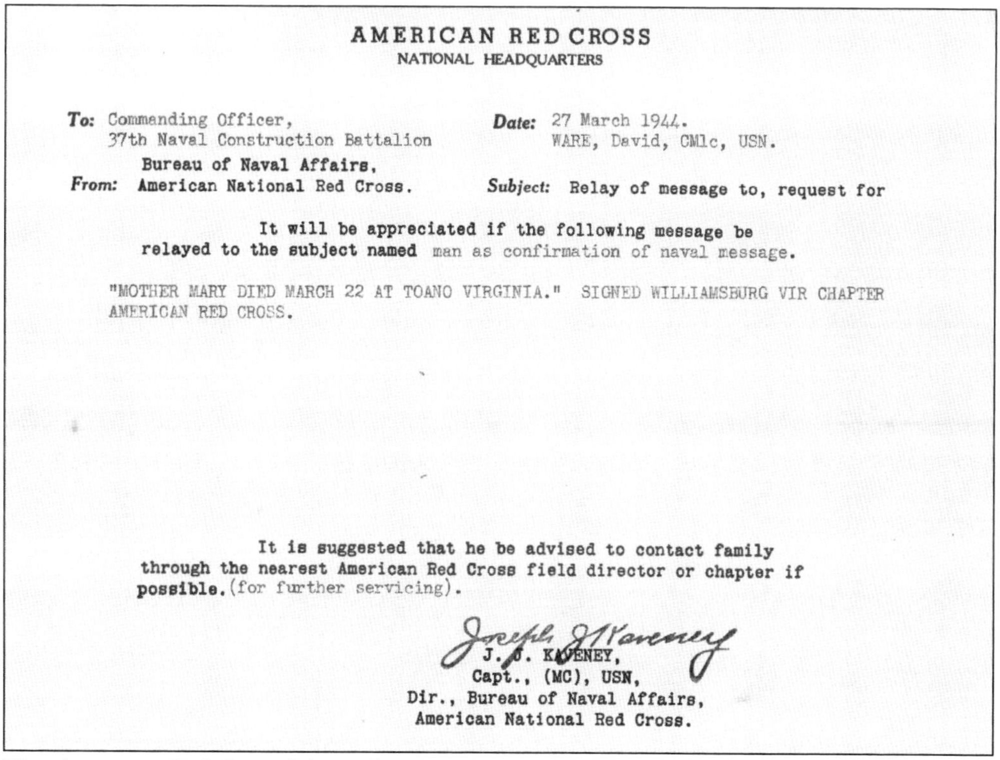

AMERICAN RED CROSS
NATIONAL HEADQUARTERS

To:	Commanding Officer, 37th Naval Construction Battalion **Bureau of Naval Affairs,**	*Date:*	27 March 1944. WARE, David, CMlc, USN.
From:	**American National Red Cross.**	*Subject:*	**Relay of message to, request for**

It will be appreciated if the following message be relayed to the subject named man as confirmation of naval message.

"MOTHER MARY DIED MARCH 22 AT TOANO VIRGINIA." SIGNED WILLIAMSBURG VIR CHAPTER AMERICAN RED CROSS.

It is suggested that he be advised to contact family through the nearest American Red Cross field director or chapter if possible. (for further servicing).

Joseph J Kaveney
J. J. KAVENEY,
Capt., (MC), USN,
Dir., Bureau of Naval Affairs,
American National Red Cross.

The American Red Cross delivered emergency news to servicemen such as David Ware, who learned of his mother's death this way. Mary Vail Ware's funeral was held at Mount Vernon Methodist Church in Toano. She was 69 and the widow of William Walker Ware. The Reverend L. L. Llewellyn, pastor, officiated and was assisted by Rev. A. Prunell Bailey of New Kent. She was buried in James City Chapel Cemetery. (WF.)

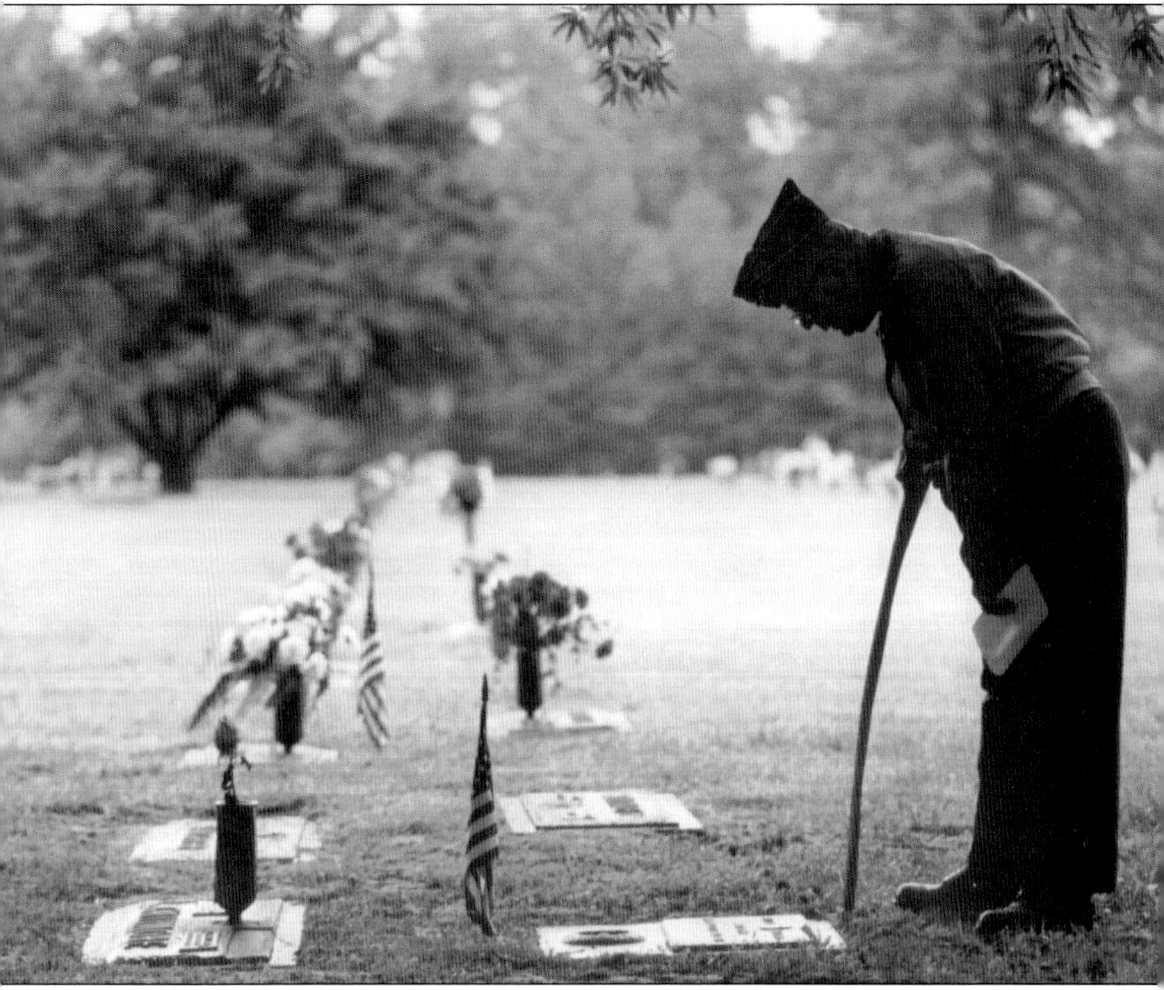

In the 1990s, a newspaper photographer snapped this touching scene of Williard S. Gilley when he stopped to read fellow veteran Robert Cottingham's grave marker during Memorial Day services at Williamsburg Memorial Park. Gilley grew up at Gatehouse Farm on Neck O' Land Road, his family's dairy farm. He attended Virginia Polytechnic Institute and State University. During World War II, Gilley served in the 26th Infantry Division of the U.S. Army and earned the Purple Heart. His division fought in France and Central Europe, and was particularly distinguished for its role in the Battle of the Bulge. (Photograph by Kenneth D. Lyons for the *Daily Press*, WSG.)

Eight

A Moment at Mid-Century

The Colonial National Historical Park's scenic byway from Jamestown to Williamsburg and Yorktown was completed and the 350th anniversary of the English landing at Jamestown was celebrated in 1957 at Jamestown Festival Park. Travel in the Historic Triangle increased, and Jamestown's temporary structures remained open. Anheuser Busch, which opened a theme park in Florida, was attracted to this area in the 1960s to scout a location. Colonial Williamsburg sold land that had been part of the Kingsmill tract for a brewery and subdivision as well as another Busch Gardens theme park. Nearby Carter's Grove was opened as a museum property. Jamestown Festival Park continued to attract tourists and was renovated as today's Jamestown Settlement.

In the 1950s, the process of public school consolidation was completed, and James Blair High School opened. In the 1960s, the promise of equal education was fulfilled as white and black systems were combined. Between 1900 and 1950, James City County's population grew from 3,688 to 6,317. By 1980, the population had increased sharply to 22,763. Today's population stands at more than 60,000 people, or nearly 10 times the population of the county in 1950. Growth that began during the era of the World Wars boomed as more people were attracted to the area to visit, work, and stay. Looking back, some longtime residents see moments at mid-century when change accelerated and a new era began.

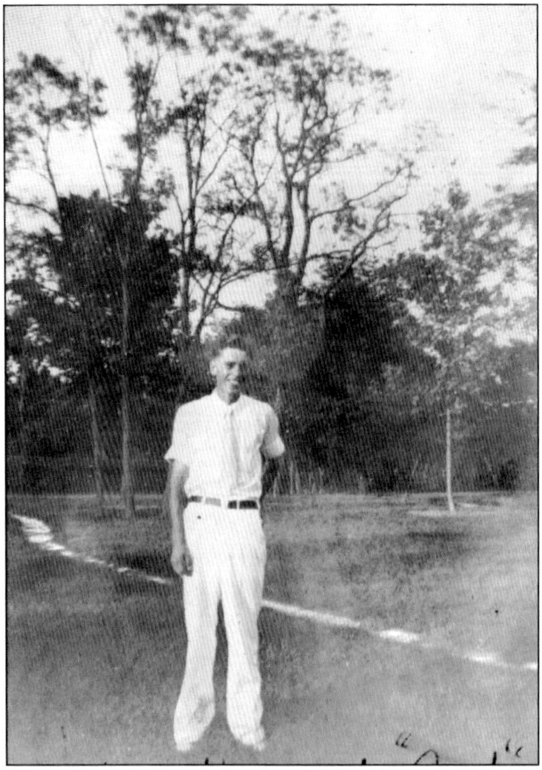

Buck Hazelwood's photograph was taken in 1936. He was a farmer who delivered orders of fresh vegetables to homeowners in the city of Williamsburg and later sold produce from his truck. His land is currently farmed by his great-nephew, Randy Gulden, who sells through a Community Supported Agriculture program and local farmers' markets. (GHD.)

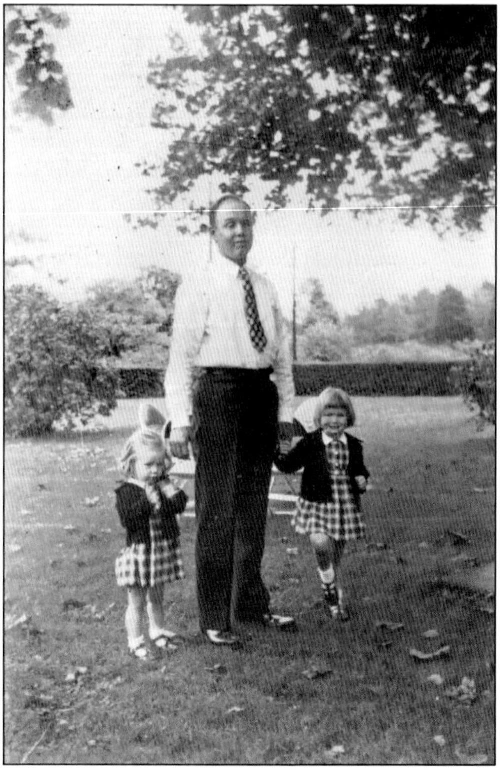

George Marston, seen here in 1949 with daughters Keith (left) and Randi, farmed land along Richmond Road near its intersection with Croaker Road. Family members still live on a portion of the property, and Marston tends a garden there. His father, George A. Marston Sr., established the family's Oakland Farm in 1917. Like Hazelwood, his family was among the earliest James City County residents. (GDMM.)

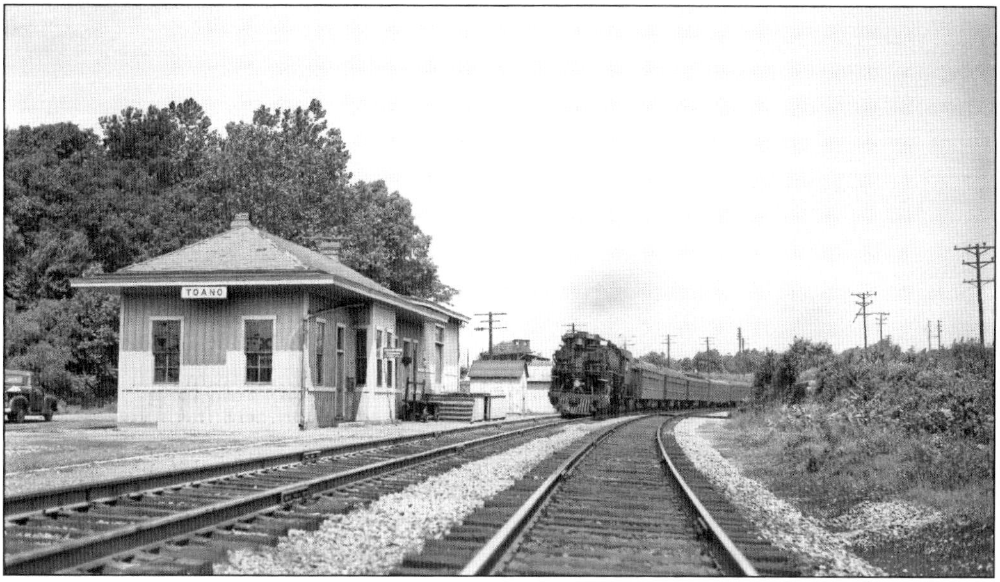

The C&O Railroad was still central to community and commerce in the mid-20th century. Above, a passenger extra passed the Toano depot in June 1951 en route to the SS *United States* cruise ship christening at the Newport News Shipbuilding and Drydock Company. Below, an empty coal train returning from Newport News and headed to the coal mines in western Virginia passed the Norge depot in June 1952. Andy Bradshaw, a former James City County supervisor who grew up nearby, said, "We got our first notions of a world bigger than our town as we saw rail cars move past covered in snow when our weather had been mild and clear for days. And our concept of community expanded as we saw coal, logs, automobiles, livestock, and freight cars whose contents we could only guess, pass by going to or from distant ports." (Both photographs by J. I. Kelly, COHS.)

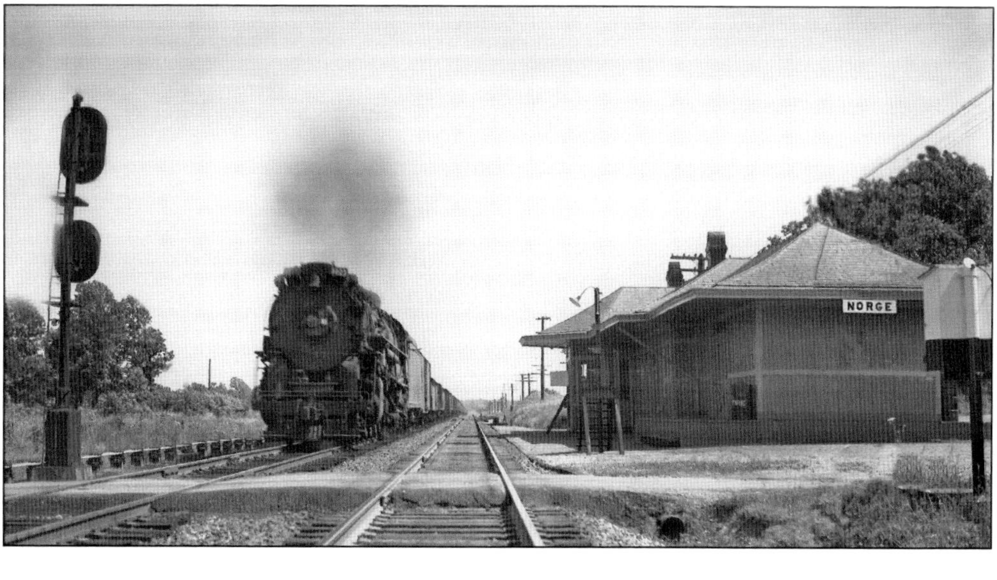

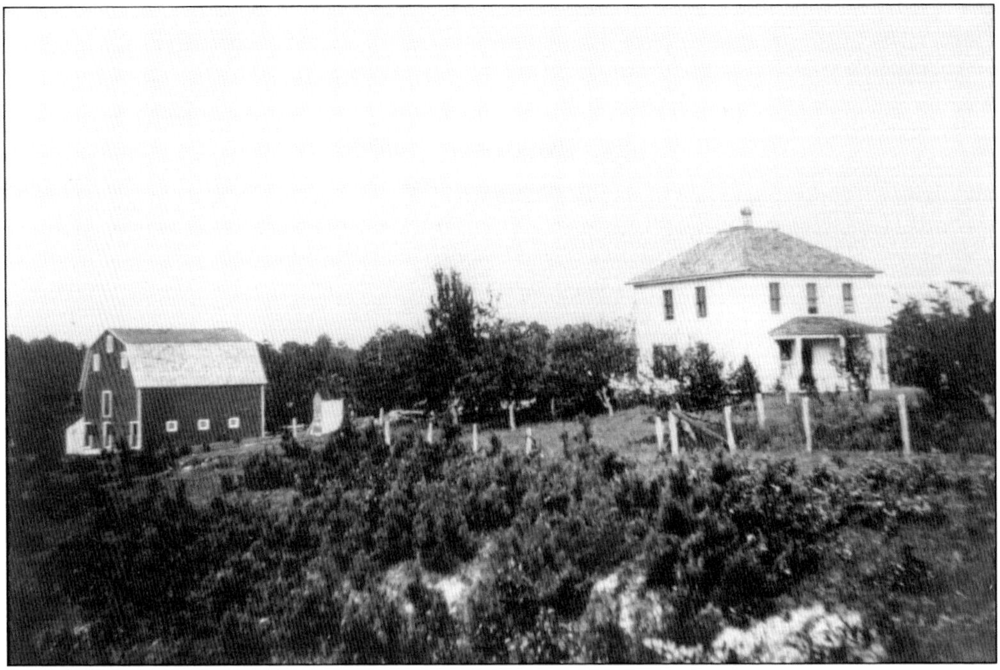

Above, the 80-acre home and farm property of Ingeborg Houg, a Norwegian emigrant who resettled from Wisconsin to Lightfoot in 1907, was left to her son Bennett Benson. In 1938, Jimmy Maloney purchased an acre of the property near the side of the road from Benson. There Maloney built his first pottery kiln and home, and sold "seconds." Gradually, Maloney bought more and more of the property and supplemented his pottery with seconds of other pottery, clothing, and decorative wares. The outlet, pictured below in a 1978 photograph, became a multimillion-dollar business and, at one point in the late 20th century, a leading Virginia tourist destination. (Both, DBW.)

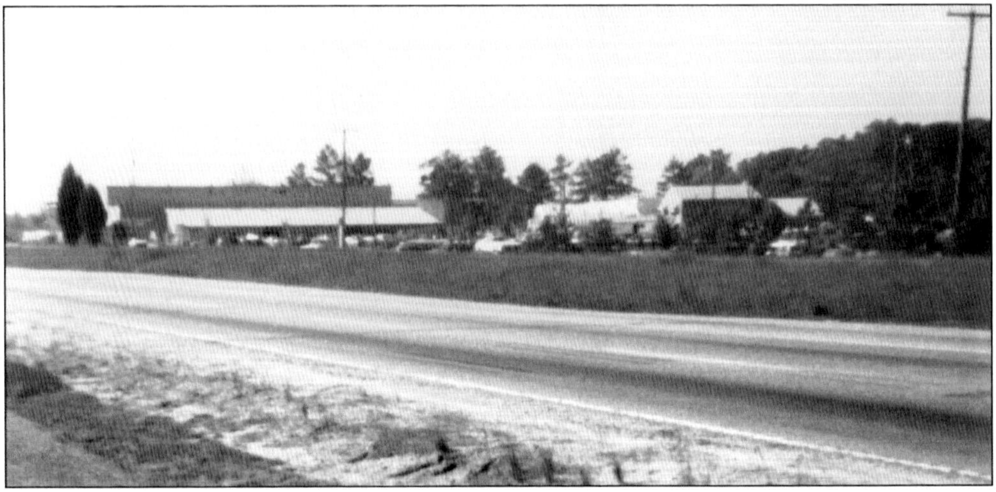

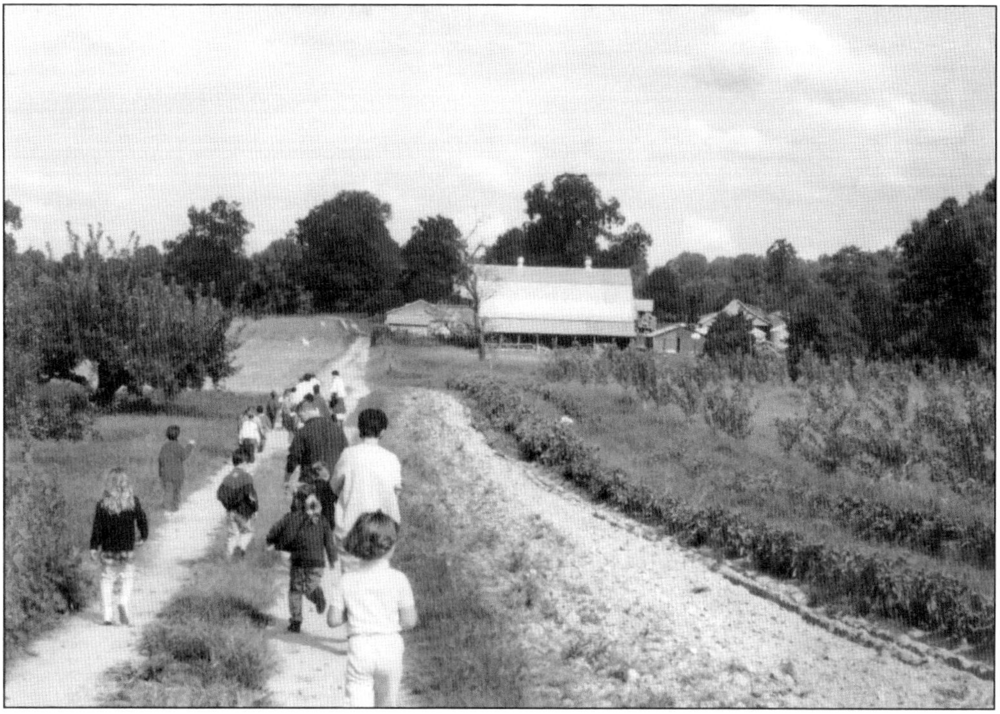

The Hunt family's Hill Pleasant Farm was one of the last working farms along Richmond Road. Many mid- to late-20th-century schoolchildren visited the farm each fall to see apple trees, pick a pumpkin from the field, and learn about food production. (SEL.)

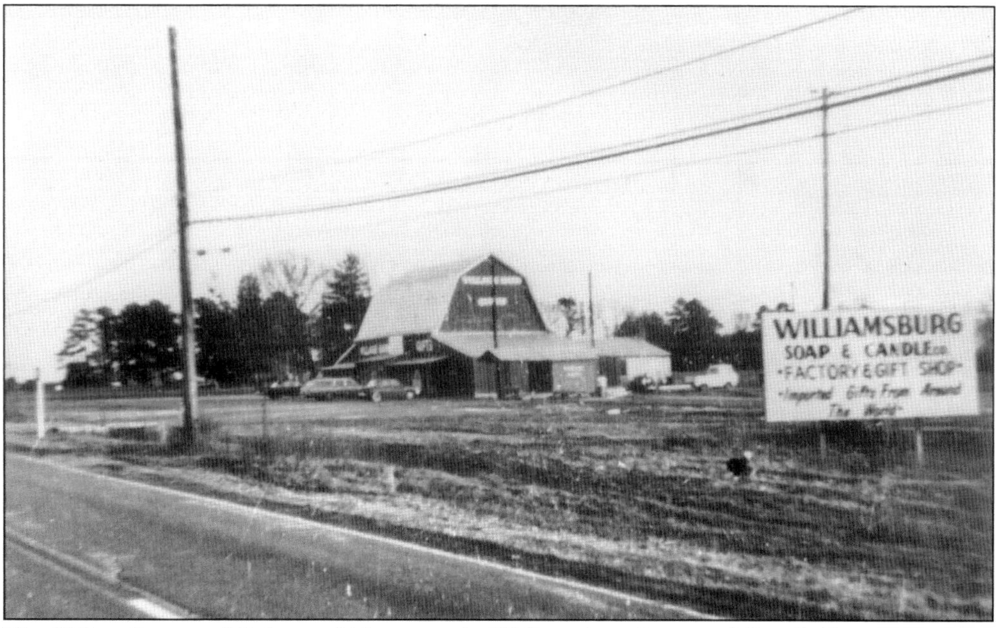

The Village Barn and Gifts would become the Williamsburg Soap and Candle Factory, another early factory "seconds" warehouse featuring "gifts from around the world." The factory produced molded and hand-dipped beeswax candles for Colonial Williamsburg for most of the second half of the 20th century. (Collection of Robin Miller, DBW.)

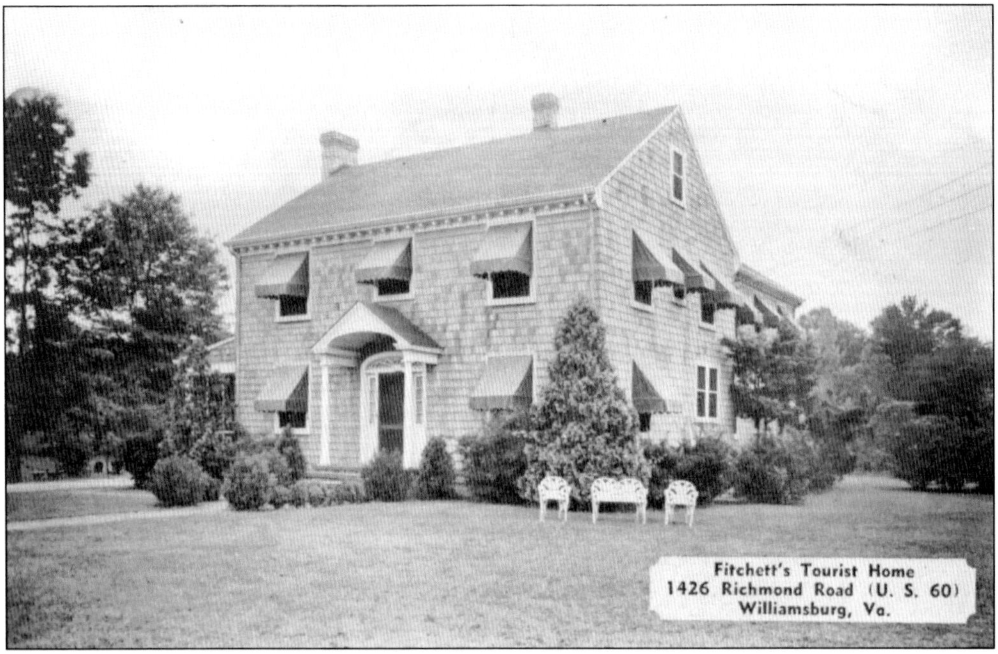

After farmer Kendall Fitchett passed away, his wife, Lura Fitchett, moved from rural western James City County to open Fitchett's Tourist Home close to the city of Williamsburg. The hostelry was located along Richmond Road where the entrance to High Street Williamsburg is located today. (GDMM.)

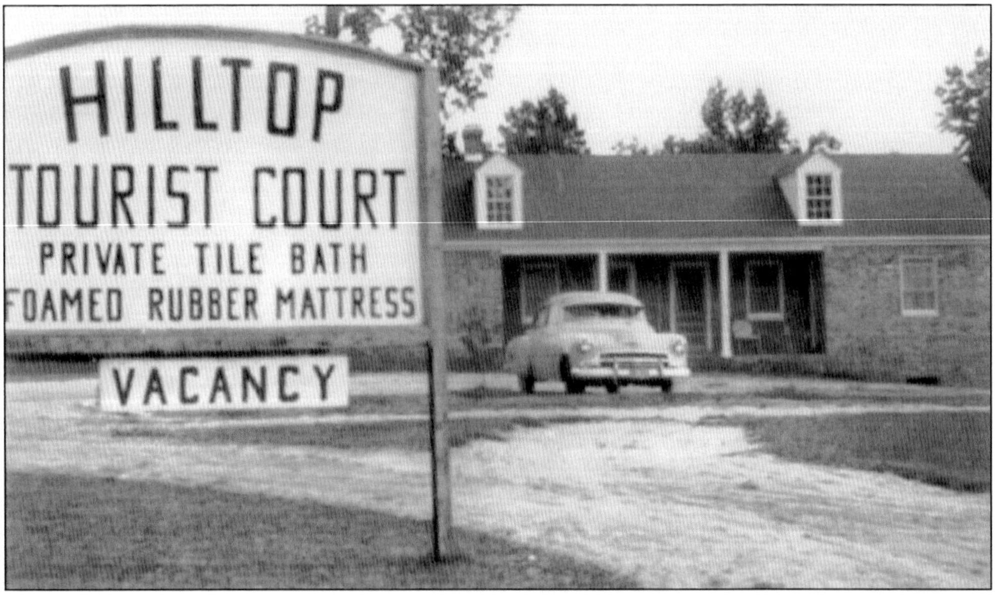

Waverly and Glennis Hazelwood Davis opened the Hilltop Motor Court in Lanexa in the late 1940s. Waverly, a brick mason, built the tourist court, and he and his family rented and maintained the rooms. Each room had one double bed and rented for $4 per night. In the mid-1950s, the rate escalated to $14 per night. The name was later changed to the Golden Key, and a restaurant and gift shop were added. The motor court was on the main highway from Richmond before Interstate 64 was built through James City County. (GHD.)

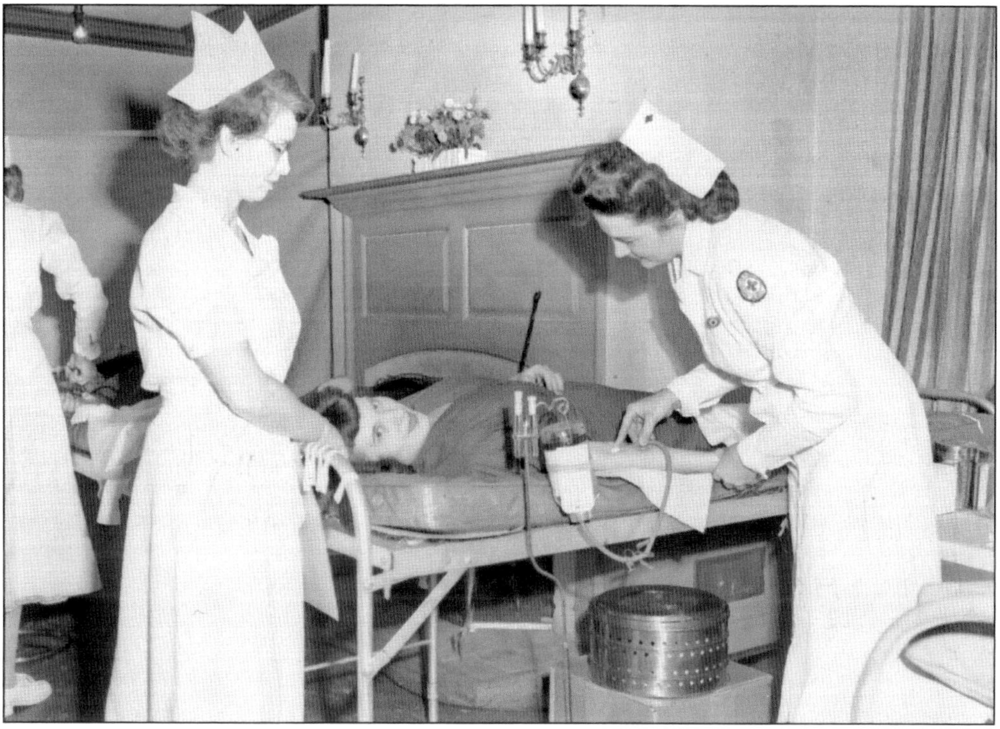

When England faced invasion in the early 1940s, a program began to prepare for the stockpiling of lifesaving blood that might be needed on a massive scale. Advances were made in blood collection and plasma processing techniques. During the postwar baby boom years, known as the atomic age because of the development of nuclear weapons, the United States' population grew rapidly. Several massive hurricanes in the 1950s increased the sense of vulnerability. Red Cross blood drives became an important means for local citizens to make a contribution to preparedness and to help in relief efforts. (CVC-ARC.)

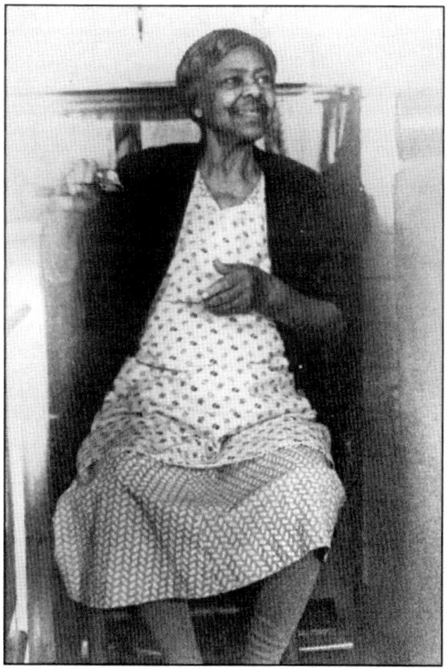

Rosa Bell Graves (1892–1978) delivered babies for local African American families all over James City County from the 1940s until the 1970s. Before Williamsburg Community Hospital opened its doors in 1961, individuals requiring hospitalization usually traveled to the Medical College of Virginia in Richmond and other hospitals in the capital city or on the lower Virginia Peninsula. Small hospitals, Bell and Blayton, were located in Williamsburg. Trained midwives such as Graves, however, were often called upon to deliver babies in the rural areas. She kept a notebook with a list of mothers and the sex of their children. (OT.)

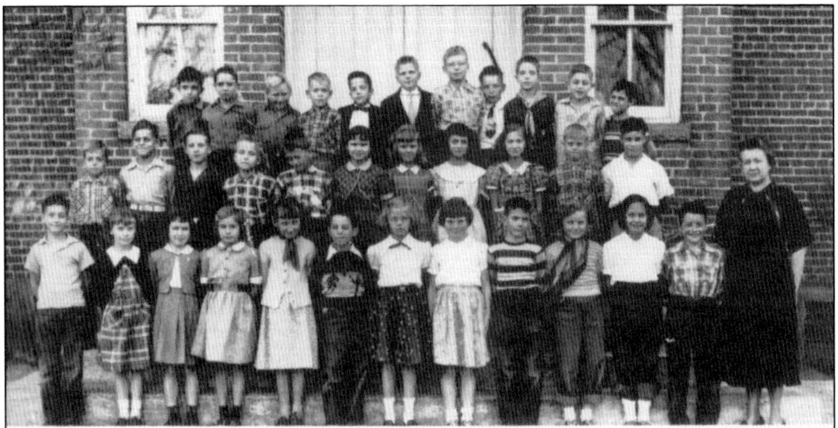

Fourth Grade

First row, left to right: Gerald Otey, Patsy Marston, Gladys Talley, Eugenia Brush, Joyce Otey, George Richardson, Lois Martin, Lucy Moore, William McAllister, Joyce Smith, Carolyn Taylor, William Cowles, Mrs. Pitman. Second row: Stanley Sears, Robert Garrett, John Parker, Douglas Bowman, Robert Clayton, Barbara Fannin, Laura Pitts, Betty Stewart, Elizabeth Ford, Clarence Stewart, Wayne Brown. Third row: John Woodward, Jerry Hazelwood, Gene Richardson, Charles Minor, James Crowell, Billy Taylor, Buck Stewart, Tommy Drewry, Bertrand Geddy, Welford Matheny, Walter Scruggs.

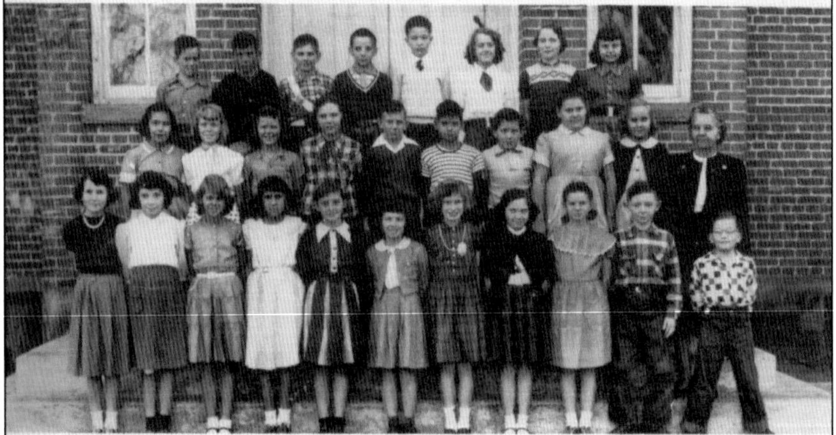

Fifth Grade

First row, left to right: Gloria Koger, Barbara Payne, Louetta Buckner, Anne Wilkerson, Virginia Moyer, Carolyn Talley, Willie Mae Hicks, Laverne Millirons, Ethel Otey, John Hoar, Dickie Nelson. Second row: Barbara Isaac, Peggy Sutphin, Eva Pearl Pitts, Joan Malone, Leslie Moore, Tommy Green, Micahel Runyans, Karen Halligan, Norma Adams, Mrs. Taylor. Third row: Pete Cowan, Earnest Richardson, Lacy Banks, Ronnie Moore, Bobby Drewry, Lillie Mae Sears, Laura Lee Fannin, Joyce Goad.

A page from the 1954 *Chieftain* offers a glimpse of a few of James City County's future citizens. The 1954 school year was the last year James City County's Powhatan and Stonehouse districts would share a school system with Charles City and New Kent Counties. During the 1955–1956 school year, the schools for white citizens of the city of Williamsburg and all of James City County were consolidated into a single school system. White and black school systems would be integrated in 1968. (WF.)

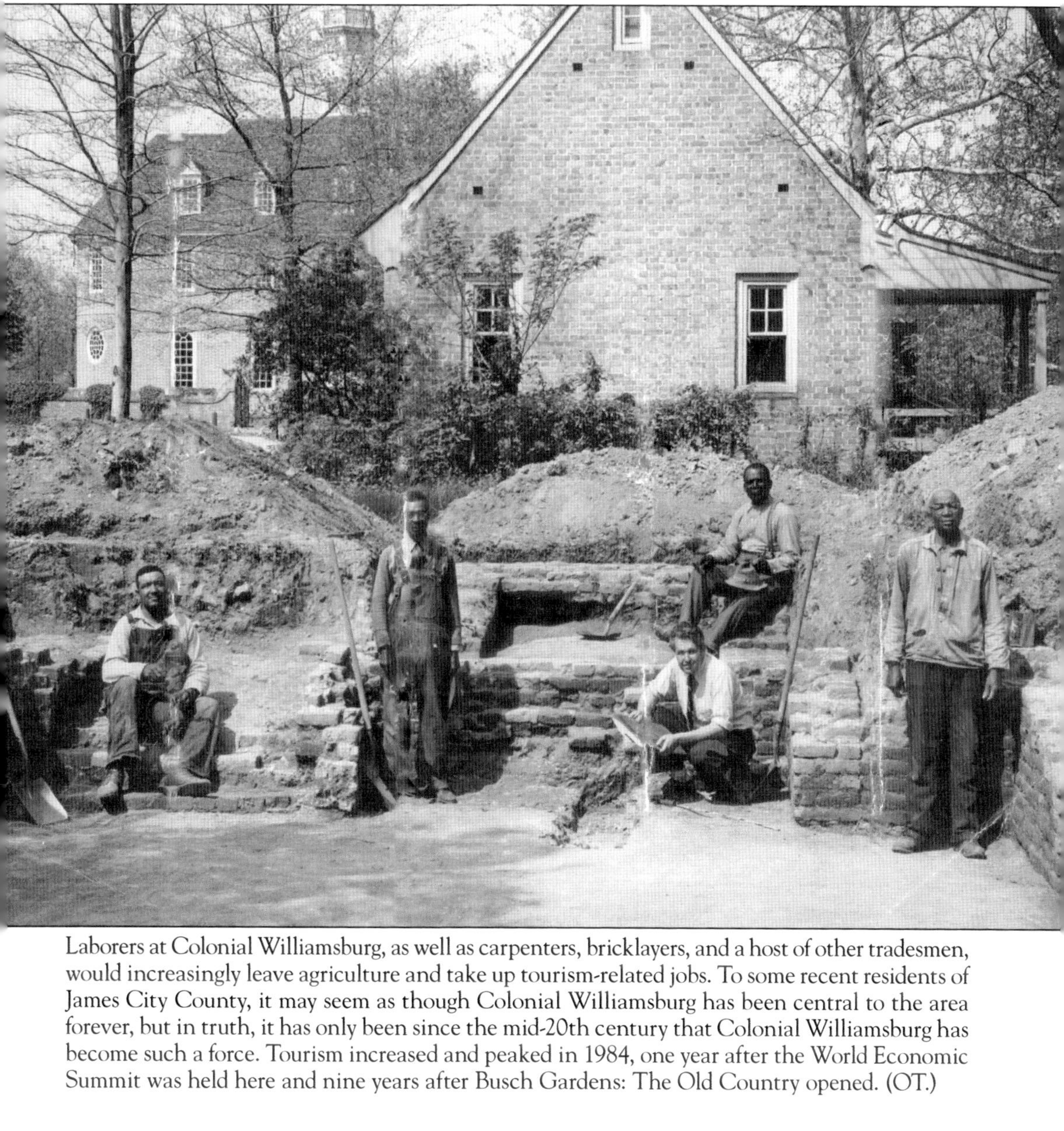

Laborers at Colonial Williamsburg, as well as carpenters, bricklayers, and a host of other tradesmen, would increasingly leave agriculture and take up tourism-related jobs. To some recent residents of James City County, it may seem as though Colonial Williamsburg has been central to the area forever, but in truth, it has only been since the mid-20th century that Colonial Williamsburg has become such a force. Tourism increased and peaked in 1984, one year after the World Economic Summit was held here and nine years after Busch Gardens: The Old Country opened. (OT.)

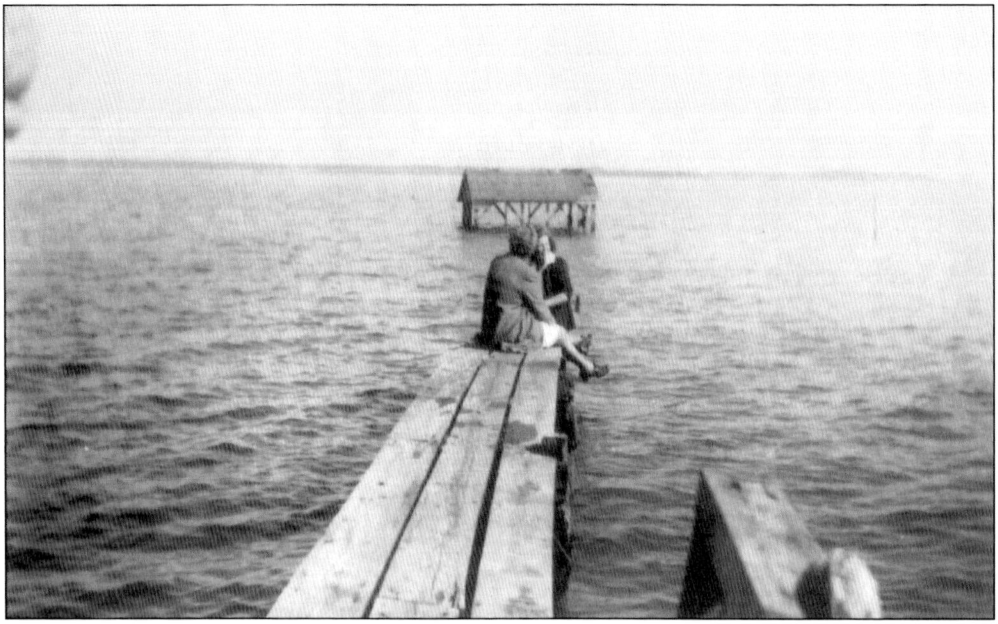

At the end of Croaker Road on the York River, Sycamore Landing was called "Little Richmond" because several of the homes were vacation cottages owned by Richmond residents. These photographs were taken during the annual fall get-together when Brunswick stew brewed in a kettle was stirred with an oar and oysters gathered from the river in front of the houses were roasted. Some of the families in attendance were the Burnetts, Joneses, Jameses, and Rivaldis. These photographs were taken in 1955 after hurricanes had destroyed part of the pier at the old landing. Across the river in Gloucester, antebellum to early-20th-century steamboats stopped regularly for travel along routes that connected West Point to Baltimore and Norfolk. (Both, SW.)

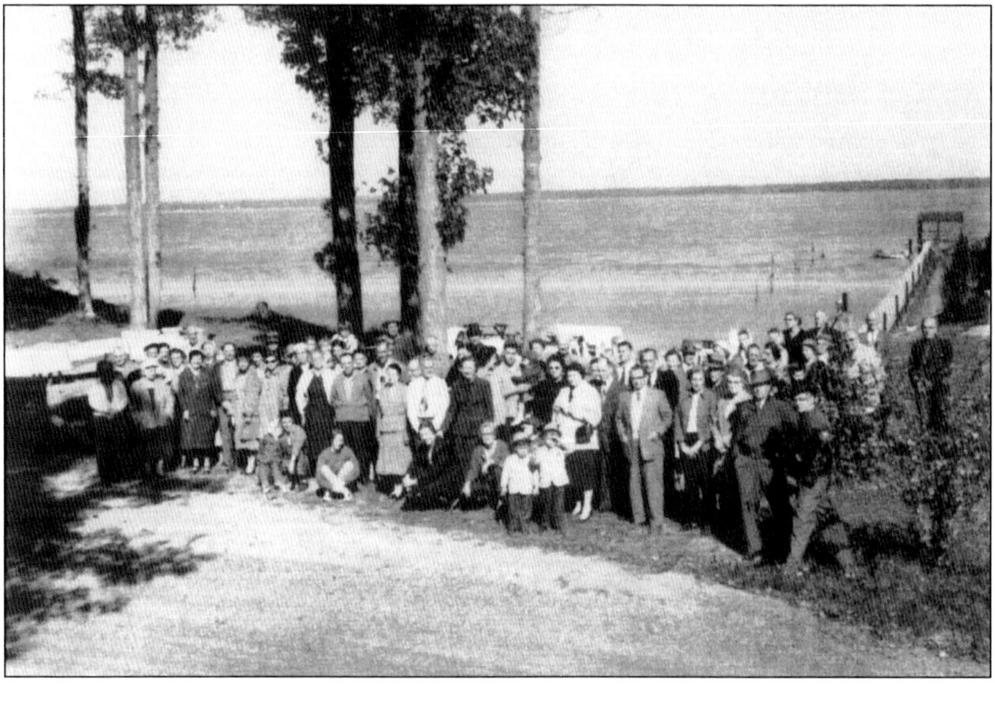

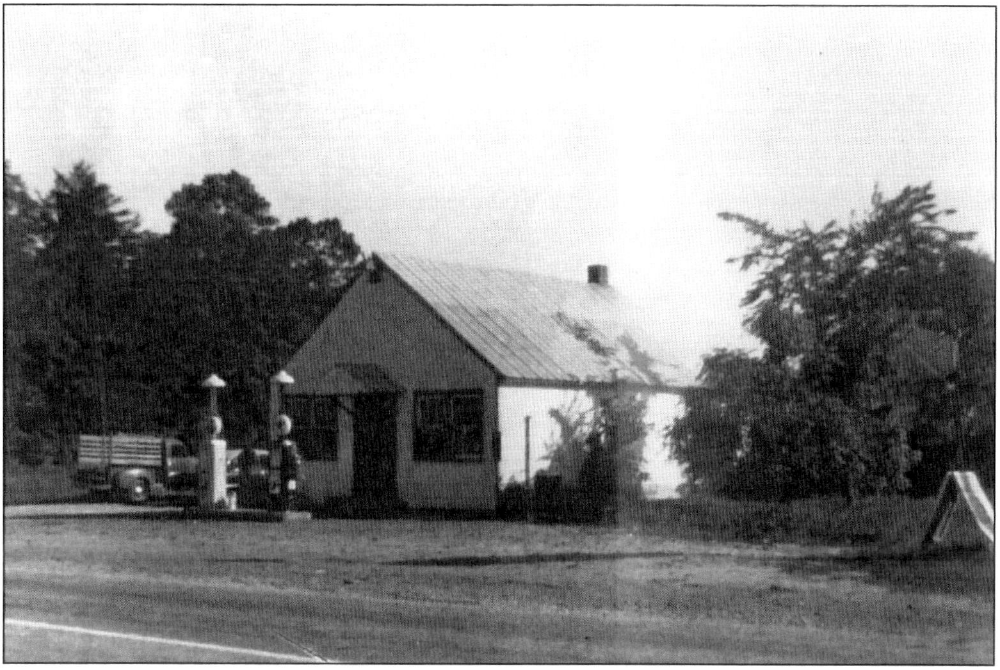

Garrett's Grocery on old State Route 168, which traveled east and west through James City County, was closed in the 1960s when the land was taken to build Interstate 64. The store operation moved to the Croaker Road intersection with Ware Creek Road. The portion of the interstate that passes through James City County was not completed until the 1980s. (SW.)

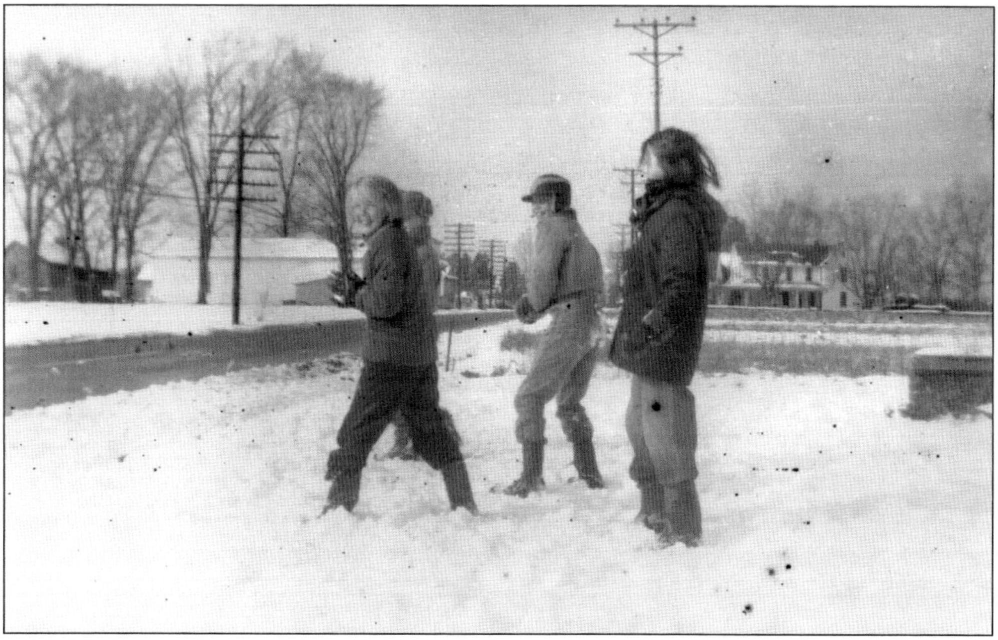

In 1957, it was possible for children to enjoy a snowball fight across Richmond Road before it was widened. The steps of Norge Hall can be seen on the far right. The H. A. Bergh Hotel, which is Williamsburg Wicker today, is the two-story building in the right background. Children include, from left to right, Judy Petersen and Neal, Gary, and Sharon Miller. (DBW.)

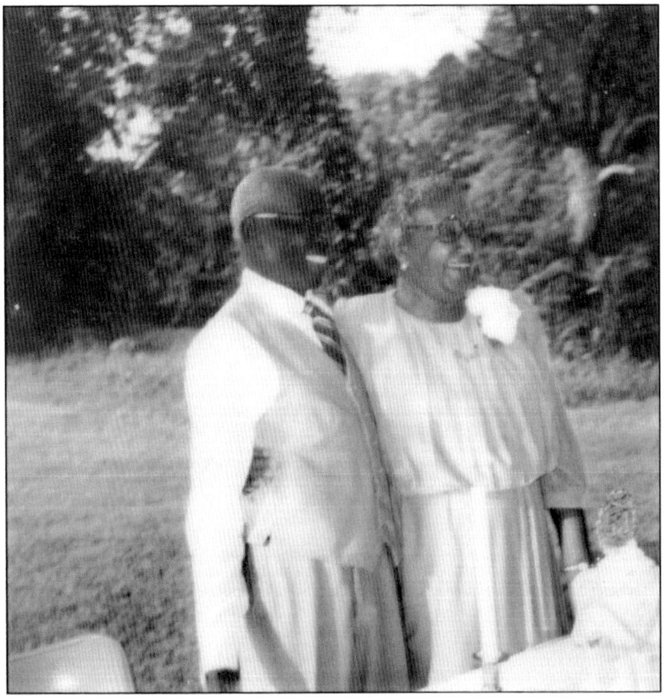

The Taylors celebrated their 50th wedding anniversary about 1985. The couple lived on Chickahominy Road, where many of their descendants live today. The area was anchored by Chickahominy School, which closed when schools were integrated, and Chickahominy Baptist Church, which continues to be central to the neighborhood. (OT.)

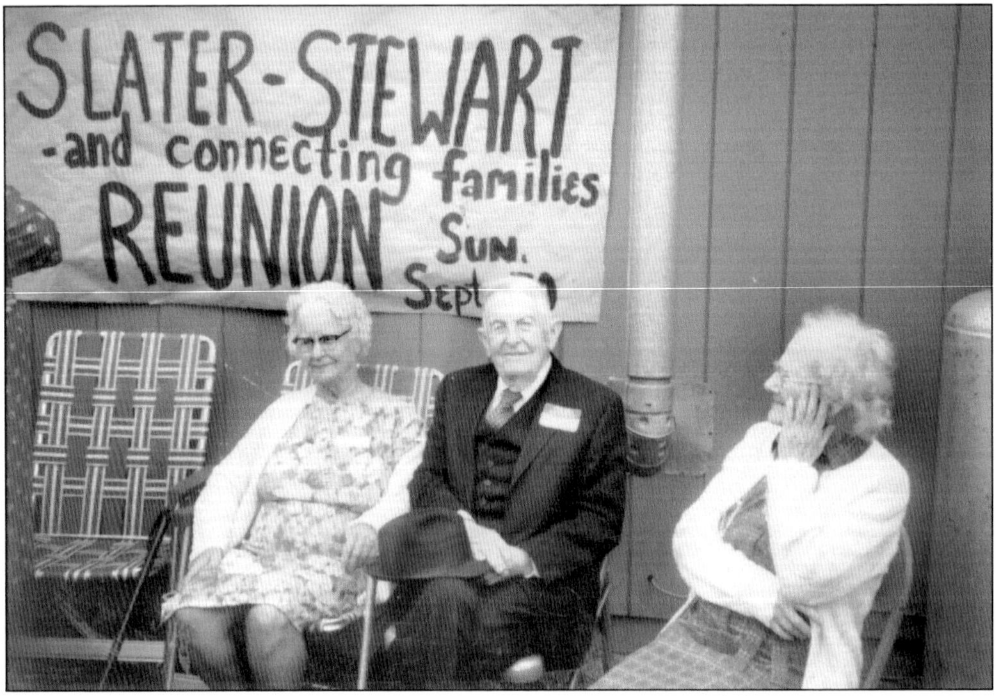

The Slater and Stewart families of westernmost James City County celebrated a reunion in 1984 at the Chickahominy Shores neighborhood recreation center. The oldest Slater in attendance was Gracie Lillian Slater Hazelwood (right), and the oldest Stewart in attendance was Edward Clifton Stewart (center). Laura Vernell Slater Stewart (left) is Hazelwood's sister. Slater and Stewart family ancestors have lived in James City County since the early Colonial period. (GHD.)

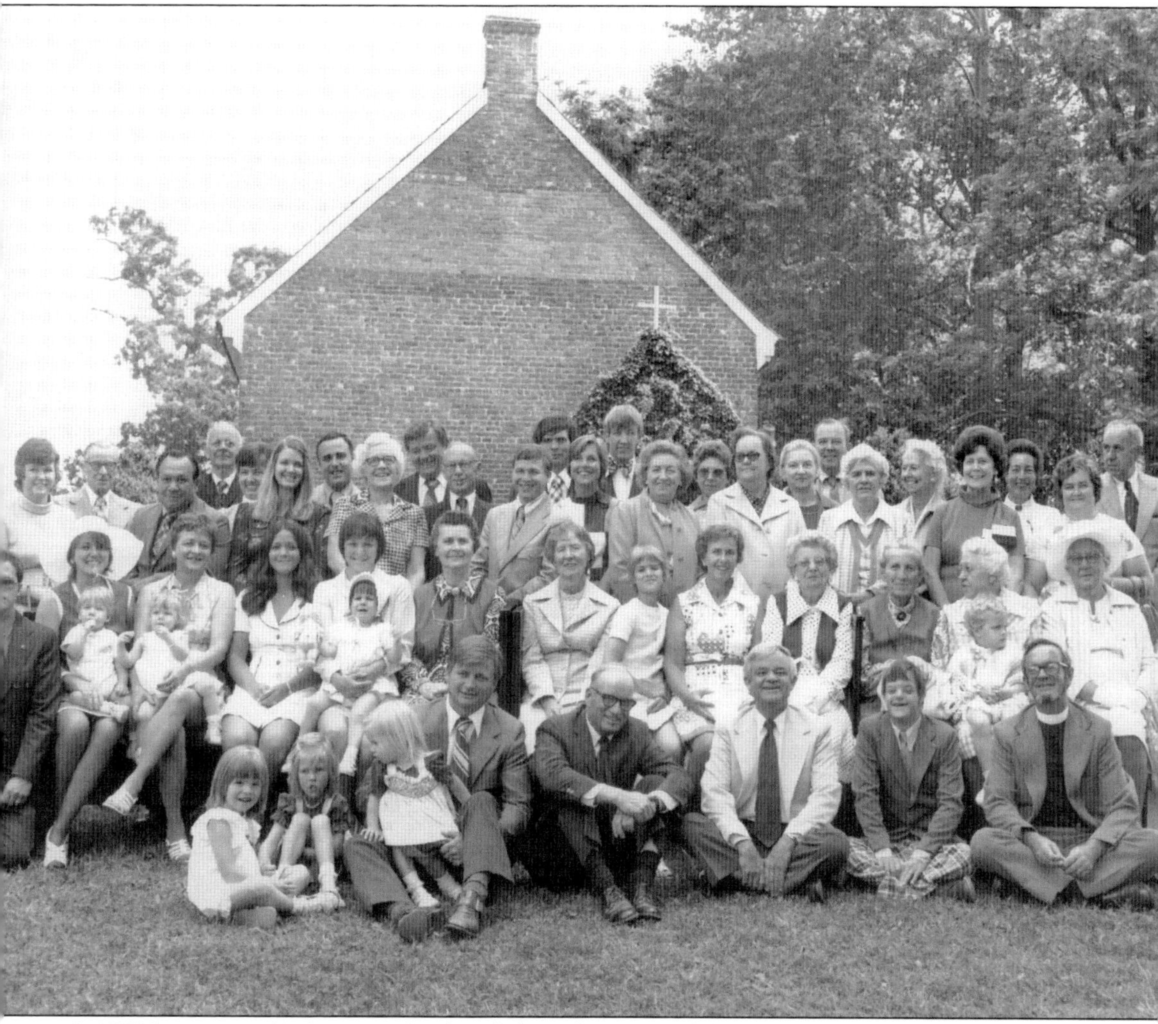

A 1975 baptism at Hickory Neck Church brought many of the area's oldest families together, including, from left to right, (first row) Mary Vail Ware, two unidentified girls, Dennis Chautier, Billy Ben Piggott, Dick Wilkinson, Tommy Wilkinson, and Rev. Harmon Smith; (second row) David Ware Jr., Laurice Ware with William Walker Ware V, Kate Ware with Martha Ware, Mary Ware, Martha Ware Petro with Jeanne Petro, Caroline Dozier, Lucy Taylor, Nancy Wilkinson, two unidentified, Margaret Harrison, Trittie Geddy with Renee Geddy, and Mary Branch; (third row) Linda Chautier, Bertrand Geddy, David Ware, Carter Harrison, Adealia Harrell, Chase Ware, Joe Petro, unidentified, Loy Harrell, unidentified, Walker Ware, D. D. Tennis, ? Tennis, Kevin Harrell, two unidentified, Pearle Miller, Christina Henderson, J. B. Cowles Jr., Genelle Cardwell, Jeanne Etheridge, unidentified, Amie Crute, Helen Piggott, and W. M. "Tar" Crute. (Photograph by Thomas L. Williams, WF.)

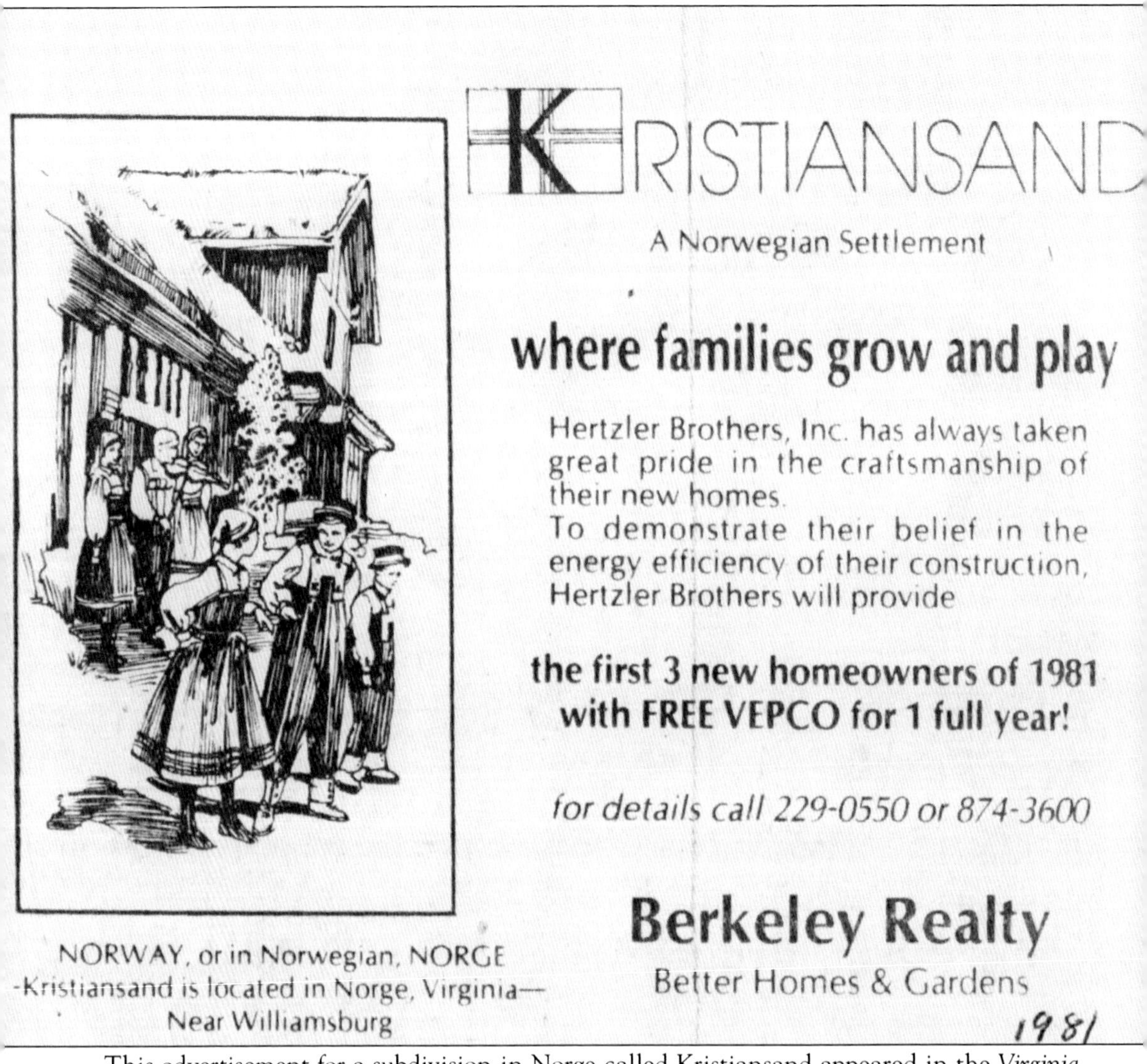

This advertisement for a subdivision in Norge called Kristiansand appeared in the *Virginia Gazette* in 1981. The housing development includes more than 150 homes today. World War II housing needs and then the postwar baby boom saw the first subdivision in James City County developed at Middletown Farms. By the 1950s, suburban clusters of modest homes on lots of one acre or less blossomed. Skipwith Farms and Indigo Park were others that were planned on former farmland. The number of farms declined as improvements in transportation and food technology meant that families no longer had to spend a great deal of their time raising and preparing food. Dependence on cars and inexpensive fuel meant people could live in areas far from work, stores, and services. Kristiansand was an early development in the former western population center of the county. Before the development of Kingsmill, the eastern end of the county was lightly inhabited. Anheuser-Busch began to sell houses there in the mid-1970s, and Kingsmill was James City County's first large-scale exurban community. (DBW.)

The James Blair High School senior class of 1973 chose Bruce Hornsby and Holly Baker as "Most Likely to Succeed." Hornsby, a pianist and songwriter, achieved his first Top 40 hit, "The Way It Is," with his band, the Range, in 1986. (SF.)

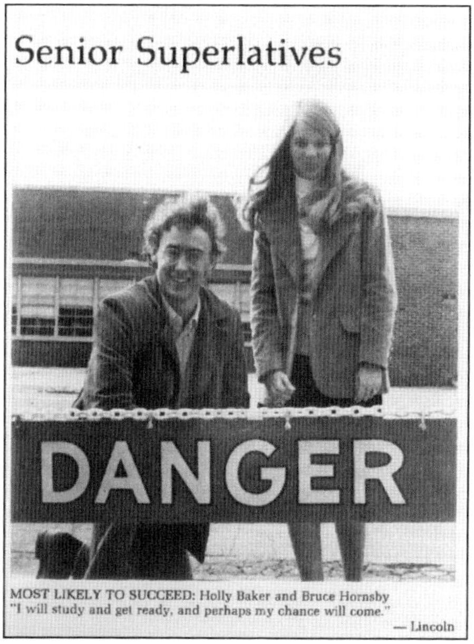
Senior Superlatives

MOST LIKELY TO SUCCEED: Holly Baker and Bruce Hornsby
"I will study and get ready, and perhaps my chance will come."
— Lincoln

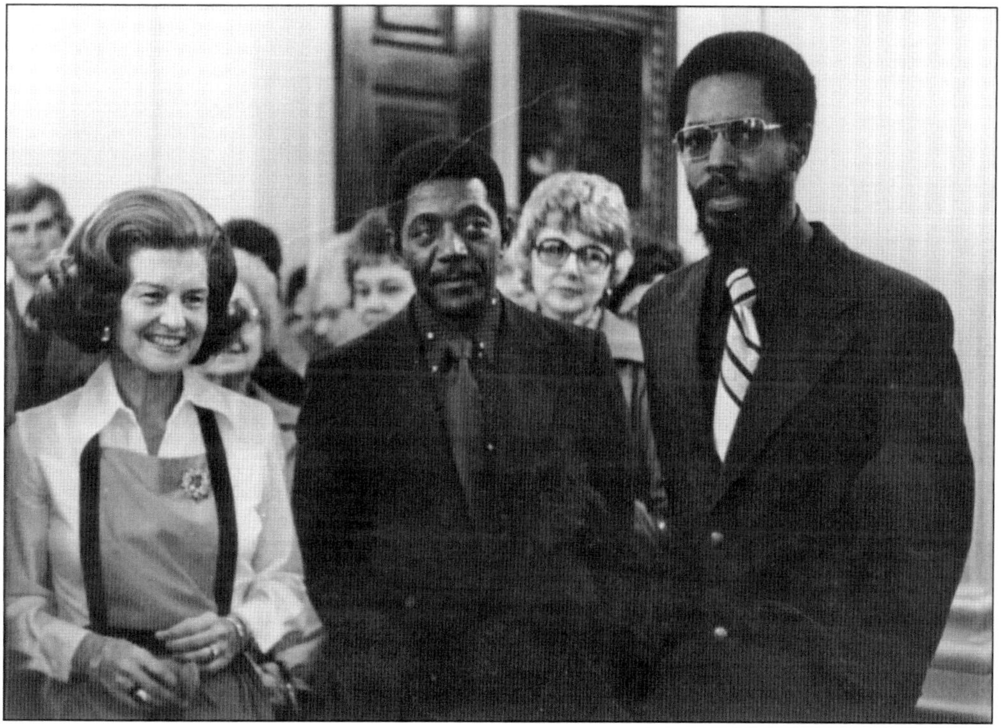

Colonial Williamsburg received national attention when 3,000 ornaments based on the Abby Aldrich Rockefeller Folk Art Collection were requested by Betty Ford to decorate the White House Christmas Tree in 1975. Posing with the First Lady in this photograph are James City County residents Douglas Canady (center) and Osborne Taylor Sr. Afterward, many people crafted ornaments inspired by the 1976 book *Christmas Decorations from Williamsburg's Folk Art Collection*, including crocheted snowflakes, fabric apples, boats made of walnut halves, and ornaments made from vines, pinecones, seashells, and other natural and found objects. (OT.)

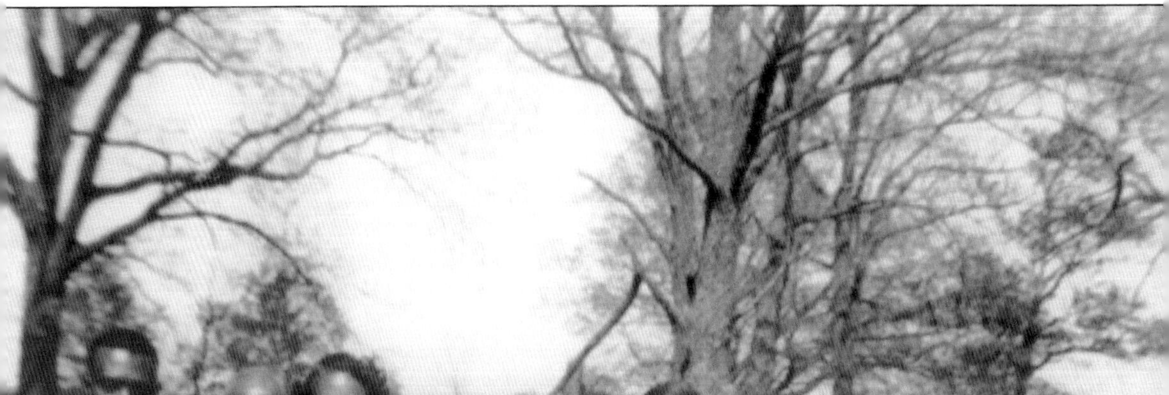

In 1998, the Virginia General Assembly presented the family of Rev. Junius H. Moody with a resolution expressing the high esteem in which his memory is held. The resolution stated, "The Williamsburg–James City community has lost a citizen of exceptional learning, talent, and dedication, one who has touched the lives, in one way or another, of virtually every member of the community." Dr. Moody, seen here kneeling in front of the Chickahominy Baptist Church choir, was pastor of Chickahominy Baptist for 56 years, New Zion Baptist for 60 years, and Ebenezer Baptist for 46 years. He taught school for 30 years and gave of his time to the James River Community Action Agency and the Williamsburg–James City Community Action Agency. Choir members pictured here include, from left to right, (first row) George White, Richard Watkins, Alfreda Lewis, Ella Mae Tyler, Carrie Jones, Hattie Cox, Doris Lee, Rosa Ashley, and Sam T. Jones; (second row) Tunis Taylor, Edna Graves, Geraldine Wallace, Gertrude Taylor, and Ernest Hawkins. (OT.)

Nine

Traces of the Past Surround Us

Get out. Explore James City County's ancient landscape. One will find, even in these modern times, traces of the past. They are best noticed while walking, paddling a boat, or riding a bicycle. These old-fashioned means of transportation are slow and do not attract attention. Drift. Follow the path or the railroad trace. A motor vehicle cannot always go there. Motor vehicles are much too fast, too insulating, and there are too many electronic distractions. If you must, turn the radio off, roll the windows down, and precede the posted speed limit. Go exploring. Look around. Find Richardson's Mill and the first Kingsmill Plantation; go inside Norge Hall and walk around downtown Toano. Turn at Croaker and proceed to Christensen corner. Find Diascund depot and Back Creek. Discover Grove and old Jamestown Road. Visit Historic Green Spring. Enjoy the best-kept secrets: the road signs that whisper the past, the shape of geologic time, and the natural places where man and nature have layered themselves one after the other. Notice the progress of time. Make connections. Look into the portals of the past and discover for yourself the things that are enduring about James City County. The past has shaped us and our surroundings. The future is the past over which new meaning is applied. An acute and mindful explorer will see how we build the new atop the old. History is the past. It is also what we contemplate, study, adjust, and resolve as we move forward.

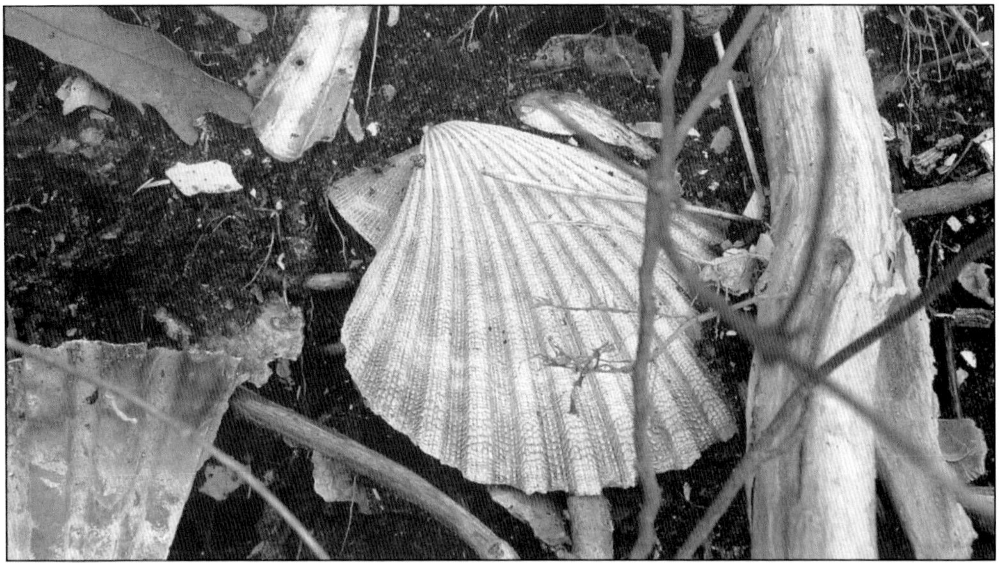

Fossils of scallops that lived between four and five million years ago can be seen in James City County's exposed riverbanks. The terraced landscape of the Virginia Coastal Plain forms stair-steps through James City County from west to east, marking former shorelines and river bottoms. It was formed during the last few million years when the sea level rose and fell as the large continental glaciers melted or grew. The cycle left creatures like the scallop high and dry and extinct. (SEL.)

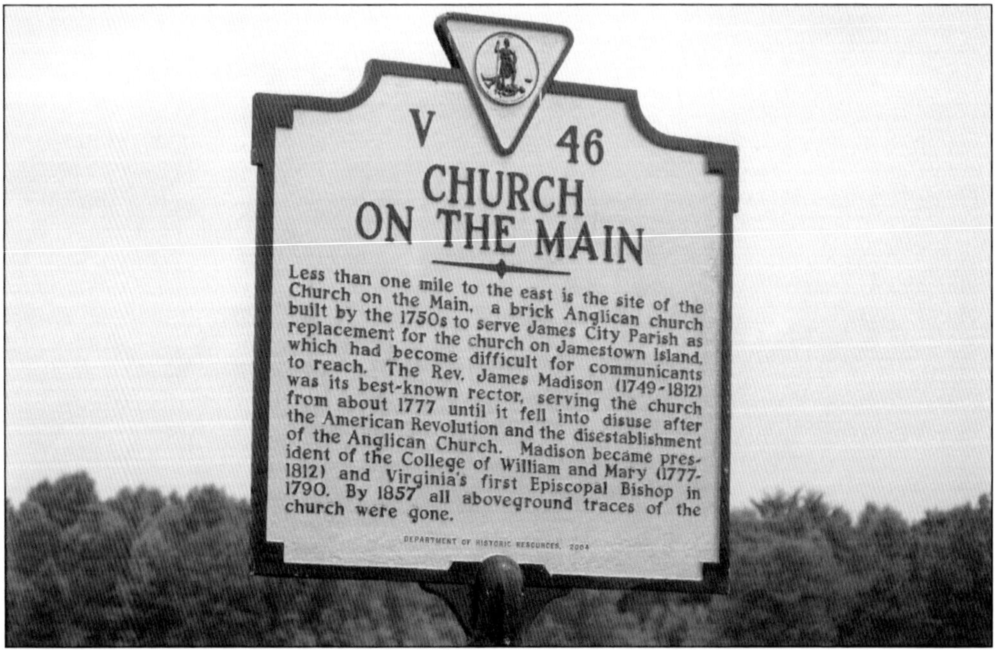

The Church on the Main historical marker is one of a group located on Green Spring Road and the Virginia Capital Trail. Virginia's historical highway marker program began in 1927, and roughly 1,200 markers have been installed along state roads, including many that mark James City County's rich history. Citizens can sponsor new markers and keep up-to-date on marker dedication ceremonies by visiting the Virginia Department of Historic Resources Web site. (SEL.)

The tides mark time and uncover the past. Bricks and pottery from James City County's earliest days can be found in creek beds at low tide, especially where wave action erodes and as sea levels creep higher. (SEL.)

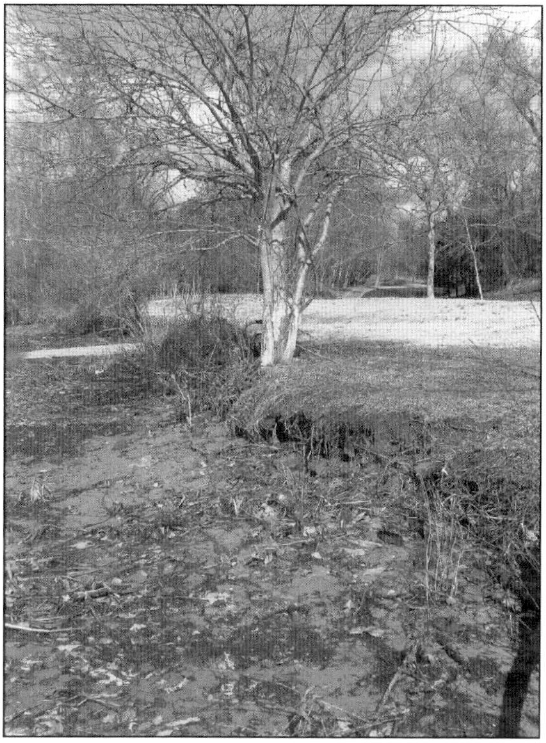

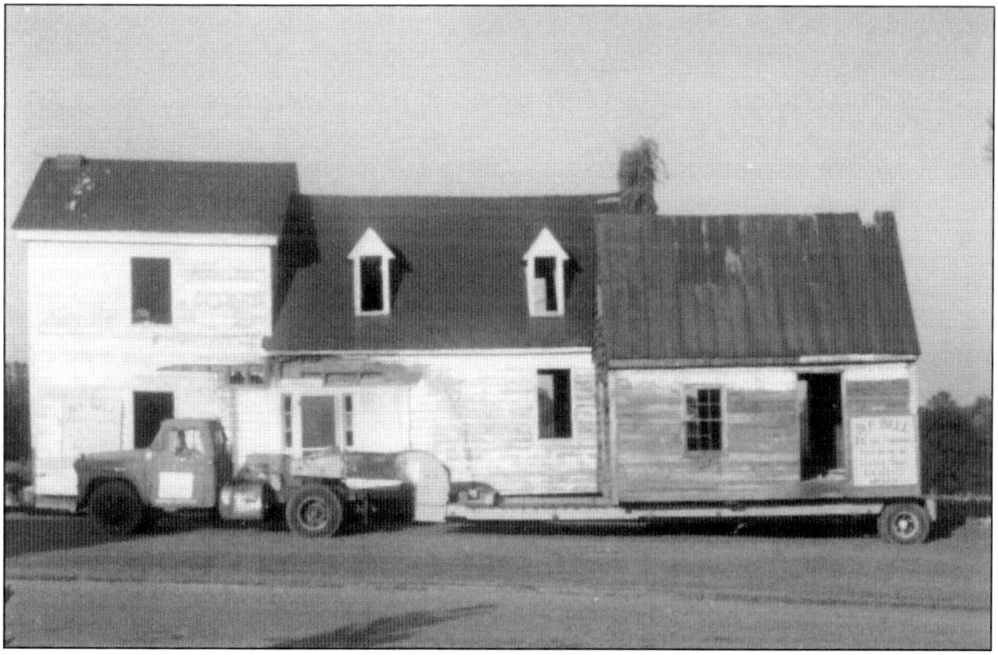

Six Mile Ordinary was moved in the late 1970s to make way for the Williamsburg Outlet Mall and McDonald's. The house mover intended to relocate the structure off of Centerville Road, but the movement caused it to crumble as the tractor trailer left the pavement and headed into the woods. Most of the boards were left where they fell and have probably decomposed—gone without a trace. (DBW.)

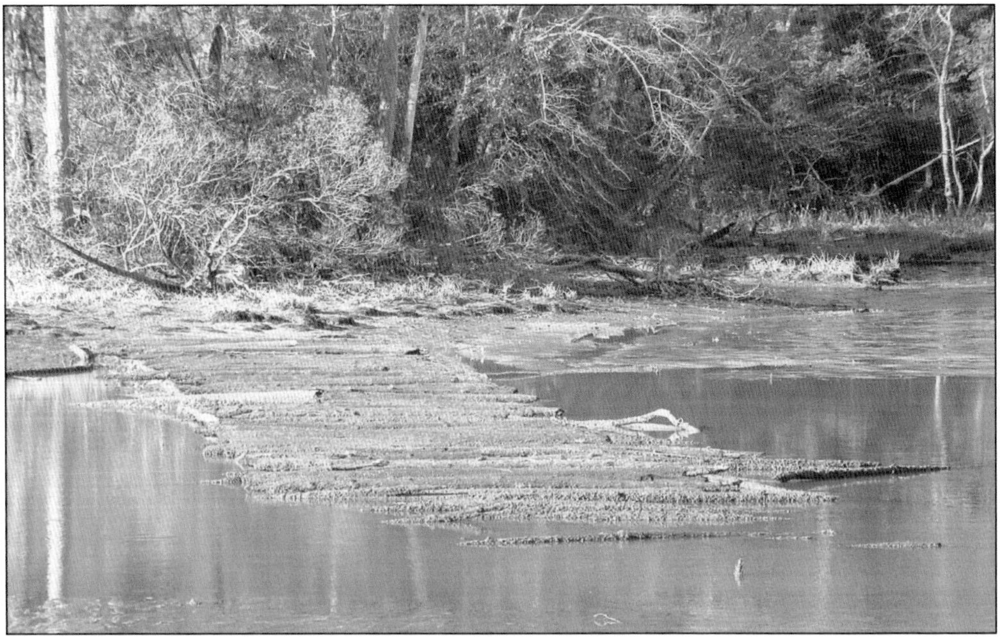

So-called corduroy roads were built by fastening logs together. Such roads appear in marshes and creeks at low tide, where they were essential to provide a bed for horses and wagons to cross. This corduroy road was built from one of the county's earliest plantations, Richneck, to College Landing. The road provided a shortcut for logging operations. (SEL.)

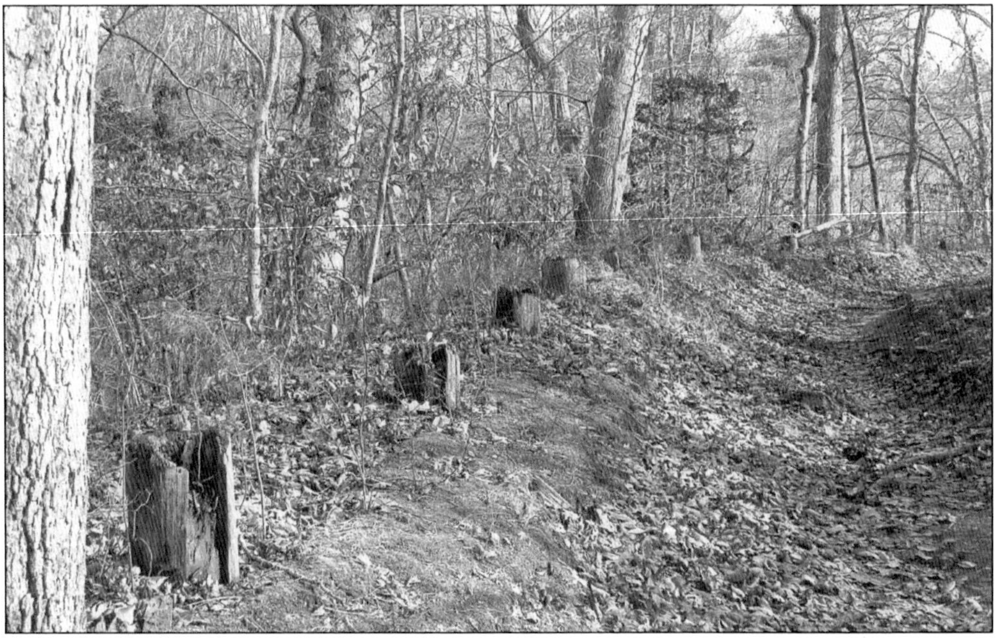

Traces of trails through the College Woods recall the era when Civilian Conservation Corps men were brought to town to build a state park and an amphitheater. They also repaired the Lake Matoaka dam, which washed out during a storm while they were there. Photographs from the period found in an old family album indicate that students from Toano were active in the William and Mary Hiking Club, whose members took hikes in the woods. (SEL.)

Willie Slater's store is nearly overgrown. It served as the Diascund railroad depot and post office many years ago. Another ghost of a building across the street reflects the growth of the complex: the depot and post office probably expanded to that location about 1940. During that mid-century period, Beatrice Slater Gray was postmistress. She hung the Diascund mailbag on a hook. When the train passed the depot, the mailbag would be snatched and another thrown off with local mail. Dave Ware Sr. remembered going to Slater's store as a boy to pick up the weekly *Grit* newspaper to sell it throughout the area. (SEL.)

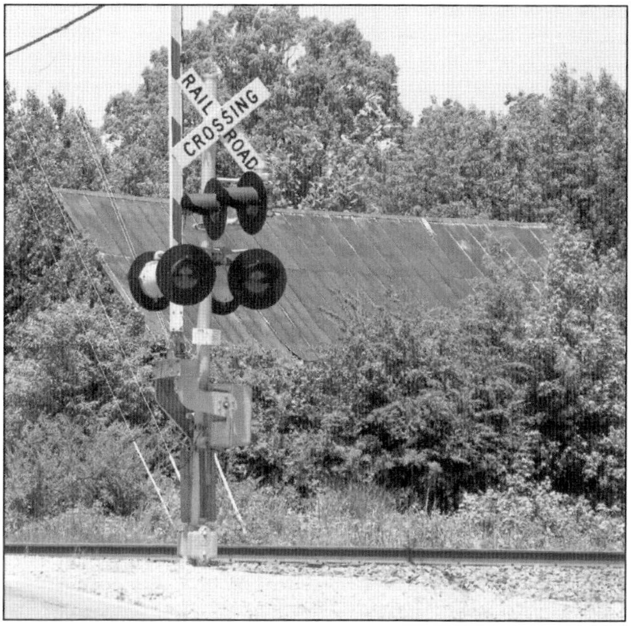

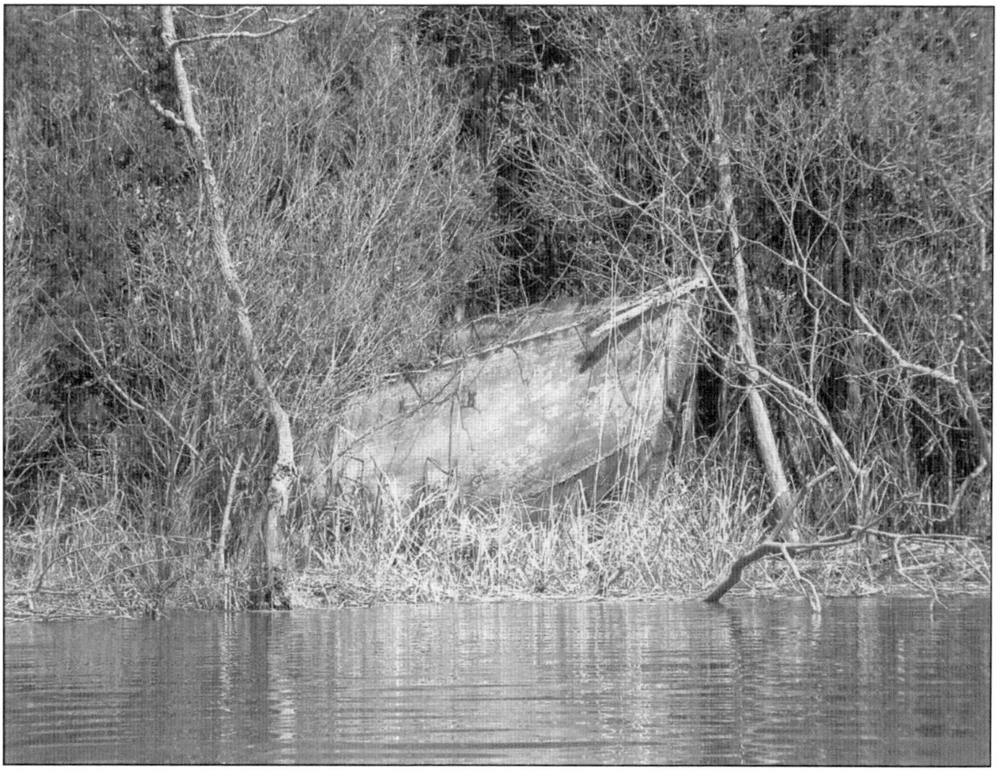

A boat rests in the brush on Mill Creek's shore. James City County watermen fished the James River and the county's creeks until the 1970s, when contamination by kepone was exposed. Afterward, the river was shut down to commercial fishing. The manufacturer of the carcinogenic insecticide was charged with improper handling and dumping of the substance into the James River. (SEL.)

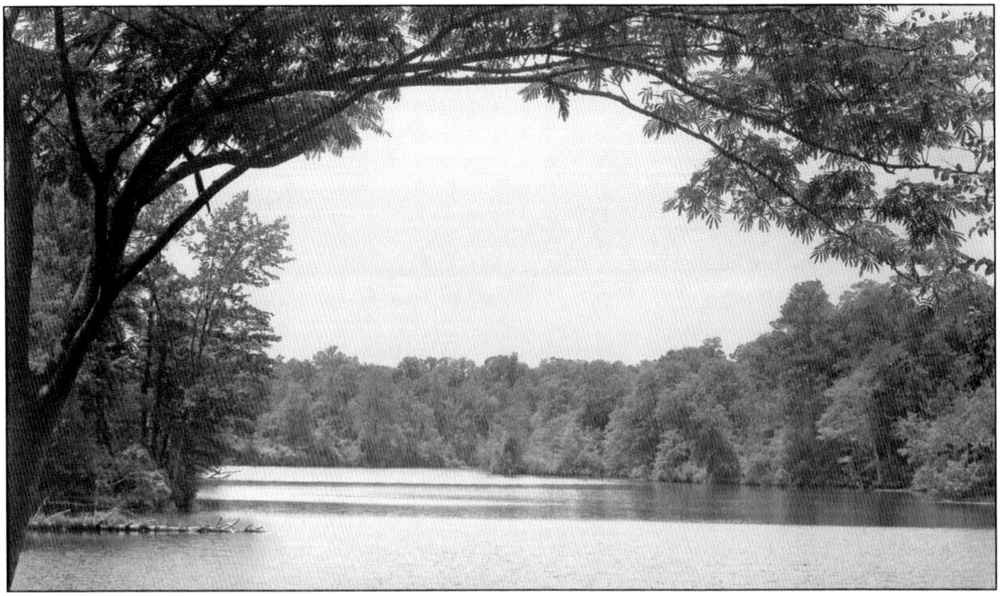

Richardson's Millpond is one of many that dot the county. This one is on Ware Creek, a tributary of the York River. Millers ground grain for flour, and older residents can remember regular visits to the mill as a responsibility when they were children. (SEL.)

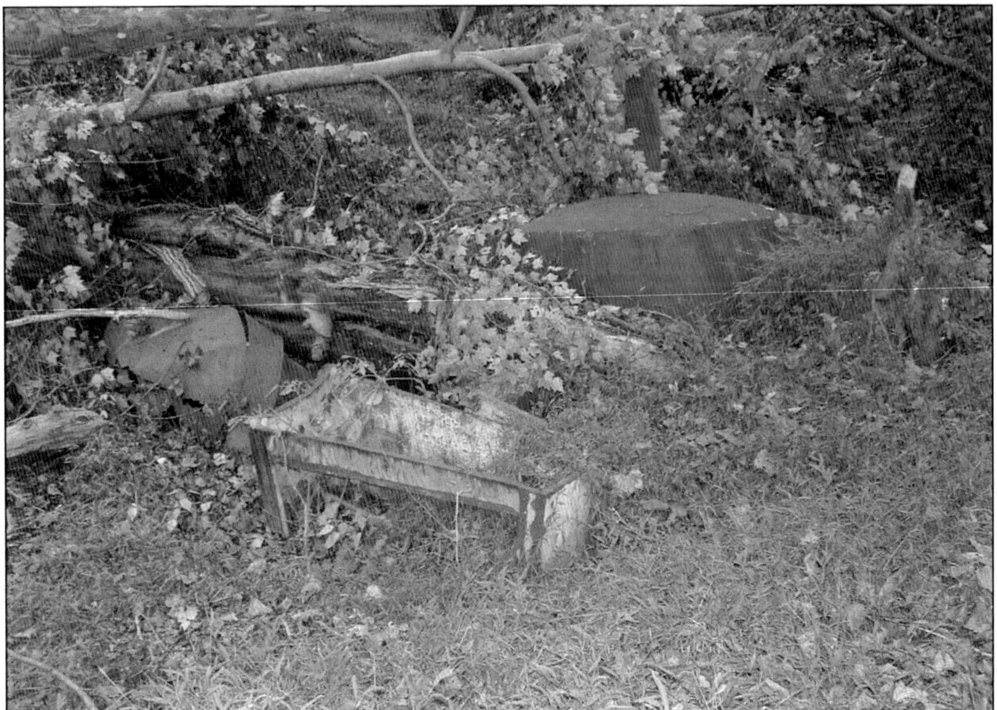

When Jamestown Road was widened, the old mill was bulldozed into the bottomland below Lake Matoaka. A mill had been active at that site for about 250 years. Traces of early structures, including pieces of brick, wood, and iron, as well as pieces of milling equipment, were still visible there in the early 21st century. (SEL.)

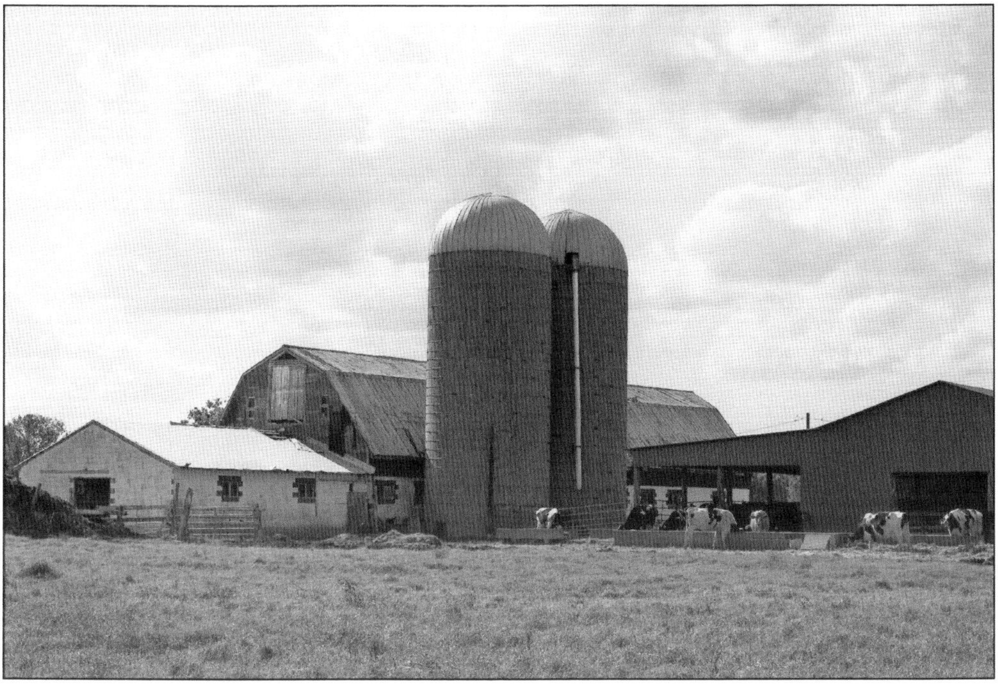

Camp Lightfoot is a camp for boys and girls founded by the Gospel Spreading Church of God. At the Gospel Spreading Farm, located along the Colonial Parkway between College and Mill Creeks on the James River, children observe and feed animals at the working dairy. (SEL.)

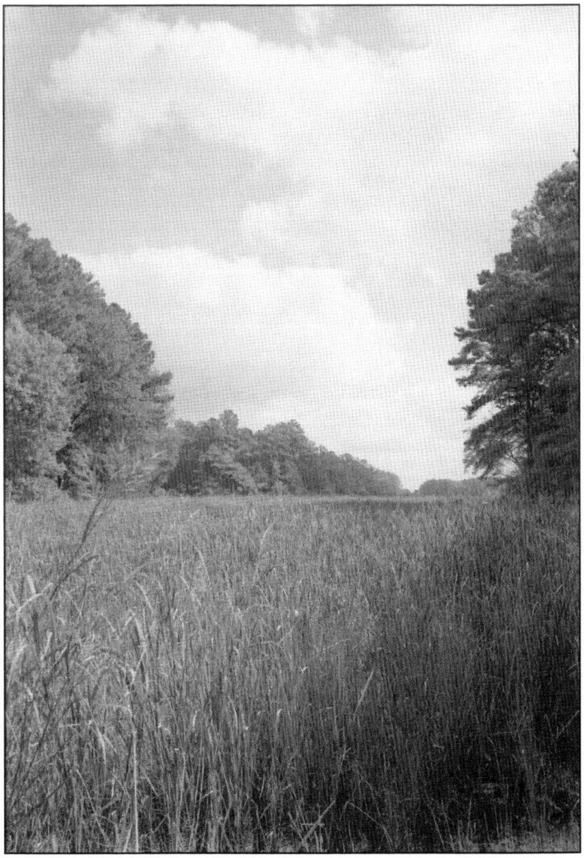

The marsh views surrounding Jamestown Island and James City County today are remarkably preserved in some areas and provide those who look for traces of the past with views that would have been familiar to the Woodland Indians and the English adventurers who lived here centuries ago. (LOC.)